KNOW.
BE.
LIVE.®

Impact 360
INSTITUTE

KNOW. BE. LIVE.®

A 360° APPROACH TO DISCIPLESHIP IN A POST-CHRISTIAN ERA

JOHN D. BASIE

Editor

Foreword by **J.P. MORELAND**

Forefront
BOOKS

Published by Forefront Books.

Cover Design by Bruce Gore, Gore Studio Inc.
Interior Design by Bill Kersey, KerseyGraphics

ISBN: 978-1-63763-021-1 print
ISBN: 978-1-63763-022-8 e-book

To all Impact 360 Institute alumni and staff who, like Daniel in Babylon, are compassionately seeking the good of the city, even as they risk intentionally in holding fast to God's loving, unchanging, revealed truth.

Soli Deo Gloria

CONTENTS

FOREWORD

J.P. Moreland

Our children are growing up in a post-Christian culture in which the public often views people of faith as irrelevant or even, in some cases, harmful extremists. In this context, the world (and the church) desperately need a new kind of Christian—a new generation of Jesus-followers who know what and why they believe; who are being formed and mentored carefully and wisely; and who are activists in whatever way God has gifted them for the cause of Christ. In our cultural Babylon, we need to raise up a new generation of Daniels to be ambassadors for Christ.

So how do we do that?

Before offering an answer to this question, let me say a word about my own journey. I received Christ as a chemistry major at the University of Missouri in 1968. Upon graduation, I served for 10 years with Cru (then called Campus Crusade for Christ). Seeing the great need for Christian thought leaders, I went to Dallas Theological Seminary, and then earned my Ph.D. in philosophy at USC under Dallas Willard. While there, I met and married Hope Coleman, and today we have two married daughters and five grandchildren. For the last thirty-five years or so, I have taught undergraduate and graduate students, with the last thirty at Talbot School of Theology, Biola University. I have also planted three churches and two Cru ministries.

During my fifty years of serving Christ, I have spoken and debated on 200 college campuses, have lectured in 400 churches, and have been featured numerous times on radio, social media, and television. Hopefully, I have accumulated some wisdom from which to speak about where we Christians need to go from here to practice and propagate a biblically-centered, vibrant form of Christianity. As I see it, we must thoughtfully and carefully re-emphasize three central needs.

Understanding Why We Embrace Biblical Christianity

Christians must be taught not only what they believe but why they ought to believe it in today's world. Scripture recognizes several definitions of *the world*:

1. the entire created order (see, for example, Ps. 24:1);
2. the entire class of human persons (see John 3:16);
3. that part of culture, especially non-Christian culture, that is contrary to the kingdom of God and Scripture (See Eph. 2:2–3).

It is this last sense I want to address.

In every culture in which the church is present, God's people are to avoid adopting particular manifestations of the world in that culture. At the same time, we are to be in the world, saturating it with a Christian worldview combined with spiritually mature, informed activism. To do so, we must understand both Scripture *and* the worldly systems of thought, practice, and value in our culture. We need to know how to help fellow Christians recognize those ungodly systems and refute them using both biblical and nonbiblical evidence (see 2 Cor. 10:3–5).

This will especially involve exposing and undermining secular ideas hostile to truth, including issues relating to science and the Bible. With glorious exceptions—and as my colleague Dr. Gene Fant points out in his chapter of this volume—the local church is a complete failure in this regard. Anti-intellectualism has derailed the church from making disciples and has made Christian parenting less effective. We practice *ostrich Christianity*—we put our heads in the sand and hope that these ideas will just go away and leave us alone.

Unfortunately, our failure to address them effectively is encouraging young people to leave the church. In an interview in *Leadership Journal*, Barna Group president David Kinnaman listed six reasons young people leave the church. Four are especially relevant to our current discussion:

- the church's shallowness of thought, including its biblical teachings and practices;
- the feeling that it is an unsafe place to express doubts and get answers to questions;
- its isolationism; that is, its failure to interact fairly with the surrounding culture;
- the church's anti-science attitude, including being out of step with scientific developments and debate.[1]

Instead of equipping disciples, especially Generation Z disciples, to understand and meet the world head-on, giving solid reasons for their Christian beliefs, the church has become its own gravedigger. The very practices that cause its numbers to rise and its budgets to be met are making the church increasingly anemic and marginalized. What are those practices? We try to grow the church by emphasizing worship and good Christian music; by offering watered-down, intellectually vacuous, simplistic preaching that is always applied to a parishioner's private life while failing to deal with the broad cultural, intellectual, and moral issues facing us all; and by trying to get people into small groups.

There is nothing wrong with the first and last practices. Clearly, they are of crucial importance. But conspicuously absent is any place in weekly church practice for people to learn; for their minds to be stretched; for learning to defend their faith; for becoming godly, intelligent ambassadors for Christ. People lack the courage to stand up for their faith in a non-defensive, winsome way because they lack the requisite knowledge for doing so. Thus, when challenged, Christians get defensive. If the church wants to avoid getting drawn into the world's way of thinking, we need to prioritize teaching Christians how to respond to pervasive cultural ideas. Knowledge confers authority and courage.

By failing to help parents equip their children with reasons for believing Christianity, the church has crippled Christian parenting. To see this, consider the following words by the great spiritual master and Christian activist William Wilberforce (1759–1833), who wrote about genuine Christianity and true spiritual growth. Whereas today, a book about the spiritual life and the cultivation of spirituality in children would likely not be considered *apologetics* (the art of defending the faith), apologetics was at the forefront of Wilberforce's mind:

> In an age in which infidelity abounds, do we observe them [parents] carefully instructing their children in the principles of faith which they profess? Or do they furnish their children with arguments for the defense of that faith?

> They would blush on their child's birth to think him inadequate in any branch of knowledge or any skill pertaining to his station in life. He cultivates these skills with becoming diligence. But he is left to collect his religion as he may. The study of Christianity has formed no part of his education. His attachment to it—where any attachment to it exists at all—is too often not the preference of sober reason and conviction. Instead his attachment to Christianity is merely the result of early and groundless prepossession. He was born in a Christian country, so of course he is a Christian. His father was a member of the Church of England, so that is why he is, too.

> When religion is handed down among us by hereditary succession, it is not surprising to find youth of sense and spirit beginning to question the truth of the system in which they were brought up. And it is not surprising to see them abandon a position which they are unable to defend.

> Knowing Christianity chiefly by its difficulties and the
> impossibilities falsely imputed to it, they fall perhaps into the
> company of unbelievers.[2]

Clearly, Wilberforce was on to something, especially when we consider how our contemporary culture seeks to make sense of reality. Training in apologetics is vital to perhaps all areas of Christian education and parenting. Failing here increases the odds that, when they leave the home, our children will leave Christianity.

Like it or not, we can't just bury our heads in the sand regarding the power and pervasiveness of the competing worldviews of our culture. It will affect Christians negatively if the leaders of the church and parents are not equipped to recognize the presence of these ideas and to provide a reasoned response to them. And that sort of equipping is exactly what this book is all about.

Taking Practical Steps to Become Like Jesus

Regarding spiritual growth, formation, and maturity, I have good news and bad news. First, the good news. In the last quarter of a century, a huge renewal of fresh, deep, practical, and life-changing approaches to growing in Christ have burst onto the scene. Returning to Scripture with fresh eyes; re-examining the best of the church fathers and the great spiritual giants throughout church history; reinvigorating a Christ-honoring integration of Christian theology and the best of psychology; and a surge in focus on biblical sexuality and the issue of our day—all of these have facilitated exciting new resources in books, seminars, social media, and more. The bad news is that so many do not know or avail themselves of these resources.

I am so delighted to say that the authors in this book provide top-notch chapters on spiritual maturity. These chapters exhibit depth, accessibility, and breadth of topics covered. You will find treasures to strengthen your soul for an intense spiritual conflict that lies before us.

Becoming Christ-centered Activists

We need Christ-centered activists who permeate the culture with humility, courage, and purpose. The Lord Jesus made it crystal clear that simply knowing his teaching, as critical as that is, will not alone get the job done. These and other teachings must be combined with action, practice, and behavior in order for them to have their maximum impact on Christians and the world.

I can assure you that the authors of this book are no mere theoreticians. All of them have years of ministry and Christian activism under their belts. These believers are Christian activists who have a long-earned reputation for integrity and action in light of the Great Commission's emphasis on evangelism and discipleship, and in light of seeking to do all that the Lord Jesus taught us to do. Let's be honest. Life is hard and our culture is, as one author puts it "slouching towards Gomorrah."[3] Thankfully, the authors of this book are of one mind in seeking to disciple members of Generation Z to be Christlike activists for the cause of Christ. This is our best hope, humanly speaking, for a long-term solution to the disorder all around us.

In light of what we have seen, I am edified and encouraged by the publication of *Know. Be. Live.®: A 360° Approach to Discipleship in a Post-Christian Era*. I have had the privilege of being involved with Impact 360 Institute since 2005. I teach there for a week every year. And I know the individuals who contributed to this book. I trust their hearts, their dedication to the Lordship of Christ, and their knowledge and skill about the things of which they write. If you ask me where you should start in order to become part of a new and growing Jesus movement, centered around the three areas mentioned, my answer would be to read carefully, study, and share the ideas in this book. This is foundational. Happily, the chapters to follow will provide direction for where to go after your reading. It is my fervent prayer that this volume will be widely engaged and used by God to spark a new and different kind of Christian revolution for such a time as this. I urge you in the name of Jesus to read and study this book carefully with your friends, family, and church community. If you do, you will no doubt become a more effective part of the solution.

J. P. Moreland, Ph.D.
Distinguished Professor of Philosophy
Talbot School of Theology, Biola University

ACKNOWLEDGMENTS

When it comes to pulling together a multi-author volume, the general editor is one person on the team. There are many others who assisted in making this project come to fruition. Indeed, without their help, this volume's publication would not have been possible.

Special thanks are due to John White, III, Impact 360 Institute's cofounder and president, for giving me the opportunity to facilitate this project. I am honored and humbled to have had the rare opportunity to serve in such a capacity.

Beth Yoe, a longtime Institute friend and author of the blog, "Bread and Butter," did a marvelous job of compiling scriptural references for appendix B of the volume.

Thanks to Kyle Dennard and the Impact 360 Institute marketing team, who did a ton of work to help with the book's cover art, as well as developing the marketing plan to get this volume in the hands of those whom it would most help.

To all contributors—you were an absolute joy and getting to know each of you better as a result of this project was truly one of my highlights of the last two years.

I am grateful also to those who took the time to read and endorse this volume prior to its publication. Time, as we are often reminded at Impact 360 Institute, is the one resource we can never get back.

Mitch Jaeger, with whom I work at the Institute on a daily basis, was of great assistance to me in keeping track of key details of the project as well as communicating with our contributors.

Heartfelt appreciation is due to my wife, Marana, and our three teenaged kids. They were incredibly understanding and patient with me as I took time away from them to finish this work.

Sincere appreciation is due to the publisher of this work, Jonathan Merkh. He and Lauren Ward and the entire team at Forefront Books were a joy to work with. On behalf of Impact 360 Institute, I want to thank them for allowing us the opportunity to get this book out to our audience.

Finally, I am grateful to all Institute team members for the various ways in which their own discipleship journeys have influenced me for the better as an image-bearer. Even in this cultural moment, when the temptations of darkness and despair surround us, their hopeful posture, sincere questions, and servant leadership remind me that the power of Jesus Christ working through us causes us to shine as stars (Phil. 2:15).

INTRODUCTION

John D. Basie

C.S. Lewis wrote in *Mere Christianity*, "Reality is . . . not neat, not obvious, not what you'd expect." At the time of writing this book, the realities that make up North American culture are vastly different from what most Christ-followers would have expected, even as recently as five years ago. Indeed, our culture is like plate tectonics; it is moving beneath our feet as we seek to maintain some semblance of an upright posture. Although this metaphorical ground has never been 100 percent stable, it is now shifting in ways that are throwing businesses, churches, and families completely off balance. Some may never recover. As the title of this volume suggests, we are clearly living in a post-Christian era.

This isn't all bad news. Much of what is falling away is what Russell Moore, formerly the president of the Southern Baptist Convention's Ethics and Religious Liberty Commission, has called "almost-Christianity," which

> . . . looks in the mainline like something from Nelson Rockefeller to Che Guevara at prayer. Almost Christianity, in the Bible Belt, looks like a God-and-Country civil religion that prizes cultural conservatism more than theological fidelity. Either way, a Christianity that reflects its culture,

> whether that culture is Smith College or NASCAR, only
> lasts as long as it is useful to its host. That's because it's, at
> root, idolatry, and people turn from their idols when they
> stop sending rain.
>
> Christianity isn't normal anymore, and that's good news.
> The Book of Acts, like the Gospels before it, shows us that
> Christianity thrives when it is, as Kierkegaard put it, a sign
> of contradiction. Only a strange gospel can differentiate itself
> from the worlds we construct. But the strange, freakish,
> foolish old gospel is what God uses to save people and to
> resurrect churches (1 Cor. 1:20–22).[1]

There is less-than-good-news as well. Many of us in the Bible-believing evangelical community are bracing ourselves for the biggest cultural earthquake this nation has ever known. The wake of the COVID-19 pandemic and rising political tensions are already changing our families, our local communities, and the way we have done church. These challenges cause us to question the ways we have traditionally done discipleship. It is extremely painful to many of us.

We should not be surprised by this. To Moore's point, we cannot expect God to "save people and resurrect churches" while we cling to a comfortable "almost-Christianity." Jesus Christ promised that we would experience our fair share of trouble and suffering for being his loyal followers. He also urged us to take a courageous stance in our work, because he has already conquered this fallen world (John 16:33).

To be faithful in such times, we need a new kind of discipleship—one that turns out to be "strange, freakish, foolish [and] old," as Moore put it. We need a discipleship model that takes into account the *imago Dei* in its totality, including the intellectual, physical, vocational, and spiritual dimensions.

This volume represents the work that Impact 360 Institute has been doing since its launch in 2006 to help young Christ-followers be courageous. Our founders, John and Trudy White, along with the board, intended to build an institute that could endure the test of time. The board knew that such an institute would need to be built on strong pillars. They knew that the apostle Paul was spot-on when he pointed out that "our struggle is not against flesh and blood, but against the rulers, against the powers, against the world rulers of this darkness, against the spiritual forces of evil in the heavens" (Eph. 6:12). With this truth as an animating conviction, the board adopted "Know. Be. Live." not only as a motto, but as the pillars of *spiritual transformation* that would provide a rock-solid foundation for discipleship for decades to come. These pillars, and this motto, were adopted after prayerful consideration of what the holy, inerrant Scriptures indicate a "curriculum of Christlikeness," as the late Dallas Willard called it, should look like. Such a curriculum would be holistic, as is fitting for those who would be apprentices of Jesus. The Institute's mission is to cultivate leaders who follow Jesus. This mission, along with the Know. Be. Live. pillars of spiritual transformation, constitute the primary organizing principle of this volume.

The Know. Be. Live. model, as the main organizing principle of this book, helps in framing the question of what a 360-degree, *holistic discipleship model* ought to look like for Gen Z in particular. My good friend, colleague, and contributor to this volume, Jonathan Morrow, has ably led the Institute's efforts to partner with David Kinnaman and the Barna Group to produce two groundbreaking studies on Gen Z from a worldview and discipleship perspective. If you have not had the opportunity to read those studies, you can find them here (https://shop.barna.com/collections/frontpage/products/the-ultimate-gen-z-collection). This volume seeks to expand upon the key questions and challenges raised by those studies and provide insight for cultivating Gen Z leaders who follow Jesus.

All contributing authors are proven experts, with many having authored their own books and articles in areas relevant to this volume's central purpose—to equip kingdom citizens to disciple Gen Z in new, more effective ways. Additionally, each author has served Impact 360 Institute in some meaningful way, whether by instructing students on campus, contributing through podcast interviews, or helping the Institute's faculty design curriculum. Most importantly, these contributors were selected because they exemplify the kind of holistic discipleship described in this volume. Their vocations include discipling Gen Z on a daily basis.

The chapters are organized into three sections—Know, Be, and Live—that respectively correspond to and highlight the three major biblical mandates: the Cultural Mandate, the Great Commandment Mandate, and the Great Commission Mandate . While some topics can easily fit into two or even all three categories, I've attempted to align the topics in a biblically faithful, as well as reader-friendly, way. All chapters seek to address a particular aspect of the Barna/Impact 360 Institute research on Gen Z through the use of real-life stories, relevant data, biblical and philosophical arguments, and each author's experiences. Additionally, authors offer timely insights on the unique challenges and opportunities for effectively utilizing the Know. Be. Live. model of discipleship in a post-COVID-19 world.

Part One emphasizes the importance of *knowledge* as a foundational plank in the platform of authentic Christian discipleship. This is the first pillar of the Institute's model of holistic spiritual formation:

> **Know Jesus More Deeply**
> Grow in your understanding of what God has revealed about reality and why Christianity is true.

Our post-Christian culture would have us believe that there is no objective knowledge apart from science, a view of knowledge called *scientism*. According to this view, everything else we think we know, including the reality and character of God, the reality of objective morality, and the reality of non-physical human souls, is relegated to the realm of the subjective. This pervasive assumption has shaken the faith of many Christ-followers, including those who belong to Generation Z. Sadly, every contributor to this volume has seen members of this generation walk away from the faith in large part because they no longer believed that these things are actually *real*. As Gene Fant argues in chapter 1, the Church has failed spectacularly in this aspect of discipleship. The contributors to this part of the book seek to make the case for rigorous worldview formation as essential to a holistic approach to biblical discipleship. Christianity is the most robust worldview that accounts for reality, and that reality is actually knowable.

Gen Zers have grown up in a virtual world that tells them their experience—rather than God's revelation—is "their truth." This creates a crisis of knowledge where people lack the confidence of *knowing* God's intention for how we should live. The fallout for Gen Z means that there is no meaningful sense in which the Cultural Mandate to fill and subdue the earth (Gen. 1) and all that this mandate entails—in terms of building culture and society according to God's good design—has any real bearing on how we choose to order our families and society at large. Morality, on this view, is based on mere *agreed-upon preferences* and how we as individuals decide to live in community. We believe that only a holistic discipleship model will succeed in replacing this false, yet increasingly pervasive, assumption.

In Part Two, the contributors cover the second pillar of the Institute's model of holistic spiritual formation—what it means to:

> **Be Transformed in Your Character**
> Discover your identity in Christ and your God-given
> calling in authentic community.

This "Be" pillar supports identity formation as image-bearers and identity formation's relationship to the Great Commandment—love of God and love of neighbor. Getting that order correct, as John Stonestreet shows in his chapter, is essential to being formed into the likeness of Jesus Christ. This part of the book addresses a number of important questions: What does it mean for humans to be made in the *imago Dei* (image of God) in a world where technology undergirds every aspect of life? How can we help Gen Z cultivate a love for God through recapturing the spiritual disciplines? What does it look like in this cultural moment to honor people of all races and ethnic backgrounds? What does a healthy, biblical understanding of sexuality look like in a world that assumes the only ethic that matters is mutual consent?

Part Three is built on the Institute's "Live" pillar:

> ### Live a Life of Kingdom Influence
> Live a life of Spirit-empowered Kingdom influence as
> you cultivate a servant's heart.

Actively developing apprentices of Jesus in a post-Christian era
requires that we take the Know and Be pillars and make them matter in
everyday life through spirit-empowered Kingdom influence. Just as the
Know pillar has its foundation in the cultural mandate (Gen. 1), and the
Be pillar has its moorings in the Great Commandment mandate (Mark
12:29–31; 1 John 4:20), the Live pillar also is anchored in Scripture, namely
the Great Commission mandate (Matt. 28:18–20). What does it look
like, in this cultural moment where the ground is like plate tectonics, to
believe Jesus's words that "all authority in heaven and on earth has been
given to me"? What does it look like to disciple *all people groups* today,
"teaching them to obey everything I have commanded you"? What could
it look like for Gen Z to adopt a posture of servant leadership in their
various callings? What does living out the gospel in a politically charged
culture look like? How can parents of Gen Zers adopt a posture of
wisdom in teaching their digital native children as they simultaneously
try to protect them from virtual space that is dangerous to their souls?

The volume's main content concludes with a convictional rally
cry-style postscript written by Impact 360 Institute's cofounder and
president, John White, III. Two appendices follow the postscript. The
first is a recommended reading list, categorized by the Know. Be. Live.
pillars of spiritual transformation. The second, utilizing the same meth-
odology, is a selection of Scripture references and devotional thoughts
that have been put together by longtime Impact 360 Institute friend and
devotional author Beth Yoe.

Here are a few things to keep in mind as you work your way through
this volume. First, the primary audience for this book is anyone who is
interested in, or is already, discipling others—specifically Gen Z—in their
faith journey. Second, by arguing for a 360-degree approach to discipleship, the contributors to this book are not claiming to cover every aspect
of discipleship in its pages. That would be unrealistic for a single volume.
The 360 in the book's title is a way of reinforcing the holistic aspect of

our Know. Be. Live. discipleship model. We have selected topics that we believe to be essential based on the recent Barna/Impact 360 Institute research of Gen Z as well as our own personal experiences in working with them. Third, be aware that some themes in the book are addressed in multiple chapters. Because the human condition is messy and rarely falls neatly into abstract categorical lines, we wanted the authors to have the freedom to color a bit outside the lines of their assigned topic, helping the reader make relevant connections. We believe this is what it will take to disciple Gen Z in a faithful, holistic way. For example, the hot-button topic of sexuality is specifically addressed in depth by Sean McDowell in his chapter. Where it is relevant and appropriate to other topics, this theme also receives treatment from other contributors. Finally, all contributors have sought to convey their messages using hopeful, clear, *and* direct language. Our assumption is that the readers of this volume are generally knowledgeable about and in agreement with the beliefs of evangelical Christianity. We therefore do not spend a lot of time defending these beliefs, but rather, discuss how best to reinforce them in the current generation of disciples.

If you have picked up this book and begun reading it, then there is a reason why you have done so. Most likely, you care greatly for Gen Z and how they will be cultivated as apprentices of Jesus. My prayer for you as you work your way through this volume is that you will gain a "heart of wisdom" (Psalm 90:12 NIV) for discipling Gen Z.

PART ONE
KNOW

Know Jesus More Deeply

Grow in your understanding of what God has revealed about reality and why Christianity is true.

CHAPTER 1

FAITH, TRUTH, AND THE PROBLEM OF IRRELEVANCE

Gene C. Fant Jr.

The Church's Need to Emulate Christ

First John 4:19 tells us, "We love because he loved us first." The simplicity of this passage belies the incredible scope of its vision of God's love and his mission for the church. At the core of this vision and mission is the central truth that God loves the pinnacle of his creation: people. People are the focus of God's redemptive purpose and actions. Repeatedly, the Scriptures underscore the incredible intentionality God has shown toward humankind:

- The announcement of Christ's birth emphasized an honorific name, " 'Emmanuel,' which means 'God with us' " (Matt 1:23, fulfilling Isa. 7:14).
- Christ's divinity was channeled into his humanity, as he "emptied himself by taking on the form of a slave, by looking like other men, and by sharing in human nature. He humbled himself, by becoming obedient to the point of death—even death on a cross" (Phil. 2:7–8).
- Christ's incarnation and death were divinely designed for salvation, in that "while we were still helpless, at the right time Christ died for the ungodly.... But God demonstrates his own love for

us, in that while we were still sinners, Christ died for us" (Rom 5:6–8).

- God is likened to a shepherd who leaves the ninety-nine in order to find the one (Luke 15:3–7).
- God is likened to a woman who searches for a lost coin (Luke 15:8–10).

If the evangelical church is to emulate Christ (and the early church), it needs to renew its commitment to relationships through incarnational grace and truth.

The advent of Gen Z (those born between 1999 and 2015) presents the evangelical church with an incredible opportunity to shape a generation. In order to seize this opportunity, it is wise to examine the failures of the past due to the exaltation of programs over people.

The Evangelical Church's Spectacular Failure

Every generation has challenges transitioning its young people into adulthood. In 1919, after the end of World War I, a song became popular that was titled, "How 'Ya Gonna Keep 'em Down on the Farm (After They've Seen Paree)?"[1] The question underscores the cultural anxiety of experienced youth trying to cope with the expectations of the older generation. This anxiety was difficult enough in the early twentieth century, when the experiential gap between youth and elders was based primarily on the experience of foreign warfare, but in our digital era, when the gaps between age, geography, ethnicity, and a wide variety of other demographic markers are so swiftly shifting, it is daunting. The advent of social media has accelerated and exacerbated this divergence between generations.

Too often critics generate jeremiads about the zeitgeist of the next generation, generalizing about laziness, entitlement, or ignorance about basic facts. Such comments are misdirected, however, because the next generation is the product of the previous generation's enculturation. If the older generation is frustrated by the next generation, whether intellectually, culturally, or theologically, it needs to look with a critical eye at its own institutions. For the evangelical church, the pivot from a high-water mark at the end of the twentieth century to minority status of the 2020s marks an important inflection point in how the faith can be transmitted to the next generation and beyond.

Evangelicalism's Cultural Moment

The evangelical church, broadly defined, generated great energy following Jimmy Carter's presidential election in 1976. Carter, at the time a Southern Baptist, attracted curiosity from the mainstream press by using the term *born again* and even using the old-fashioned-sounding term *lust* in an interview with *Playboy* magazine. Attention turned to evangelicals like never before, as long-standing names such as Billy Graham merged with new options for voices in national conversations: Pat Robertson of The 700 Club, Jerry Falwell of the Moral Majority, and Jim Bakker of the Trinity Broadcasting Network. Evangelical theologians gained new traction. The heady combination of conservative politics, corporate and economic successes, and cultural popularity gave churches increased attendance, and church-related institutions, such as schools and para-church organizations, increased enrollments, donations, and influence. The loosening of denominational ties launched non-denominational megachurches that overlapped with the explosion of media outlets via cable television and the subsequent advent of the internet.

The American impulse toward marketing and business strategies yielded a movement that aimed to bring new techniques to church life. Evangelicals in particular tied in with these impulses, and a wave of non-denominational churches launched in parts of the U.S., with denominational churches deeply impacted as well. One of the founding institutions of the church growth movement was Willow Creek Community Church, founded by Bill Hybels. Willow Creek was the epicenter of many things—hosting conferences, influencing worship trends, and holding itself out as a model for evangelism and community formation. Eventually its leaders grew curious about spiritual formation and growth among its members, conducting an extensive internal study to see if heavy involvement in the church yielded improved maturity and theological orthodoxy.[2] Hybels himself noted that the results, published in 2007, were "earth-shaking." The church admitted that its programs, activities, and structures apparently led to little improvement in spiritual maturation; it further suggested that personal relationships (such as coaching) are the best platform for spiritual growth.

In the eyes of many evangelicals, this study coincided with an avalanche of data that revealed what many would call the spectacular failure of evangelicalism to leverage its moment into a lasting effect on its young, particularly in the transition from Gen Y to Gen Z. For example, in 2005, sociologist Christian Smith published an extensive study of American teenagers in *Soul Searching*. Smith coined the phrase "moralistic therapeutic deism" to describe the dominant theology of the study's young people.[3] In Smith's analysis, religion is important to teenagers but holds no special authority. Morality, broadly defined by the individual, is important, and adhering to it makes individuals feel good about themselves, which is the highest good. Smith notes, importantly, that religion (and therefore theology) is sublimated to individual preferences.

Similarly, in 2010, Tim Elmore published *Generation iY*, an analysis of the transition between Millennials and what would become Gen Z.[4] Elmore focused on the problems posed by the relentless digital nature of American youth culture. In 2012, David Kinnaman of the Barna Group sounded an alarm about the loss of biblical faith in young Christians and warned about their exit from the church.[5] In 2018, the Barna Group, in conjunction with the Impact 360 Institute, produced the first-ever in-depth survey analysis of Gen Z students.[6] The Barna Group identified trends and attitudes in Gen Z that reveal just how few Gen Z members (about 4 percent) adhere to what could be called a biblical worldview. While other chapters will be more thorough in their treatment of the study, it is worth noting just how weak the theological transmission from previous generations has been in this overwhelmingly secular generation.

How You Gonna Keep 'Em in the Youth Group, Now That They've Seen Tik-Tok? (or Mortal Combat, or Netflix, or . . . .)

The cultural moment of evangelicalism led to an explosion of programs for youth. From well-prepared retreats to apologetics institutes to free-ranging Bible studies and community groups, there was no dearth of religious activities for students. Larger events such as the high-energy Passion Conferences, starting in 1997, combined the exegetical mastery of high-profile speakers with highly produced worship music. Larger churches began to renovate educational facilities into slick worship spaces, with concert lighting and live worship teams. Some churches introduced gaming facilities aimed at attracting unchurched or casual attendees.

The competition for attention between secular events and religious events was amped up and created angst for leaders and parents alike. From my position as a denominational leader, I have seen countless videos and highlight reels from events that emphasized the cool factor. I have heard many youth leaders describe their activities as being "the place to be" in ways that sounded less evangelistic and more commercial. Some faith leaders expressed concerns that content was being watered down, with controversial topics being avoided or handled so cautiously as to be deceptive or unfaithful to Scripture and doctrine. I once counseled a church staff member who was incredibly frustrated when he tried to increase the theological content of his teaching on Wednesday nights only to face pushback from parents demanding that games and music be the primary content.

The opposite challenge has been that of dealing with controversial topics such as sexuality, gender, and politics. With the gap between historical Christian views on subjects and those of the increasingly secular culture at-large, Christianity is viewed as judgmental and out of step. While "relevance" was a clarion cry in evangelical youth culture for two decades, relevance in one time or culture quickly morphs into irrelevance in the next, once hipness becomes self-parody and trendiness becomes unfashionable, eyerolling ennui.

At the start of the third decade of the twenty-first century, the evangelical church was moving into a new status in the larger U.S. culture.

Weary of bombastic politics, out of favor with the larger Big Tech culture, and looking ahead to strong headwinds that oppose evangelical Christian beliefs and values, the evangelical church faced substantial anxiety about American culture as a whole and the church's own ability to thrive—or even survive—in the coming years. In live time, the year 2020 loomed large in the evangelical horizon, as if an ominous black swan were paddling waters between 2019 to 2020.

The Post-Pandemic Pivot

The pandemic related to the COVID-19 virus has been a disruptive event that has affected every aspect of human culture on a global level. Reminiscent of the Spanish flu outbreak of 1918–1920, the coronavirus has yielded economic, political, and social effects that will be long-lasting and far-reaching. The church has not escaped these disruptions, as many congregations have been shuttered for months, members have been placed into conflict, and staff members have been stressed to their breaking points. The rhythms of church life—services, Bible studies, retreats, and other gatherings—have been omitted for nearly a year as I write this chapter.

This loss of rhythm is particularly true for youth. For those who were actively engaged in church, Sunday mornings meant Bible study and worship. Often Sunday nights included more focused youth-oriented events. Weekends may have offered more gatherings, and some communities even offered afterschool events, providing a sense of connectedness. There were weekend-long retreats, summer camps, choir tours, athletics, and other longer immersions of shared experiences that cultivated identity, along with opportunities for spiritual growth and discipleship. Even minimally engaged youth had opportunities for contact and potential evangelism or mentorship. In many parts of the U.S., evangelical churches offered much enrichment to their communities on a day-to-day basis. And that is not even mentioning volunteerism at nonprofits and service organizations.

And Then 2020 Happened

The pandemic has resulted in an unparalleled mental health crisis in the U.S. According to a Zogby poll conducted in late 2020, 56 percent of students reported having friends who had considered suicide or other self-harm. Similarly, 58 percent reported that they no longer felt safe anywhere but home. Seventy-five percent of teens living in urban areas reported being more anxious about their well-being than they were six months previously. Zogby observed, "[T]oday's Gen Z teens are known for not trusting familiar institutions and leaders. The current crisis only seems to have exacerbated that rejection, especially toward school leadership and their ability to keep students safe. Unaddressed, this could have broader outcomes on Gen-Z's future."[7]

These results are contiguous with those found in the adult population. A Boston University study, published in *JAMA Network Open* in September 2020, revealed that depression had tripled in some areas, rising from 8.5 percent to 27.8 percent; severe depression rose from 0.7 percent to 5.1 percent, a seven-fold increase. These rates far exceeded increases following other major national traumatic events, such as the 1993 World Trade Center bombing and other terrorist attacks.

Notably, in a long-standing Gallup poll related to mental health, the sharp increase in anxiety in 2020 is an amplification of a long, steady decline in mental health. As Gallup reported, "The only demographic subgroup who didn't report a decline were those who attend religious services weekly. [In fact], that group showed an increase of 4 percent compared to 2019."[8] As commentator Joe Carter observed, "Frequent churchgoers aren't merely benefiting from a useful delusion or a sense of community. They are finding the relief—the psychological and spiritual relief—that comes from aligning oneself with the true and ultimate reality."[9]

The relationship between digital screen time and mental health is likewise well documented. Pre-COVID, counselors and healthcare workers were already sounding alarms about the increase in moderate or severe depression that accompanies increased use of digital screens. One study, for example, specifically warned about the factors of "workplace sitting, social relationship, and family history" in the anticipation of increased mental health challenges.[10] In children, even more concerns have been noted. During COVID, the pivot to online learning, commercial shutdowns, and social distancing have all dramatically increased the screen time of children, young adults, and adults in general. Even kindergarteners have encountered online learning for the first time. Isolation and unusual amounts of free time have resulted in increased media consumption. All of this has combined to devastate mental health, spiritual formation, and satisfaction with pat answers to existential questions.

What Must I Do to Be Saved?

Sometimes our obsession with our own era causes us to forget that the great questions of humankind have been the same since the creation of the world.[11] Death, suffering, and brokenness ultimately cause every person to face their own mortality. Realizing our impotence in dealing with the ultimate reality of death and what lies on the other side of this life, every person deals in some way with how to make sense of this existential question.

In Acts 16, the Macedonia jailer who was responsible for Paul and Silas faced an existential crisis when an earthquake struck the city. The jail's security was breeched, and the jailer assumed that the prisoners had all escaped. Preparing to kill himself, he heard Paul calling out with a loud voice, "Do not harm yourself, for we are all here!" (v. 28). In response, the jailer articulated the heart cry of every single human: "Sirs, what must I do to be saved?' (v. 30). Paul answered quickly, "Believe in the Lord Jesus and you will be saved" (v. 31); the entire household was baptized that night, and the jailer "rejoiced greatly that he had come to believe in God, together with his entire household" (v. 34).

What must I do to be saved? is a question I personally hear on the lips (and see implied on the social media accounts) of so many members of Gen Z. After a year of pandemic isolation, the loneliness is unbearable. After witnessing so-called cancel culture ruin lives and futures, the fear of being discovered in the worst moments is overwhelming. After a lifetime of intuiting the weight of their sins, and without even having a vocabulary to articulate this intuition, Gen Z's longing for transcendence and meaning is soul-stirring. The same question has lingered on the lips of every person who has faced up to the basic question of human existence.

In Christianity, salvation is tied to relationship between God and humankind. As Paul told the jailer, "Believe in the Lord Jesus and you will be saved." The New Testament constantly reiterates this. In Acts 16, the reader can feel the personal intensity of the moment. The jailer was suicidal. Paul and Silas were soothing. This wasn't evangelism by program. This wasn't a marketing strategy on how to grow the church in Macedonia. This wasn't a well-reasoned apologetic argument rooted in presuppositional truth. This was one man, the jailer, talking to another man, Paul, and realizing that truth had been articulated and grace had been offered.

The Grand Opportunity: Incarnational Grace and Truth

An Incarnational Church

The Gospel of John's opening verses emphasize the historical inbreaking of Christ, exploring the philosophical and theological ramifications of his role in creation and his mission to serve humankind. The culmination of history itself, the fulcrum of God's relationship with humankind, came in the birth of Christ, as the supernatural transcendent Savior entered into human flesh:

> Now the Word became flesh and took up residence among us. We saw his glory—the glory of the one and only, full of grace and truth, who came from the Father....For we have all received from his fullness one gracious gift after another. For the law was given through Moses; but grace and truth came about through Jesus Christ. No one has ever seen God. The only one, himself God, who is in closest fellowship with the Father, has made God known. (John 1:14, 16–18).

Christ, then, "the Word became flesh" who "took up residence among us," embodies the glory of the Father who had sent him. John then offered a powerful declaration of Christ's plenary power as the Savior: he is "full of grace and truth" (verse 14, repeated in v. 16 for emphasis). This grace is both relational and salvific, just as this truth is clarifying and transcendent.

As if to underscore the incarnational essence of the church, Romans uses the metaphor of the body: "For just as in one body we have many members, and not all the members serve the same function, so we who are many are one body in Christ, and individually we are members who belong to one another" (12:4–5). First Corinthians 12 reiterates this throughout the entire chapter, including vv. 12–14:

> For just as the body is one and yet has many members, and all the members of the body—though many—are one body, so too is Christ. For in one Spirit we were all baptized into one body. Whether Jews or Greeks or slaves or free, we were all made to drink of the one Spirit. For in fact the body is not a single member, but many.

Ephesians 4 repeats this image, as does Colossians 1. If the church is the body, it must be incarnational; and if it is incarnational, it must be relational. In a post-COVID world, particularly in dealing with Gen Z students, the evangelical church has not merely the calling to be incarnational; it has the privilege and responsibility to be so. And if it is part of our nature to be relational, it needs to be intentional, full of both grace and truth.

Incarnational Grace

When Christ returned from the wilderness and began his public ministry, he visited the synagogue at Nazareth and read from the scroll of Isaiah a declaration of his calling from God:

> The Spirit of the Lord is upon me, because he has anointed me to proclaim good news to the poor. He has sent me to proclaim release to the captives and the regaining of sight to

the blind, to set free those who are oppressed, to proclaim the year of the Lord's favor. (Luke 4:18–19).

Throughout his ministry, Jesus brought healing and reconciliation to people, to bring what had been out of balance, through sin and the fallen nature of the world, back into balance, through healing and grace. James put as fine a point on this as any of the New Testament writers: "Pure and undefiled religion before God the Father is this: to care for orphans and widows in their adversity and to keep oneself unstained by the world" (1:27). The question of widow-care, along with ethnic prejudice, was a large part of the initial creation of the diaconate in Acts 6.

Early church history bears out that the church was deeply concerned with the poor, the voiceless, and the outcast, as it grew from its earliest days in the shadows of the Roman Empire to a place of greater prominence.[12] The church was an agent of common grace, the non-salvific blessing that blunts the effects of sin on all people and ultimately points toward the saving grace of Christ. By being agents of grace in a culture, the church prepared that culture for the complete gospel of Christ—that forgiveness of sin was available and that the restoration of balance in this world merely foreshadowed the ultimate transcendent restoration of all things for all time by Christ himself.

The early church practiced incarnational grace, emphasizing the relational value of neighbor and fellow citizen. They took the words of Romans 12 to heart; in the face of persecution, they lived out Paul's instructions:

> Bless those who persecute you, bless and do not curse.
> Rejoice with those who rejoice, weep with those who weep.
> Live in harmony with one another; do not be haughty but
> associate with the lowly. Do not be conceited. Do not repay
> anyone evil for evil; consider what is good before all people.
> If possible, so far as it depends on you, live peaceably with
> all people....(I)f your enemy is hungry, feed him; if he is
> thirsty, give him a drink; for in doing this you will be heaping

> burning coals on his head. Do not be overcome by evil, but
> overcome evil with good. (vv. 14–21).

These actions became the trademark of Christians in their communities. The powerful sometimes persecuted them, but their reputation in their communities belied the accusations of those who sought to slander them. Just as God had loved them first (1 John 4:19), they loved and served their communities with the expectation that they would be viewed askance, rather than embraced—at least in the interim.

As the United States moves into a post-Christian, post-truth, post-pandemic culture, the evangelical church has an opportunity to act with incarnational grace in the larger culture, particularly where Gen Z is concerned. This all starts with relationships that produce transformation in individuals and communities, rather than slick programs aimed at generating statistical affirmations for institutions.

Gen Z craves authenticity in relationships and service in communities. Just as the early church served widows and defended orphans (literally!), particularly those who were abandoned in a culture that allowed passive infanticide, the evangelical church must advocate for the underserved and the voiceless in ways that are biblically faithful, economically effective, and culturally transformational. In a post-pandemic culture that feels like it is constantly grinding up and destroying people, particularly ordinary people who find themselves in public controversies, grace is a powerful antidote to a relentless, graceless secular culture that feels more powerful each day.

Incarnational Truth

In John 14, Jesus offered the disciples the promise of a place for them in heaven and that he himself would return in the future to gather them. Thomas, always the skeptic, asked, "How can we know the way?" (v. 5), to which Christ made an incredible, existential statement: "I am the way, and the truth, and the life. No one comes to the Father except through me. If you have known me, you will know my Father too. And from now on you do know him and have seen him" (vv. 6–7).

Christ's claim here is epistemic: if he is the truth, or rather, the Truth, the very Incarnation of Truth, and the Source of Truth, then all truth is his truth, and he is all truth. This means that philosophical and theological claims may be vetted by the light of Christ's life and the revelation of God's word as found in Scripture.

The evangelical church has an opportunity to cultivate relationships that are based on incarnational truth, meaning intense and even intimate Bible study, mentorship, and apologetics. By refocusing on God's Word and the truths of God's Word, it can reconnect people with an understanding of the ultimate reality: God's Lordship and Sovereignty over his creation. In a culture that is increasingly detached from reality and transcendent, non-personal truth, the careful cultivation of the mind of Christ (1 Cor 2:16) can be transformational. In a culture that emphasizes individualistic, conflict-avoidant ethics, emphasizing the authority of God over the world can be empowering over and against a soul-crushing culture.

Similarly, apologetics can provide foundational courage to resist that larger culture. In the early 2000s, apologetics tended to be institutionalized, by which I mean it was systemic and often impersonal. It was about abstraction or even ideological competition. Apologetics, however, is an incredibly powerful tool to change individual minds and remove personal doubt. Biblical truth is a deep well from which transformation may be drawn, and apologetics often is a way of channeling that truth into refreshing rivers of confidence. When it is applied in a discipleship context that is deeply relational, it is an important tool of spiritual formation.

Because Gen Z values relationships with peers so deeply, along with social acceptability and approbation, they tend to be conflict-avoidant and often subordinate revelation to relationships. By this I mean God's revelation as found in the Scriptures is ignored or customized in order to avoid a disruption in the relationship. This means that a conflict between biblical truth, values, or perspectives and the opinions of another person must always be resolved by the elevation of opinion over revelation, even if it means silencing the voice of revelation. In a discipleship mode, a safe space can be cultivated to allow for true-faced questions, open wrestling with doubts, and appropriate responses from Scripture and the Christian intellectual tradition. This kind of embracing of biblical truth is liberating, just as the modeling of biblical grace is empowering for individuals. For a culture, these twin commitments are transformational.

Conclusion

In 2017, Rod Dreher proposed that the church return to the practices of sixth-century Christianity, following St. Benedict of Nursia in retreating from the larger culture and creating intentional communities that foster and protect faith.[13] Dreher's proposal has many elements that would serve the evangelical church well, particularly where it comes to the cultivation of community and intensely personal and intimate relationships.

The global pandemic of 2020–21, along with numerous cultural and political challenges that coincided with the period, has created a time of angst and turmoil outside the walls of the evangelical church, as well as inside of it. The isolation produced by the pandemic, the deeply felt existential questions, and so many other factors have combined to produce fear and deep divisions; but they have likewise created an opportunity to change how we cultivate the faith to the next generation.

Because of the global pandemic and political and cultural turmoil, there is discussion among secular leaders about a Great Reset in terms of global economics and governance.[14] The evangelical church likewise faces a moment when a reset is possible, but its "great reset" is perhaps best identified not as a new initiative but rather as a return to its roots. In relationships that model God's love for his creation, it is able to embody the grace and truth that are central to the fulfillment of God's glorification in our lives and in our work, as it lays a Kingdom claim on every life, one at a time.

CHAPTER 2

THE CRISIS OF KNOWLEDGE AND THE THREE Rs OF WORLDVIEW FORMATION

Jonathan Morrow

Appearances can be deceiving, and the crisis that most urgently needs to be addressed is not always the most obvious at first glance. As Elton Trueblood prophetically wrote, "The terrible danger of our time consists in the fact that ours is a cut-flower civilization. Beautiful as cut flowers may be, and much as we may use our ingenuity to keep them looking fresh for a while, they will eventually die, and they die because they are severed from their sustaining roots."[1]

All of us are inundated every day with headlines, posts, and tweets that highlight growing distrust, moral and spiritual confusion, outrage, anxiety, loneliness, racial tension, skepticism, tribalism, and division in our culture. But these effects are symptomatic of a much larger cause. Echoing Trueblood's words, the resources for a unified vision of knowing and living today have been severed from the root of a biblical worldview, and the flower is dying right before our eyes. One major aspect of this withering is a crisis of knowledge, even as a new generation is trying to navigate our chaotic world and find their place in it.

The Moral and Spiritual Confusion of Gen Z

Before I begin to unpack this idea, I want to address a potential misunderstanding. Let me clearly state that I love Gen Z—the generation after Millennials and born between 1999–2015—and spend most of my days working with them.[2] I love talking with them, laughing with them, learning from them, teaching them, and am truly hopeful for who and what they can become as a new generation of Christ-followers.[3] But we won't just passively drift into that hopeful future.

In the groundbreaking generational research that we at Impact 360 Institute partnered with the Barna Group to produce on Gen Z, we learned some uncomfortable truths about the moral and spiritual confusion of the next generation. As a starting point, it's important to recognize that only 4 percent of Gen Z have what we would consider a biblical worldview; a continued downward trend from previous generations.[4] This should remove any illusions that we live in a Christian culture. Here are just a few ways this plays out:

- 58 percent (now 65 percent) believe many religions can lead to eternal life; there is no "one true religion."[5]
- Only 34 percent believe lying is wrong.[6]
- Only 29 percent believe abortion is wrong.[7]
- Only 21 percent believe sex before marriage is wrong.[8]
- Only 20 percent believe homosexual behavior is wrong.[9]
- Only 38 percent believe marriage should be a lifelong commitment between a man and woman.[10]
- 33 percent say gender is "what a person feels like."[11]
- 24 percent (now 31 percent) agree that what is morally right and wrong changes over time based on society.[12]

Sharing these statistics is not about casting blame. It's about our awareness of reality and how it should motivate and inform our actions—the way we teach, preach, parent, mentor, and disciple.

Make no mistake, Gen Z is merely living out what Boomers, Gen X, and Millennials have modeled for them. Gen Z has been discipled by their smartphones, taught sex education by Google and YouTube, and conditioned to assume that believing something makes it true. Furthermore, they've been sold the lies that freedom is getting to do whatever you want and that happiness is found in emotional pleasure and comfort. Generationally speaking, if we have an issue with the state of moral and spiritual confusion in Gen Z, we as a culture need to look no further than the mirror.

The Crisis of Knowledge Explained

Without the possibility of divinely-given knowledge—once that flower is cut off from the root of revelation—ultimate truth withers and wilts. Then we are left with trends, opinions, preferences, and feelings to build our lives upon. This is shifting sand, and it does not provide a firm foundation on which to build a life or fulfill our God-given purpose.

Reflecting on a longitudinal study of Gen Z's older brothers and sisters (in other words, emerging adults), sociologist Christian Smith made a powerful observation:

> "Very many emerging adults simply don't know how to think about things, what is right, what is deserving for them to devote their lives to. On such matters, they are often simply paralyzed, wishing they could be more definite, wanting to move forward, but simply not knowing how they might possibly know anything worthy of conviction and dedication. Instead, very many emerging adults exist in a state of basic indecision, confusion, and fuzziness. The world they have inherited, as best they can make sense of it, has told them that real knowledge is impossible and genuine values are illusions."[13]

If that was true for the youngest of the Millennials then, it's even more true for Gen Z today. I can certainly affirm this trend in the teens and young adults with whom I regularly interact. Smith goes on to note further:

"It is difficult if not impossible in this world that has come to
be to actually know anything objectively real or true that can
be rationally maintained in a way that might require people
actually to change their minds or lives ...So most simply
choose to believe and live by whatever subjectively feels
"right" to them, and to try not to seriously assess, much less
criticize, anything else that anyone else has chosen to believe,
feel, or do."[14]

One of the most important gifts that the Christian worldview gives
us—from its root system unified in the reality of the Triune God—is
moral and spiritual knowledge (see Col. 2:3). In other words, God's revelation gives us knowledge of what is right or wrong, good or bad, true or
false, and real or illusory. In the absence of this divinely-given knowledge,
Gen Z is left with unanchored emotion and feelings to guide the way. For
a whole host of reasons, this does not work. Do we really want to base
the most important questions of life on how we are feeling from moment
to moment? In order to find our way out of this crisis, we need to better
understand the post-Christian culture in which Gen Z is situated.

Growing Up Post-Christian

We are living in an age of information overload. Unsubstantiated claims
come fast and furious with each swipe of the thumb. Clickbait is winning
the Internet; activist journalism and scholarship are the new normal; and
social media algorithms create ever-increasing ideological echo chambers
sold to the highest bidder.[15] If you don't say the right things fast enough,
you run the risk of getting canceled. And if you say what are deemed
to be the wrong things, well, there seems to be no hope of redemption.
(Keep in mind that we Christians can also be guilty in this regard.) This
new reality creates unprecedented pressure to conform to the spirit of
the age rather than to hold fast to what is true, good, and beautiful. And
it is certainly true that "whoever marries the spirit of this age will find
himself a widower in the next."[16]

In many ways what we are experiencing today has been in the making for a long time. The trajectory was set as certain ideas were accepted and embedded in cultural institutions and artifacts—the timetable for when they would be ultimately and broadly applied in broader culture and dominate the cultural imagination was the only thing still uncertain. The anti-intellectualism of the past century—both inside and outside the church—coupled with some of the more harmful assumptions of post-modernism are converging to overwhelm a general public ruled by feelings and unarmed with the protection that comes from careful thinking and reflection. Unfortunately, discernment is in short supply.

Modernism's misguided quest for 100-percent, absolute, "bomb-proof" certainty in knowledge through reason or experience alone eventually buckled under its own weight. It then gave rise to the postmodern project, with its skepticism toward and often outright rejection of all metanarratives and ideologies—whether science- or faith-based—as merely attempts to gain power and keep control of the masses. The fact that postmodernism is self-contradictory did not stop it from gaining a significant amount of influence.[17]

Scientism, the view that the "sciences alone have the intellectual authority to give us knowledge of reality,"[18] cleared the way for the moral and spiritual relativism we are seeing today. If scientism relegated moral and spiritual knowledge to the realm of blind faith by narrowing all absolute knowledge claims to the sciences, then postmodernism came along and finished the job by replacing objective truth altogether with power dynamics and social location. Sure, there are some exceptions, but this basically describes where we are at today. Scientism cleared the path for postmodernism to overtake many of the disciplines and departments in our universities and captivate the attention of many of the storytellers in Hollywood. Consequently, advocacy for social justice, with its emphasis on power dynamics, defined and understood in secular terms, has become the animating force for a new generation. To be clear, a desire for justice is good and resonates with us all, as humans made in God's image, but the vision for social justice being championed by our larger culture today is at odds with God's vision of justice in significant ways.[19]

Gen Z is now living through a conflicted historical moment where relativism, both individual and cultural, is encountering new and shifting power dynamics that have their own gatekeepers and set of moral absolutes and imperatives. To put it bluntly, the pursuit of objective truth has been replaced by the postmodern pursuit of power for the individual.

In addition, true tolerance is dying as well—a mere shell of its former self. True tolerance affirms that, while all people are equal, all ideas and behaviors are not. Still, you can be friends with and love people with whom you disagree about important questions. This should seem obvious, but in a culture with its feet firmly planted in midair, many have lost the courage to say what is obviously true. And this failure of nerve is leading to disastrous effects. As my colleague and volume contributor John Stonestreet rightly said, "Ideas have consequences and bad ideas have victims."[20]

In this increasingly confused context, we see people attempting to build a good, just—even Christian—society, but doing so based on secular assumptions and categories that do not provide the necessary foundations for moral and spiritual knowledge. The flower has been cut and is dying. People made in God's image are still trying to find the true, the good, and the beautiful; they're just trying to do it without God. As Mark Sayers put it so well, "Post-Christianity is not pre-Christianity; rather post-Christianity attempts to move beyond Christianity, whilst simultaneously feasting upon its fruit."[21]

It is in this wasteland that we are called to make disciples and fulfill the Great Commission (Matt. 28:19–20), and it is this context that is forming the worldviews and shaping the moral and spiritual imagination of a new generation. So what can we do to give Gen Z confidence that moral and spiritual knowledge exist? How can we help them flourish as disciples of Jesus in a post-Christian culture?

Three Approaches that Won't Work

Good intentions do not necessarily lead to good outcomes. Whether in church youth groups, the home, or Christian schools, there are three approaches we know will not produce confidence or conviction in a new generation.

Entertainment

First, entertainment is not enough. Providing fun environments will not ground teenagers and young adults in their faith or keep them from abandoning their faith as they leave the home. As Nancy Pearcey observed, "There's nothing wrong with good clean fun. But the force of sheer emotional experience will not equip teens to address the ideas they will encounter when they leave home and face the world on their own. Young people whose faith is mostly emotional are likely to retain it only as long as it is making them happy. As soon as a difficult crisis comes along, it will evaporate."[22] I am not suggesting we make teenagers miserable for Jesus. However, sin always seems more fun for a season—until the harvest of consequences comes in and its false promises are exposed.

Overprotection

Next, overprotection will not work. We have to take off the bubble wrap. There is no way to keep people from hearing false ideas or encountering people who deeply believe things and live in ways at odds with what is true and God's good design. Not only is this not possible, it's not even good for them, and it certainly won't build resilience.[23] In age-appropriate ways, we need to expose and inoculate people to the false ideas they will be inundated with on a daily basis and train them to interact with those who believe differently than they do with confidence and clarity (see 2 Tim. 2:24–26; Col. 4:4–6).

Blind Faith

Lastly, blind faith is not the answer. When it comes to the word *faith* there is mass confusion both inside and outside the church. Faith has come to mean anything and everything. Unfortunately, the most common assumption is that faith by definition is a blind leap in the dark that is opposed to reason and evidence. As Gen Z comes of age in a post-Christian culture, asking them to have more faith that is detached from reality will not help. They will see the disconnect. Some will hold on longer than others by sheer willpower, but eventually they need to see that what they believe is rational. The Bible is clear that faith is not a substitute for knowledge; it acts on knowledge. The more we know of and about God, the more faith we can exercise. God is pleased with this kind of faith (see Heb. 11:6); and this is the kind of faith we need to pass on to Gen Z disciples.

The Three Rs of Worldview Transformation

Culture is what people come to see as normal, generally without even thinking about it. Whether we realize it or not, forces are at work every second of every day in our society, schools, and screens, shaping us and normalizing various aspects of our culture. As we have seen, there is no way for teenagers—or any of us, for that matter—to grow up in a culture and not be shaped by it. Here is the opportunity and challenge: What is true and good can become normal for a generation, but so can what is false and harmful.

A person's worldview is a web of habit-forming beliefs about the biggest questions of life that helps them make sense of all their experiences. Everyone has a worldview. And as followers of Jesus, we are not to passively allow ourselves to be shaped by our culture. We are not to conform to the ways of this world; we are to be conformed to God's ways and become more like Jesus (see Rom. 8:29; 12:2).

As I have worked with Christian teenagers over the past sixteen years, I have developed a framework that I call the "Three Rs of Worldview Transformation." In order to build a strong and lasting faith, students need *reasons*, *relationships*, and *rhythms*. God, in his providence, will do what he will do, and teenagers will ultimately make their own choices, but these are the things we have the opportunity to influence directly.

Reasons

First, Gen Z needs *reasons* for faith—to know why they believe what they believe (see 1 Pet. 3:15). Apologetics training is not optional.[24] Young people who merely profess an unexamined or ungrounded belief will be easily swamped by the emotional, intellectual, and social challenges they encounter online, in the classroom, and in our culture. J. P. Moreland's observation was spot on when he said:

> Instead of equipping people to understand and meet the world head-on, giving solid reasons for its Christian beliefs, the church has become its own "gravedigger"—the very practices that cause its numbers to rise and its budgets to be met are making the church increasingly anemic and marginalized. What are those practices? We try to "grow the church" by using watered-down, intellectually vacuous, simplistic preaching that is always applied to a parish owner's private life while failing to deal from the pulpit with the broad cultural, intellectual, and moral issues facing us all . . .[25]

Teenagers and young adults need to know that truth exists and is knowable. They need to know why Christianity is true—why it's reasonable to believe that God exists, Jesus was raised from the dead, and the Bible can be trusted as God's Word. There is powerful evidence for each of these claims. Because our culture dismisses the Bible as authoritative, they not only need reasons based in Scripture and the authority of the Bible, but also reasons that don't simply assume "the Bible says so." Both types of reasons are essential to developing a mature and lasting faith (See Rom. 1:19–20; 1 Thess. 2:13).

Moreover, they need to be inoculated against false ideas while they are younger and in environments where we can help them discover reasonable responses to objections to their faith. This requires safe spaces where true tolerance is practiced for them to ask questions and explore doubts. In addition, they need to be trained how to think critically, carefully define terms, and not fall for dismissive slogans. In an age of power plays and cancel culture, this muscle really needs to be developed, along with a healthy dose of encouragement to have the courage to stand out. In short, teenagers need a grown-up worldview, not a coloring-book Jesus. On a personal note, it's so gratifying to see teenagers' confidence grow and their faith come alive when they discover that Christianity is actually true!

Relationships

Next, teenagers need wise *relationships*. The research is clear that Gen Z increasingly feels isolated and alone, but they hunger for real relationships. There are four strategic relationships we can help them cultivate: God, parents, mentors, and friends (see Prov. 13:20). Do they have a growing personal relationship with God (hearing from God in his Word and talking to God in prayer)? So far as is possible, do they have healthy relationships with their parents? Do they have older Christians in their lives who will listen, encourage, coach, and challenge them to pursue Christ during these pivotal years? Do they have some friendship circles where they can belong and also pursue God together (see 2 Tim 2:22)? I am convinced that relationships are the most powerful shaping influence during the teenage years, as their worldview is galvanized in real time, based in part in which groups they experience belonging.

Rhythms

Lastly, students need rhythms to help them practice their faith. We become what we repeatedly do. Gen Z can't build a strong worldview if they never practice it. We must help students ask who they are becoming. Formation of virtue is more than just doing the right thing—it's about becoming the kind of person who loves what is good. Through rhythms and spiritual practices rooted in God's Word, we can indirectly affect our desires, loves, and character (see Heb. 5:14). As C.S. Lewis put it so well, "That is why daily prayers and religious readings and churchgoing are necessary parts of the Christian life. We have to be continually reminded of what we believe …Neither this belief nor any other will automatically remain alive in the mind. It must be fed …."[26] This intentional effort and focus is always to be empowered by the Holy Spirit, motivated by God's grace, and done in the context of community. As a result, these rhythms help shape us over time.

Cultivate Faithfully and Do Not Grow Weary

It can be easy to become discouraged if you only focus on the headlines. But don't give up, because God is at work! I am encouraged by the words of Paul, "So then, dear brothers and sisters, be firm. Do not be moved! Always be outstanding in the work of the Lord, knowing that your labor is not in vain in the Lord" (1 Cor. 15:58). We need to do the hard work of cultivation and have the patience to see the results take root years down the road. We must labor together to recover moral and spiritual knowledge and point to a better way. In this post-Christian context, we have the opportunity to live counterculturally. While the flowers are withering, it is not enough just to acknowledge this reality. We need planters and gardeners for a new generation. Will you join us?

CHAPTER 3

"YOU DO YOU": POSTMODERN RELATIVISM AND GEN Z

Ed Bort and Dana Bort

Recently we were given Andy Andrews's book, *How Do You Kill 11 Million People? Why the Truth Matters More Than You Think*. Intrigued—and who wouldn't be, given that title—we immediately read his brief commentary on political divisiveness and whether it is possible for citizens to find common ground. Although compellingly written and thought-provoking, once we had finished it, it occurred to us that throughout the book he had operated off of one view of truth. Young people today would easily query, perhaps with some skepticism, "Whose truth?"

Written and verbal communication rely on certain meanings associated with the words we use. Often misunderstandings occur, and communication breaks down over unrealized, diverse definitions of the words we are using. We have learned over the years that when someone asks us if we are Christians, we politely ask what they mean by that term before answering. *Christian* can be linked to a particular denomination, occasional church attendance, belief in a God along with some knowledge about Jesus, an oppressive view of the world, or as an aspect of one's familial or regional identity. How sad it is to walk away from a seemingly meaningful conversation only to realize that those conversing were operating on different definitions of the same word! What is more disturbing is the ubiquity of words being used, without clarification, with the intent of creating a hazy atmosphere.

How did we get here? Certain tenets that are indicative of what we now call *postmodernism* have been around for centuries. Yet as a movement, it is much more recent. In order to understand postmodernism, we need to begin with what preceded it, that is, modernism.

What Is Postmodernism?

Postmodernism is extremely challenging to define. The term itself means "after" or "anti" modernism, which we will explain in what follows. In general terms, it holds that no one narrative or account can be trusted to give meaning to all of life, thus it is particularly skeptical of views that make claims to have *the* truth, such as Christianity or science. Given that Christianity provides a story of the nature of human beings and conveys a very robust story of the world, morality, and meaning of human history, postmodernism rejects it. Science is also rejected in its attempt to account for everything in the world. Postmodernism does not necessarily reject truth. What it rejects is any view that claims to have a corner on the truth market. A view that presents an objective truth, "this *is* the way things are," incites the postmodernist to begin looking for holes in that view. She is strongly skeptical of people who speak about truths to which all people must conform. It is easy for Christians to wrongly categorize postmodernists as simple relativists. Typically, they do not believe that everything is relative, but they are against the *totalizing* of truth.

This may seem like an odd distinction, but we think failing to notice it contributes to speaking past each other. A sophisticated postmodernist would agree with a Christian that truths exist in the world. Neither the postmodernist philosophers Jacques Derrida, Jean-François Lyotard, nor Michel Foucault would deny the existence of truth. However, they would argue that it is either very difficult to know the truth or that it is trapped behind the meaning of words that cannot be accessed. Before we get too far down this road, it is important to understand where postmodernism came from in order to understand what it is about.

A Reaction to Modernism

Both *modernism* and *postmodernism* refer to time-defined eras in history, as well as broad views about the world. Modernism began with the Enlightenment, with thinkers such as David Hume and Immanuel Kant, and continued until the late 1950s when it was overtaken by postmodernism. Modernism may be referred to as rationalism, given that was the dominant ideology of that time. The prevailing thought held that, through reason, humanity can create a utopian society by overcoming the atrocities of the world.

We recently came across an excellent example of this. In the Marvel movie *Iron Man 2*, Tony Stark is watching old movies of his dad, Howard, and sees him filming an intro for a forthcoming technology expo. Howard claims, "Everything is achievable through technology—better living, robust health, and for the first time in human history, world peace." This is classic modernity. There is strong confidence in what science can accomplish and optimism about what humanity can achieve. Modernists have a high view of humanity. In their view, given the philosophy of David Hume and the challenge of Darwinian evolution, which provided a story about the origins of the universe that didn't need God, humanity can make things better on its own.

The main tenets or principles of modernism are rationalism, individualism, and scientism. Rationalism is the belief that any acceptable theory or thought must be based on reason and knowledge, as defined by what we can experience by our five senses. Individualism holds that the individual is sovereign and is the authority over knowledge and action. Scientism is the belief that only through the sciences can one truly gain knowledge and have authority. Ironically, this is not a scientific claim but one based in a philosophical assumption about what is and isn't knowable.[1]

Another dominant belief during this era was that knowledge requires a high standard of certainty. This view assumes an extremely high view of what humans are capable of knowing. These thoughts from modernity provided amazing advancements in society, ushered in the industrial revolution, and led to medical breakthroughs due to the aggressive ambitions of people in modernity. However, when thinkers such as Derrida,

Lyotard, and Foucault viewed modernity, they saw oppression and injustice. This leads us to the reaction toward modernity and the launch of post-modernity, that is, postmodernism.

Beyond Modernism

Although it overlapped with modernism, postmodernism began to gain momentum in society in the late 1950s, and it continues to be the governing ideology today. The dominant view within postmodernism is relativism, and more specifically, moral relativism. It is important to remember that within both of these eras, several different worldviews, including Christianity, Islam, empiricism, and others, were competing for dominance. Not all who lived in the era of modernism agreed with all its tenets, just as not everyone today adheres to the precepts of postmodernism. Among the competitors, the one that exerts the most influence over culture becomes dominant. This influence pervades the culture and affects art, architecture, literature, theatre, media, government, and education.

The modern era culminated in multiple wars, including two world wars, the Korean War, and Vietnam. When America dropped the atomic bombs on Hiroshima and Nagasaki, vaporizing an entire culture in minutes, it generated fear that gripped the world. It became clear that, rather than achieving a utopian society, we were destroying our world. The advancement made by the wars of the twentieth century was taking us in the wrong direction. This manifestation of destruction led thinkers such as Derrida, Lyotard, and Foucault to reject notions of ultimate truth. Why? What the world was experiencing was the war to end all wars followed by another gruesome war, leaving tens of millions dead. Society was not improving; people were just getting better at killing those with whom they disagreed or who were in their way. And who are "they"? They were those in power who saw the world through a modernist lens. They were people who believed in an ultimate truth.

For the postmodern thinker, the most compelling reason why a culture would destroy another is because of an adherence to some overarching truth that they believe everyone else must follow in order to reach a utopian state, and they wield power in order to make that happen.

Postmodernism, then, is an attempt to seek justice by eliminating any view of a totalizing truth. Unfortunately, this justice project lacks grounding in a robust and meaningful worldview. Jacques Derrida demonstrated this drive for justice when he said, "deconstruction is justice." Postmodernists have a strong desire for justice. They want to make the world a better place, and in their view, the way to do this is to eliminate the oppression of any and all people groups.

Postmodernism, Justice, and Oppression

We hope you caught the definition of justice—the elimination of oppression. But who gets to define what oppression is? The answer is, the postmodernists do. Ironically, the way many postmodernists go about this project is by silencing any group that disagrees with them. They are not driven by a desire to seek the truth but a desire to end oppression. They oppose people in power who use a metanarrative to dictate what counts as truth with a capital T.

What are postmodern thinkers opposed to? They are opposed to a person or group in power that believes in an ultimate truth of some sort and begins oppressing others, primarily minority groups, into following "their truth." When the postmodern thinker perceives minority groups such as the LGBTQ+ being bullied by the Christian community with the Christian truth—and unfortunately, such bullying does occur, though perhaps not as often as it is perceived—they view it as oppression. Since on the postmodern view we are not able to discern the ultimate truth, they are seeing one dominant worldview bullying a minority group and they cry out to stop the injustice. In their minds, these wars begin with the idea of one overarching truth. This gives some background to the motivations and ideology of postmodernism from a big picture view.

Postmodernism's Problematic Principles

What are the tenets or principles of postmodernism, and why are these principles problematic? When thinking about the tenets of postmodernism it is important to note that there are many views, and it is difficult to capture them all. You might read this chapter and ask, "Why didn't they include X when talking about postmodernism?" Largely, this is due to the nature of the view, that there are many *truths* and not simply the *truth*. A friend once described postmodernism like chasing Jell-O around in a bowl. Just when you think you have it cornered, it wiggles away from the spoon and the chasing begins again.

The basic tenets of postmodernism that we are chasing around the bowl are derived from Derrida, Lyotard, and Foucault. Derrida was not so interested in whether truth exists, but he was concerned about meaning. How did he view meaning? Derrida believed there is no meaning outside of the text. He went to great lengths to explain that words carry meaning, but words must be defined by using other words, and those words are defined by other words, and so on. On this view, the meanings of words change over time, and so the use of language is a living and changing adventure. It's not stable and fixed. For example, the word *gentleman* was once a derogatory term, yet now it is a term describing a man who has a positive influence on society. The same can be said for words such as *tolerance*, *gay*, and many others.

Derrida's point was that to be able to really know what someone is saying or intends to say, one must know the web of historic meaning of that word and all words associated with those words. Thus, it is questionable whether we can know with absolute certainty what someone else is saying. This means right now you are not able to understand definitively what I am intending to say. As the reader, you can only create meaning by interpreting the words you have read. This is a dangerous idea. Why? Truth can no longer be discovered. Rather, it is something that each individual creates. This leads to communities being formed around agreement or adherence to similar ideas and that becomes "their truth." This truth is not grounded in objective reality, but rather in the agreement of the community.

Ironically, Derrida used the French word *différence* to explain this concept with the expectation that the reader can understand it. *Différence* is the idea that we should defer or put off something—namely that we fully understand the truth. He argues that we should realize that the individual only has part of the truth and must defer an ultimate meaning, so it becomes impossible to truly understand an author's intent. If Derrida is right, then truth is not one thing that we discover. Rather, there are many views on a given truth and one person or group of people do not have the truth but, only a viewing of it. While he would agree that the author had thoughts and wrote a book, the meaning for the author stops there. When a reader picks up the book the reader now constructs their viewing of that or those truths. This is the beginning of deconstruction. Why? *Because it leads to the authority of meaning resting with the individual perceiver and not the source.* This opens a Pandora's box because the number of interpretations of texts becomes relative to the number of readings of the text, and ultimate truth is lost. A biblical worldview holds that when we read a book, we are trying to understand the author's meaning or intended meaning, and we can actually get to the author's intended meaning. This is authorial intent.

A second important concept when thinking about Derrida is *logocentrism*. It simply means that the individual is the ultimate authority of truth for herself, because the individual is in control of her thought, speech, writings, and, more importantly, the meaning of them all. *Différence* is the idea that ultimate meaning must be deferred and not settled on. *Logocentrism* is the idea that individuals are the authority to meaning.

A final concept to understand in postmodern thought is that truth is not discovered; it is created. To be more exact, meaning is not discovered but created from within the individual.

In short, the three tenets of postmodernism are as follows: 1) that there are no ultimate truths that we can fully understand, 2) the individual is his or her own authority on meaning and truth, and 3) truth and meaning are created, not discovered. To end our account of postmodernism, Lyotard's contribution must be considered as it is an important one. Lyotard primarily attacked ideas that a metanarrative exists, arguing that there is not one narrative, but there are many narratives. Although these thoughts can be seen from Derrida's work, Lyotard was the main thinker undermining the idea of an overarching metanarrative.

Can Anything Good Come from Postmodernism?

Turning from the negatives of postmodernism, let's address some of the good and healthy ways that postmodernism has benefited humanity, beginning with the concepts of epistemic humility and soft skepticism. First, *epistemic humility* is the understanding that, as a human person, I do not have all knowledge, and even collectively, we will not exhaust knowledge. This is freeing and encourages collaboration, as we naturally learn from one another. It also is a benefit in that one does not need to know something with certainty in order to truly know it. The unrealistically high standard of certainty is brought to a proper place where one can have knowledge of something without having to be certain of it or know all things about that topic. It allows for us to continue learning and being open to learning more about the world or people.

This leads to the second benefit, which is encouraging *soft skepticism*. What we mean by soft skepticism is having a curious mind that asks appropriate questions with the intent to seek truth. *Hard skepticism*, on the other hand, is requiring absolute certainty of knowledge in order to know something, which can lead to doubting all or most things, especially if its source is another person. Doubting itself need not be all bad. In his book, *God in the Dark*, Os Guinness explored different kinds of doubt, how doubt is helpful, and the best way forward when we encounter doubt.

Not everything about postmodernism is bad. It corrects some of the extremes of modernism and provides benefits such as knowing without the high standard of certainty and the encouragement of developing a curious mind.

Three Harmful Ideas

Despite some helpful corrections to radical modernist thinking, there are three destructive ideas stemming from postmodernism that must be overcome in order to achieve a healthy and accurate worldview. These are the destruction of (1) ultimate truth claims, (2) moral knowledge, and (3) authority.

Earlier, we addressed the deconstruction of truth in the description of the origination of postmodernism. Deconstructing truth claims is dangerous because it leads to the conclusion that truth does not exist or that truth is completely subjective.

This naturally extends to the second harmful idea—the destruction of moral knowledge. When truth claims are deconstructed, then all moral statements are reduced to statements about what people think or believe. This means that statements such as "rape is evil" are reduced to "I don't like rape." There is no room in the postmodern framework that allows for the overarching claim that all rape is evil at all times, in all places, and in every instance. The postmodern worldview is lacking the necessary structure to bear the weight of this statement.

When you begin to compile the list of atrocities that the postmodern worldview is unable to accurately account for, it quickly becomes unlivable. Here is a short list: murder, adultery, pedophilia, sex trafficking, slavery, and oppression. Where would postmodernists be without their drive toward justice that must have the oppression of people to fuel it? You see, oppression gets reduced as well. It is reduced to the claim, "I don't like oppression," but it can never actually be wrong or evil. Talk about sawing off the limb you are sitting on! A robust worldview will be able to distinguish between truths that are objective and are true regardless of the individual and truths that are subjective.

Subjective truths exist and are easily understood when we consider things such as taste. It is true that I think Blue Bell's Butternut Crunch ice cream is the best. When I say it is "the best," I'm making a true statement about my subjective tastes or preferences for a certain kind of ice cream. It does not follow that everyone else must think the same or have the same preference. It is a truth about the subject (me), but it does not follow that it is true about everyone in the world.

By way of contrast, an *objective truth* is a claim that is true at all times and in all situations. For example, "torturing babies for fun is wrong" is a morally objective statement that is true at all times and in all situations. What makes this statement objectively true? Given a Christian worldview, where a wholly good, omnipotent, and omniscient Being (God) created all of space, time, and matter with purpose and meaning, that being is in position to say what is morally acceptable and what is not. Those moral statements become objectively true for all creation. Why? Because, by God's design, it is true for all human beings in all times and in all situations. These moral truths are not open to preferences by individuals.

A third destructive idea that comes with postmodernism that must be overcome is the deconstruction of authority. When hard skepticism is heightened, the intent is to cause doubt, and accepting the thought that nobody has the truth leads to an undercutting of authority. Clearly, there are both good and bad authority figures. What makes one good and one bad? A different approach says that a good authority seeks to make wise choices that work toward the ultimate good of the people they are leading. The good authority knows where we are going and how to get there. They have the power to remove obstacles and do what they promise. They also have a genuine desire to do what is good for others. On the other hand, a bad authority seeks to use authority for selfish gain or to harm those being led. History is replete with multiple examples of both.

The Importance of Truth

First, a few broad introductory comments about the misconceptions of truth are needed.[2] The primary terms used in the Old Testament and New Testament for truth are 'emet and alētheia, which together convey the idea of faithfulness and conformity to fact. Faithfulness is exemplified when a person acts according to her word, manifesting genuineness and integrity. Throughout Scripture, truth is ascribed to propositional statements. In Isaiah 45:19, God stated, "I the LORD speak the truth; I declare what is right" (NIV). Proverbs 12:17 addresses truth in contrast, "The faithful witness tells what is right, but a false witness speaks deceit." Jesus declared himself to be truth (see John 14:6) and ensured that knowledge of the truth sets one free (see John 8:32). These are but a few of hundreds of verses that can only be understood on an objective view of truth.

Disparate understandings of truth yield significant confusion. While the objectivist holds that truth is discovered, the relativist holds a claim to be true if he or the group accepts it, thus it is created. Considering the relationship between the nature of truth and the three fundamental laws of logic provides a clarifying standard. First, the law of identity says that A is identical to itself and different from other things. Second, the law of noncontradiction says that A cannot be both true and false in the same sense at the same time. Someone cannot be legally be married and single at the same time. Third, the law of the excluded middle says that A is either true or false, that either A or its negation, not-A, is true. It is important to note that these laws say nothing about one's ability to verify the truth of A. If my son is unable to hear the doorbell because he has his gaming headset on, it in no way discounts the fact that the doorbell is ringing, only that he is hindered from hearing it. Absolute truth conforms to three fundamental laws of logic.

For at least two reasons, those who hold to an absolute view of truth have the upper hand on the nature of truth. One, by its very nature, relativism itself is either true or it is false in the absolutist sense. If it is true that relativism is true, then it is self-refuting. If it is false that relativism is true, then it is merely an expression of preference.

Relativism confuses truth claims in various ways. A nature show we recently watched featured an animal called a guanaco. Although we had been completely oblivious to the existence of that llamalike creature prior to seeing this show, the animal had been in existence for a long time. Equating *what is* (ontology) with *how we know what is* (epistemology) generates a great deal of confusion. As our example shows, a thing can exist without any recognition of that thing's existence.

What Is Truth?[3]

A robust biblical worldview of truth will prioritize correspondence theory. Simply stated, the correspondence theory of truth says that "a proposition is true in just the case it corresponds to reality, when what it asserts to be the case is the case."[4] Truth is a matching relationship between a person's thought and reality. When the thought correctly matches reality, you have truth. As seen previously, Scripture consistently recognizes some form of the correspondence theory of truth as well as contrasts truth with lies or deceit. It requires a truth-bearer, the truth-maker, and the correspondence relationship between the two. The *truth-bearer* is a proposition that is true or false, such as, "the current time is six o'clock." The *truth-maker* is the set of facts or state of affairs that render the proposition true, namely that the time on my computer shows 6:00 p.m. The proposition about the time being six o'clock either does or does not adhere to the actual state of affairs. This historically predominant view of the nature of truth assumes there is an objective reality that is accessible to human beings. It does not mean that we can know the truth about everything, but it does mean that there is a tight connection between truth claims and the way things really are.

Postmodernism's Influence on Gen Z

The influence postmodernism holds on Gen-Z runs vast and deep. While it is beyond the brevity of this chapter to adequately address the majority of them, three in particular stand out: (1) truth, (2) morality and values, and (3) identity.

How does Gen Z view truth? According to the Barna Group's report, "For many teens, truth seems relative at best and, at worst, altogether unknowable. Their lack of confidence is on pace with the broader culture's all-out embrace of relativism."[5] While not surprising, this is deeply concerning and inconsistent, especially for those who are content to live consistently with the physical laws of the universe. Is gravity true? Is the medicine we take for a headache what the bottle claims it is? The way physical laws of the universe operate and pharmaceutical labels are among many claims that are verifiable and thus not relative. The abundant confusion experienced by this generation is evidenced in this statement from a focus group participant: "There is no such thing as truth, but there are facts. People can believe whatever truth they want. [There is] always room for truth to change."[6] *Truth* in this statement is so nebulous it is hard to know where to begin. What might you say to this young person?

There is a gaping divide between Gen Z as a whole and a thorough-going biblical worldview on how to know what is true, especially in light of the former questioning if there even is such a thing. The fact that they experience uneasiness with the relationship between science and the Bible, as almost half identify with needing factual evidence to support their beliefs, is both challenging and encouraging. The challenge for us as we work with Gen Z is to deepen our own understanding of the relationship between science and the Bible and refuse to let that intimidate us or yield to the temptation to oversimplify.[7] As for encouragement, their stated desire to have evidence to support their beliefs, or verification, indicates that in spite of their confusion they are still seeking truth.

Recognition of the interrelatedness between truth and morality surfaced in the concluding section of the Barna Group report: "It's conceivable, even likely, that the relativism ascendant in Gen Z is based less on a general deficit of moral values and more on thin, insufficient ideas about what truth is and how to find it. More broadly, buying in to scientism and hostility toward religion doesn't so much prove the failure of Christian belief and ways of knowing, as it reveals careless, unexamined assumptions about knowledge and truth."[8]

When one-quarter of Gen Z strongly agrees that what is morally right and wrong changes over time based on society, our first response tends to be one of shock and even fear. Additionally, the fact that only 34 percent of Gen Z agrees that lying is morally wrong can have the same effect.

How Should We Engage Gen Z?

We need to be aware of the Babylon in which we live. None of us lives and operates in the culture around us unscathed. Yet we would be fools to ignore the invitation to explore what they mean by their answers and for what reasons they hold them. Engaging in conversations about the relationship between truth and morality, as well as how to discern between objective and contextual truth, can bring much needed understanding that leads to freedom. We believe the concepts in this chapter have been largely lost with Gen Z, and we need to give attention to teaching and discussing these ideas with them.

Sexuality, in particular, is a hotbed of controversy and confusion as some of the other contributors to this volume point out. Gen Z tends to hold more liberal views on issues of sexuality and are generally opposed to challenging the beliefs of others. Given the rapidly changing landscape about sexual identity, particularly in the last couple of decades, this comes as no surprise. Thinking through and discussing these issues can be very difficult and painful, yet it is also very needed to engage with their ambivalence and hyper-attentiveness to their public image.

Guiding Gen Z to discover truth and understand the nature of morality and values will inevitably lead them back to the question of their core identity. Who am I? Who or what defines who I am and how I see myself? These are crucial questions, especially in this day of hyper social media. If a young person seeks her identity from what others think about her, she is at the mercy of the group, class, or social media mob of the day. Anxiety and depression are on the rise among Gen Z due to the pressure of maintaining a certain self-image. Identity can never be anchored this way, because people change their minds all the time, and they are also wondering about their own identity.

Scripture is very clear that every human being is made in the image of God, which is what gives every one of us dignity (see Gen. 1:27; 5:1–2.). A bedrock value in social justice fields, such as human rights or racial reconciliation, is that humans have dignity. But when activists are probed as to why, what is their answer? Their answer will derive from the worldview from which they live. For believers, this is just the starting point. God has said much about who we are and how we should live, but the question remains if we trust him as the ultimate authority and live in the light of his revelation.

DISCIPLESHIP FOR A DIGITAL GENERATION: CULTIVATING A HOLISTIC WORLDVIEW THROUGH A SYNTHESIS OF TRUTH, NARRATIVE, AND THE AFFECTIONS

Nathan A. Finn

The Case for a Holistic Model

A few weeks ago, my glasses began to bother me a little bit. Like many people who wear glasses, I still keep a couple of older pairs in my bedside drawer, just in case there is an emergency. My previous pair were replaced only about eighteen months ago, so I decided to wear them for a couple of days. This turned out to be a terrible idea. Everything was just a little bit blurry, especially if the room was a tad too dark, a smidge too bright, or anything in between. The problem is that my older glasses are a slightly different prescription than my current glasses. It isn't a very big difference. But the variance is just enough to distort my perception of the world around me. I returned to my newer glasses and all is right with the world.

Glasses or spectacles are commonly used as an analogy to help us understand the concept of worldview. One recent textbook defines a worldview as "the conceptual lens through which we see, understand, and interpret the world and our place within it."[1] Everyone has a worldview, even if you are ignorant of it, don't think much about it, take it totally for granted, or just ignore it completely. Your worldview is always there, informing how you make sense of everything. If your worldview is on point, then you see things pretty clearly. But if something about your worldview is wonky, then your vision of life becomes distorted, much like wearing a pair of glasses with the wrong prescription.

Our goal as Christians should be to conform our innate worldviews to the biblical worldview. This is not something that happens naturally. In fact, it begins supernaturally when we become new creations in Christ (see 2 Cor. 5:17) whose minds are transformed (see Rom. 12:2). Our regeneration is the beginning of our worldview reset. As we follow Christ as his disciples (see Matt. 16:24), grow in godliness (see Col. 1:9–10), and are conformed increasingly to his image (see Rom. 8:29), our worldview reflects the biblical worldview more and more. We learn to think rightly about God and his world for the sake of living rightly before God in his world.

Every generation in every culture embraces worldview assumptions that are simply "in the air" and taken for granted. Because of the distorting power of sin, many of these assumptions are twisted at best and openly antithetical to the biblical worldview at worst. Every unbiblical world-view needs to be confronted with the biblical worldview, both in the lives of individuals and in the public marketplace of ideas. Worldview trans-formation is a key component of authentic discipleship and is crucial for Christ-centered cultural engagement.

This aim of this chapter is to help ministry leaders think about how to pass on the biblical worldview to Gen Z followers of Jesus Christ. I will begin with an overview of the Gen Z worldview based primarily upon the 2018 study published by the Barna Group and the Impact 360 Institute.[2] Then I will survey three competing ways of thinking about the biblical worldview that, when rightly understood, are really comple-mentary perspectives. Finally I will show how a synthesis of these three approaches leads to a holistic understanding of the biblical worldview that challenges the fragmented, digital worldview of Gen Z.

Worldview Assumptions of Gen Z

According to research conducted by the Barna Group in partnership with the Impact 360 Institute, Gen Z defaults to a worldview that is highly inclusive and individualistic. They emphasize diversity and want to be perceived as open-minded. They value the feelings and experiences of themselves and others. They are hesitant to make exclusive claims about right and wrong.[3] Gen Z is the "you be you" generation. What is right for me might not be right for you, but that is okay, because variety is the spice of life. What matters most is authenticity. This worldview is digital, fragmented, and decidedly post-Christian.

At least six trends contribute to the Gen Z worldview.[4] I'll call these the six worldview assumptions of Gen Z. The first is that they live their lives on their screens: computers, tablets, and especially smartphones. Their public identities are carefully constructed, meticulously curated, and intentionally promoted via social media. Some have trouble making meaningful, real-life connections. The hours of screen time often contribute to a heightened sense of loneliness and depression. Because their relationships revolve around screens, they evidence less interest in learning to drive and are often ambivalent about dating—two phenomena that older generations often find baffling. This worldview assumption is so prevalent that Jean Twenge refers to Gen Z as the iGen in her informative (and often troubling) book of that title.[5]

The second worldview assumption is a post-Christian view of life. Only 4 percent of Gen Z has a biblical worldview as defined by Barna. While observers have discussed the rise of the religious "nones" for more than a decade, the rate of atheism among Gen Z is double that of the national average. But unlike many older atheists, Gen Z often does not actively reject the existence of the biblical God so much as they assume a universe devoid of the supernatural. Many of them have limited exposure even to cultural forms of Christianity. As James Emery White argues, "The most defining characteristic of Generation Z is that it is arguably the first generation in the West (certainly in the United States) that will have been raised in a post-Christian-context. As a result, it is the first post-Christian generation."[6]

A desire to avoid all that is bad, negative, scary, or unsafe is a third Gen Z worldview assumption. Theirs is a world of safe spaces, trigger warnings, and hate speech. They don't like to have their feelings hurt or cause offense, and thus they tend to be reticent about taking hard stands on controversial issues (or appreciate it when others do so). In many ways, the first commandment of Gen Z is, "Thou shalt not offend." They embrace what an older generation considered political correctness and are not afraid to "cancel" those whose contrary opinions are deemed out of step with what is considered appropriate by mainstream shapers of culture. While evidence shows Gen Z is less inclined to be sexually active at a young age, use illicit drugs, smoke, or drink alcohol underage, they are not socially conservative by conviction. They are simply slower to embrace adult decisions (even rebellious ones) than their generational predecessors.

Ironically, a fourth worldview assumption is a concern that genuine safety and security is a myth, leading some to note that Gen Z sees the present moment as a complex, anxious age.[7] Gen Z has an affinity for the dystopian, having come of age in a world of financial recession, the opioid crisis, the War on Terror, racial injustice, resurgent white nationalism, global threats to cybersecurity, and uncertainties about gender identity and sexuality. There is a reason Gen Z gravitates to post-apocalyptic novels and shows about zombies or oppressive future regimes. Gen Z is not an optimistic generation that believes the world is gradually getting better.

Fifth, Gen Z places great value on diversity. They suspect white male heterosexuals have too much influence in culture and are sensitive to oppression of minority groups and suppression of alternative opinions. Many members of Gen Z hail from multi-ethnic homes, so they often resonate with superheroes such as Wonder Woman and Black Panther who break from white male stereotypes. They have come of age during a time when progressive advocacy groups pressure studios to include a certain number of LGBTQ+ characters and storylines in their shows. It is common to reject (or at least question) binary understandings of gender and to experiment with more than one sexual identity. Homosexual marriage has been legal in the USA for over half of their lives.

Finally, as my colleague Stephanie Shackelford argues in her chapter of this volume, Gen Z has been raised in contexts where their parents evidence a peculiar mix of overprotectiveness and underprotectiveness. On the one hand, parents try to solve their children's problems, determine their hobbies, and map out their academic and vocational futures, hindering independence and initiative. As a university chief academic officer, I get to witness this sort of parental overprotectiveness first-hand on a fairly regular basis! On the other hand, parents provide few boundaries related to screens. As Twenge and other observers note, this results in an unhealthy obsession with social media, an unhealthy amount of time spent consuming digital media, such as video streaming and gaming, and the ubiquity of pornography and threat of cyberbullying among Gen Z. While an older generation of parents might have worried that their kids' friends were undermining their vision for child-rearing, the parents of Gen Z should be more concerned about the detrimental effects of screens.

Gen Z is a fragmented, anxious, post-Christian generation. They live their lives between the fake, or at least artificial, world of screens and the real, or at least embodied, world around them. They desire safety and security, but fear there is no such thing. They love diversity, but not a genuine pluralism where every idea—including ideas with which they disagree—is given a fair shake. They live in a world devoid of the supernatural and enchantment but are drawn to apocalyptic narratives. They believe they are empowered sexually, but in practice, the prevalence of pornography has actually led to fewer teens having sex with one another. They want to be independent thinkers who make a difference, but they want their parents to be close by to protect them while they do so and catch them if they fall. Such is the worldview of Gen Z.

Three Approaches to the Biblical Worldview

Worldview language originated in nineteenth-century German idealism before it was imported into Christian circles around the turn of the twentieth century through the writings of theologians Abraham Kuyper and

James Orr.[8] Postwar evangelical scholars such as Gordon Clark and Carl Henry promoted worldview thinking among evangelical pastors and theologians, while Francis Schaeffer helped to popularize the concept among Christian college students during the Vietnam era. By the 1980s, there were two different approaches to the biblical worldview.

The first approach emphasizes the importance of propositional truth claims in the development of a biblical worldview. These writers tend to write from a more philosophical perspective that is concerned with countering false worldviews with truth claims that are rooted in Scripture. They tend to be deeply concerned with apologetics and cultural engagement, and they value the role of logical consistency and rational coherence. Many worldview thinkers who emphasize the importance of truth are particularly concerned about postmodernism, especially deconstructionist versions that reject metanarratives or claims of absolute truth.

James Sire is one of the key authors to write from this perspective. Sire served as the longtime editor of InterVarsity Press in the USA. In his 1976 book, *The Universe Next Door*, Sire offered an overview of the Christian worldview and contrasted it with seven other rival worldviews. He followed up this work with a 2004 volume titled, *Naming the Elephant: Worldview as a Concept*. In each book and their subsequent revisions, Sire developed a list of basic worldview questions based on what one believes to be true of the world.

1. What is prime reality—the really real?
2. What is the nature of external reality, that is, the world around us?
3. What is a human being?
4. What happens to a person at death?
5. Why is it possible to know anything at all?
6. How do we know what is right and wrong?
7. What is the meaning of human history?[9]

Wheaton College philosopher Arthur Holmes is another author who popularized this approach to a Christian worldview. Holmes was especially keen to apply the biblical worldview to Christian higher education in his 1985 book, *The Making of the Christian Mind*. Largely because of Sire and Holmes, the importance of the Christian worldview has become one of the animating ideas within evangelical colleges and universities.

Two other works from this perspective are worthy of note. The first book is coauthored by my colleague, J.P. Moreland, who supplied a compelling foreword for this volume. *Philosophical Foundations of a Christian Worldview*, which J.P. co-authored with William Lane Craig, was first published in 2003 and revised in 2009. Moreland and Craig are two of the most influential philosophers and apologists among evangelicals today. They identified the biblical worldview with an explicitly Christian approach to philosophy. A second work, *Making Sense of Your World*, was first published in 1996 and revised in 2008. The authors treated the concept of worldview as synonymous with a "philosophy of life" and included both beliefs about certain truth claims (the biblical view of) and the faithful application of those beliefs to particular issues (the biblical view for).[10]

A second approach to the Christian worldview became popular in the 1980s as an alternative to accounts that were considered overly philosophical. Many of the key writers identified with the Dutch Reformed tradition and focused upon the role the grand narrative of Scripture plays in shaping a biblical worldview. For these writers, the biblical narrative is "the true story of the world" that frames how we understand our own individual stories, as well as the various cultural narratives around us.[11] Proponents believe this approach is arguably more amenable to a postmodern context, since people often resonate more with stories than they do propositions.

The pioneer of this line of thinking was Al Wolters, a Canadian philosopher and Bible scholar whose 1985 book, *Creation Regained*, offered a "reformational worldview," building upon the biblical narrative of creation, fall, and redemption. Following the Kuyperian tradition's emphasis on the lordship of Christ over all things, Wolters focused his attention on how the biblical worldview leads to faithful engagement with culture. More recently, Reformed theologians Michael Goheen and Craig Bartholomew have teamed up to write two books that expanded on Wolters approach and put it in dialogue with the writings of Bible scholar N.T. Wright and missiologist Lesslie Newbigin. In *The Drama of*

Scripture (2004), Goheen and Bartholomew divided the biblical narrative into six acts that expanded upon Wolters's earlier paradigm and discussed how this narrative shapes a biblical worldview. In their follow-up book, *Living at the Crossroads* (2008), Goheen and Bartholomew more explicitly applied that biblical worldview to cultural engagement.

Some worldview authors recognized that a combination of propositional truth claims and an emphasis on the biblical narrative is helpful in understanding the biblical worldview. In 1984, Brian Walsh and Richard Middleton authored *The Transforming Vision: Shaping a Christian World View*. Walsh, a Reformed theologian, and Middleton, a Wesleyan scholar, contrasted the biblical world with the modern world, drew upon the narrative of Scripture, and sketched out an outline of a Christ-centered philosophy. In 1999, Charles Colson and Nancy Pearcey combined philosophy, the biblical narrative, and contemporary and historical anecdotes in *How Now Shall We Live?* Pearcey followed up with her 2004 book, *Total Truth*, which was weighted more toward philosophical arguments, while still taking narrative into account. In the case of all three books, the emphasis was upon application to Christian cultural engagement.

In more recent years, philosopher James K.A. Smith has challenged both approaches to the Christian worldview for being overly focused on how we think and not enough on how we feel. Following classical Christian thinkers such as Augustine and Thomas Aquinas, Smith argued that humans are directed by their loves more than they are directed by their brains. As such, our worldview speaks to our desires as much as it does our convictions. We are worshiping creatures whose affections are formed by our habits. Smith laid out his proposal across the three volumes of his Cultural Liturgies series (2009–2017), while he offered a more lay-oriented summary of his views in the 2016 book, *You Are What You Love: The Spiritual Power of Habit*.[12] Smith's views are still being assessed and processed by scholars of Christian worldview thinking. However, at least one recent textbook, the multi-authored *An Introduction to Christian Worldview: Pursuing God's Perspective in a Pluralistic World* (2017), attempts to take his perspective into account.

Cultivating a Holistic Biblical Worldview

In recent decades, missiologists have argued for the value of contextualization when it comes to communicating the gospel to various people groups. As Timothy Tennent argues, "The historic deposit of the gospel is unchanging, but contextualization acknowledges the need to 'translate' the message into forms that are meaningful and applicable to peoples in their separate cultural settings in such a way that the original message and impact of the gospel is communicated."[13] I would suggest this principle applies to worldview formation among Gen Z. Gen Z believers need to be discipled in a way that meets them where they are and helps them to follow Christ faithfully in the context of the particular challenges their generation faces.

In the previous section, I discussed the three different approaches to the biblical worldview among those who have written on the topic. While the stakeholders in those debates sometimes have a vested interest in the reception and application of their particular paradigms, I suggest they should be seen as complementary rather than competing. Furthermore, when they are synthesized into a more holistic, "thick" understanding of the biblical worldview, they address the various worldview assumptions of Gen Z in a way that makes the gospel and its implications understandable and, ultimately, transformative. This thick understanding of the biblical worldview simultaneously gets the facts straight (propositional truth claims), tells a better story (the grand biblical narrative), and reorients human desires (affective habits). For the sake of space, I will apply this holistic biblical worldview paradigm to two topics prominent in Gen Z worldview assumptions: screens and sexuality.

As discussed, a screen-centered existence is often identified as the single most defining feature of Gen Z. Confronting this worldview assumption can be a challenge, especially when many parents and ministry leaders struggle with at least some of the same addictions and temptations as the young people whom they are discipling.[14] However, a holistic biblical worldview can help lead Gen Z toward a more rightly ordered understanding of screens and their place in the world.

Gen Z needs to get the facts straight about screens. Digital realities, whether on social media or in a video game, are just that—simulated reproductions of real life. Screens are an artificial, if often meaningful, construct invented by humans that exist within the real world of created by God. As such, how one relates to others in embodied relationships is a better gauge of character than whatever virtues are being signaled in a simulation, though, of course, the two are related. Furthermore, God is truth, and he created us to value what is true. Screens complicate our ability to discern truth from falsehood. This could be as insidious as so-called fake news intended to deceive or as mundane as the teenager on Instagram who creates the impression that her life is a modern-day fairy tale.

Gen Z also needs to hear a better story than what a grand digital narrative can provide. People are more than the sum of their social media presence. They look to their screens for relationships, when in reality they are created in God's image and intended to be in a covenant relationship with the Creator and Lord of all things. This relationship, entered into by grace through faith in Jesus Christ, in turn redeems and reframes every other relationship, whether in person, online, or both. Also, while the misuses of science can be scary, and though such misuse is evidence of the fall, science is part of God's creation, and it is good. We need not despair over the fictitious, apocalyptic scenarios depicted in the digital media we stream, but rather we can have hope that everything that is broken will be redeemed because of the perfect life, atoning death, victorious resurrection, and triumphant future return of Jesus Christ. There is a *telos* to this world that is better than any Hollywood screenwriter could dream up on his own.

Gen Z also needs to have their screen-driven desires reoriented. The facts and the story are reinforced by redeemed habits that are consistent with and confirm the biblical worldview. The spiritual discipline of fasting could be applied to digital media so that there are times of the day, days of the week, or seasons of the year where one unplugs from screen usage. Perhaps a student ministry could encourage teenagers to fast from screens on Sundays or to give up social media during Lent. While Bible apps are a wonderful resource for gospel proclamation and the promotion of biblical literacy, Gen Z believers might benefit from cultivating the habit of using a physical Bible in their personal devotions and corporate worship gatherings as a way to put their smartphone aside and allow Scripture to speak to them from outside of their screens. Such habits serve as earthy reminders that embodiment matters, and screens, though an important part of our world, are not ultimate.[15]

Another defining feature of Gen Z is a more fluid understanding of gender and sexuality. Gen Z has come of age in a world of transgendered celebrities, rejections of a binary understanding of gender, the promotion of homosexual cultural icons, and legalized homosexual marriage. Again, a holistic biblical worldview has much to say to Gen Z (and others) about these cultural phenomena.

Gen Z needs to get the facts straight about gender. Scripture teaches, and science confirms, that there are only two genders: male and female. Scripture teaches, and science confirms, that the only natural way for humans to procreate is through sexual intercourse between a man and a woman. Scripture teaches that the marriage relationship is intended for one man and one woman, ideally for life, while both history and social science confirm that stable, traditional marriages are the best for children and for the overall flourishing of a society.[16] Scripture teaches that one's gender is determined, and while the misuse of science would suggest otherwise, surgeries and hormones do not change one's gender, but rather suppresses evidence of such.

Gen Z also needs to hear a better story than the grand sexual narrative. The marriage relationship is a creation ordinance the predates the fall. Marriage between a man and a woman is an embodied picture of the gospel. Sex was created by God, has been distorted by sin, but has been redeemed by Jesus Christ. Many people experience phenomena such as gender dysphoria and homosexual attraction, including some who are trying to follow Christ faithfully. But these tragic experiences are effects of the fall that have been redeemed through the finished work of Christ. Gen Z believers who struggle with gender dysphoria and homosexual attraction have been freed from the power of sin and one day they will be freed from its presence. People are more than their sexual desires.

To that end, Gen Z needs to experience a reorienting of their sexual desires. Though the context for Gen Z's struggles is unique, their temptations are not new. Young people have always struggled with their sexuality. One of the costs of discipleship will always be embracing a sexual ethic that reflects the facts and is reflected in the biblical narrative. Students should be encouraged to understand sex to be a wonderful blessing from God, but this blessing should be reserved for marriage. Abstinence should be defined holistically as refraining from masturbation, copulation, and activities that are intended to result in copulation. Sex and screens are often entwined in the digital worldview, so one reason Gen Z should be taught to use screens properly is to protect themselves from pornography and online sexual predators. Students should be encouraged to memorize Scripture, have open and frank conversations with parents and ministry leaders about sexuality, and establish accountability relationships with other believers who are pursuing sexual virtue in a hyper-sexualized culture.

In conclusion, these two case studies are intended to spur careful reflection and faithful action about all of Gen Z's worldview assumptions. The task of worldview renovation and formation will always be an important aspect of discipleship. Embracing a thick approach to the biblical worldview will help Gen Z to navigate the complexities and anxieties of the digital age and be "blameless and pure, children of God without blemish though [they] live in a crooked and perverse society, in which [they] shine as lights in the world" (Phil. 2:15).

PART TWO
BE

Be Transformed in Your Character

Discover your identity in Christ and your
God-given calling in authentic community.

CHAPTER 5

DEFINING AND ORDERING LOVE

John Stonestreet

The Greatest Commandment and Our Fundamental Identity

The greatest commandment, Jesus said, is to love. The entire Law and the Prophets "depend on," first, loving God with heart and mind and soul and strength, and second, loving our neighbor as ourselves (see Matt. 22:36–40). With this definitive answer to a legal questioner, Jesus clarified that God's extensive instructions for his Old Testament people were, in fact, means to a greater end. That the commandment to love is elevated by Christ in this way reflects, not only what God expects of us, but also a fundamental truth about the kind of creatures humans are. Members of Gen Z know, at some level, that we as humans have natures that are fundamentally different from animals or machines. What fewer of them affirm than older generations, however, is a thoroughgoing biblical worldview that says we are *imago Dei*—made in the image of God—the only created beings in the universe endowed as such by the Creator.[1] As his image bearers, our relationship with God is of a different kind than that of anything else in the created order, even the angels. They, we are told, "long to catch a glimpse of" these things (1 Pet. 1:12). The purpose of this chapter is to help disciplers of Gen Z understand how the *imago Dei* and ordered loves are related, and why that relationship is important in coming alongside members of Gen Z.

Created to Know God

In his *Confessions*, St. Augustine described his own journey to God through a variety of exploits and philosophies, "You have made us for yourself, O God, and our hearts are restless until they find their rest in You" (1.1.1). Human restlessness—our curiosity about why we exist and who we are—is both a distinguishing mark of the human condition and a revealing clue about the answers we seek. Human curiosity starts small, about shapes and faces and voices, but expands to the existential as we mature, to questions concerning the meaning of the universe and our place in it. Eventually, not even the most amazing projects of human creativity or the most astounding realities of creation can ultimately satisfy what Blaise Pascal famously called "the God-shaped hole" in every human heart. Only God himself can.

The dramatic rise of the so-called "deaths from despair," especially in the time of the COVID-19 pandemic and especially among Gen Zers, reveal how dangerous perpetually restless hearts can be, if they fail to find what they seek.[2] Meaninglessness is, indeed, a "pre-existing condition" that is exacerbated by times of disruption, isolation, and disconnection. The majority of British young people, for example, considered life meaningless, even before the pandemic stole employment, human contact, and many of culture's distractions.[3] For too many young people in 2020, COVID was a comorbidity that worsened an already potentially deadly underlying condition.

That we were made for God is, then, more than a matter of personal inspiration, religious preference, or even mental health. It is matter of our fundamental identity as human beings. Even then, we were made to not only know about God, but to know God himself. That God has gone to such great lengths to make himself known, not just what he wants but—in Scripture and in Christ Jesus—who he is, is a distinctive of a Christian worldview and reveals something fundamental and profound. God clearly wants to be known. If he didn't want to be known, the greatest commandment would be nonsensical.

Instead, the greatest commandment makes good sense. By loving God and our neighbor, we not only fulfill God's expectations for us, we also become, in a sense, more human. To love God is not only to know him; it is to know ourselves. Because it is the truest reflection of who we are, and not just a personally helpful slogan, the greatest commandment is the only adequate starting point for Christian education. Whether for the home, for the church, or for the school, upon these two commandments hang every Christian educational endeavor that is truly Christian. Helping Gen Zers behave, believe, and learn, while important, are only means to helping them love as God created them to love.

The Problem with Love

A crucial battle for the heart and mind of any individual or any society is over the definition of words. "The most dangerous ideas in any society," says a quote often attributed to C.S. Lewis, "are not the ones that are argued, but the ones that are assumed." Definitions, especially ones that go unchallenged, effectively smuggle ideas into hearts and minds, and eventually shape the cultural imagination.

Often in a pluralistic culture such as ours, Christians will use the same *vocabulary* as everyone else but not the same *dictionary*.[4] Though *love* is used ubiquitously across so much of culture, it is rarely defined. To fulfill the greatest commandment, we must first know what love is. This is not a given in a world where silly slogans such as "love is love" have largely won the day, controlling both the cultural imagination and public policy.

In the present cultural moment, love is often used either in a *sentimental* sense or in a *sexual* sense. Locating love in fickle and fluid emotions destabilizes relationships, especially within marriages and families. And if this defined-down understanding of love cannot secure the most intimate of human relations, it offers no hope for holding together larger society. Put differently, if love is a feeling, the tasks of loving God when we don't *feel* he is there or loving our neighbors (especially the unlikeable ones) are doomed from the start. If the emotive takeover of relationships has proven to be destabilizing, then the hyper-sexualization of love has proven to be destructive. Built not only on abandoned moral norms but a redefined understanding of the human person, more and more relationships that were never designed for sex—such as casual friendships, performers and audiences, and individuals of the same sex—are made sexual.

Even worse, human beings are defined down to their sexual inclinations and urges. As a result, not only are previously unthinkable behaviors with others justified and called love, they determine, we are told, our most essential identities. Even inherent physical realities are mutable and under the authority of the sexual impulses. Sentiment and sex are, in the biblical worldview, legitimate ways to express affection, even love. However, to define love down to either of these things is to fundamentally miss the truth about love communicated in the greatest commandment. Love, as God designed it, is to be directed toward another. To reduce love to feelings or sexual instinct is to turn love wholly inward, rendering it nothing like it was created to be.

There is a trend, in fact, to turn almost *all of life* inward.[5] External relationships are increasingly seen as mere means to the ends of a sort of "you be you" impulse, one which is consistent with recent research demonstrating that a large portion of Gen Z's members embrace moral relativism.[6] This impulse is ultimate in our current cultural moment, and it is not to be questioned or challenged. When *expressive individualism*, a term coined by philosopher Charles Taylor to describe this inward turn and pursuit of self-realization, becomes the *modus operandi* of a cultural moment as it has in ours, love is only one of many concepts essential to our human existence to be redefined.[7]

In this broken context, all efforts to disciple followers of Christ, especially any aimed at members of younger generations who've never experienced a culture *not* dominated by expressive individualism, must begin by overtly and properly defining the word *love*. Think about it. Gen Z is growing up in a world of legalized same-sex marriage, Disney princess movies, and social media. Most have *only* experienced the word *love* used sentimentally and sexually, *every* time it is used. What do we think someone catechized in these cultural norms means when they express love to a friend or significant other, or when they sing "Jesus loves me this I know"? The Bible might tell them so, but that doesn't mean the definition being assumed is biblical in any real sense.

Clarity is helpful in any cultural context, but it's absolutely necessary in this one. Not only will defining love carefully reinforce essential truths about who God is and who we are as *imago Dei* but doing so offers an ingredient essential to pursuing our *telos*, the true end for which God designed us.

Defining Love

C.S. Lewis said that for every new book, we should read three old ones. I say reading three C.S. Lewis books would be a great start in following this advice. Of all the very important books written by Lewis, including the ones even more relevant now than when they were written, *The Four Loves* may be the most important for our cultural moment, and for Gen Z in particular.

The sentimentalized and sexualized notions of love from our cultural moment are not equivalent, or even close, to any of the four notions Lewis described in his book. Even worse than poor substitutes, they are corruptions, escalated by the dramatic culture-wide inward turn described earlier.

Each of the loves that Lewis described requires an outward posture.[8] Affection (*storge*) is the appreciation we have for God's good gifts of people, things, and the creation around us. These good gifts ultimately point our affections to the giver of these good gifts. Friendship (*philia*) is a uniquely human love with powerful potential to shape and stabilize individuals and entire societies. Romantic love (*eros*) can only be properly understood as a giving of self for another, and not as a "falling in love." In the marital context, this kind of love protects human sexuality from devolving into a mere pursuit of personal pleasure. Charity (*agape*) is the highest love, known to us only because it is how we are loved by God. "We have come to know love by this," the apostle John wrote, "that

Jesus laid down his life for us; thus we ought to lay down our lives for our fellow Christians" (1 John 3:16).

These four are gifts of God as well as callings to be embraced and embodied in whatever cultural moment in which he has placed us. By clarifying each, Lewis helpfully illuminated which are to be directed to God and which are to be directed to our neighbors. God loved us first, and he calls love out of us as a way of further loving his world.

This clarity also helps love the right things. As St. Augustine said, we are what we love. Because our loves shape us, we become more fully human when our highest love is directed to God himself. The converse is also true. When our affections are directed "to things below," when our love and worship is aimed at idols, we become, in a very real sense, less human.

As the Psalmist wrote:

> The nations' idols are made of silver and gold; they are man-made. They have mouths, but cannot speak, eyes, but cannot see, and ears, but cannot hear. Indeed, they cannot breathe. *Those who make them will end up like them, and so will everyone who trusts in them.* (Ps. 135:15–18; emphasis added)

Ordering Loves

Not only must we love the right things, we must love the right things in the right order. As a father, I love it when my children are happy. Any parent will attest to the joy they experience in those moments of unbridled laughter with their children, or when they see a child deeply engaged in a story, sport, or activity, as if they were made for it. The only thing (I hear) that tempers the sadness of giving a daughter's hand to another is the happiness seen in her at the moment of marriage.

I also love it when my children grow in holiness. I love seeing their own faith and love for God deepen. Many parents appropriate the words of the apostle John, "I have no greater joy than this: to hear that my children are living according to the truth" (3 John 4).

Holiness and happiness must be properly ordered. My loves for seeing both of these things in my children must be properly ordered as well. Perhaps you've met someone whose parents loved their happiness over all else. Perhaps you've sat beside that child on an airplane. Elevating happiness over holiness never ends well. Perhaps this is why the greatest commandment is given to us already ordered. We are to, first, love God with heart, soul, mind, and strength, and second, to love our neighbor as ourselves. This order reflects the order of reality: "In the beginning God" (Gen. 1:1). "God said, 'Let there be …'" (Gen. 1:3). The ordering of the greatest commandment corresponds to the contours of reality itself.

Further, our ability to obey the greatest commandment is dependent on this ordering. We will only love God well if we love him first, recognizing his primacy over all other relationships. We will only love our neighbors well if our love for them is shaped by our love for God. Misordering the love of God and the love of neighbor will inevitably corrupt both. This truth is key for Gen Z as they are highly likely to reverse this God-ordained order in the name of maintaining harmony with their friends and family who are choosing to live out alternative lifestyles.

Rightly ordering the love of God and neighbor is as profoundly countercultural as defining them properly. As cultural notions of love are turned increasingly inward and defined down to sentimentality and sexuality, Christians are tempted to elevate the love of neighbor over and above the love of God. Emptied of any real substance, the love owed our neighbors is replaced by flimsy concepts such as tolerance and inclusion, both of which are words redefined in their own respects. The result is a wholly gutted Gospel.

The Gospel offers forgiveness of sin, a way to move from being an offender of the holiness of God to one of his children because of the obedience and sacrifice of Christ Jesus. Instead, when love of God and love of neighbor are misordered, people hear, often from well-intended but misguided Christians, that they have not offended God at all. Rather than hearing the good news that they need not remain in their sin and brokenness, they hear that God made them that way, and that their sin and brokenness were his intent for their happiness.

To pit the love of God, the God who has gone to such great lengths to make himself and his will known against the love of neighbor in this way is a "devil's bargain."[9] God's Gospel and God's morality are not in conflict. The God who so clearly demonstrated his love for us in Christ is the same God whose character determines the unchanging moral norms of the universe.

Often the gutted Gospel is presented in an attempt to remain relevant, but actually accomplishes the precise opposite. As cultures shift, adjusting to newly dominant ideas and worldviews, they either more closely correspond to the eternal truths about who we are or move away from those truths. For example, as American culture continues to confront its racist history, our collective ideas are being pruned and sharpened and, hopefully, coming closer to aligning with the truth that every single person is endowed with infinite value because of who they are as image-bearers. On the other hand, the normalization of pornography has taken us further from that truth, deceiving us with platitudes such as "victimless crime" and "right to privacy."

In other words, attempts to remain relevant to the shifting of culture actually leave us less relevant to reality. Christians should always self-correct beliefs, traditions, and conduct that are not in line with the God whom we are called to love first. We should never correct those things aligned with God but in conflict with the culture. We must love God first if we are to love our neighbors well. If at any point we do successfully love our neighbors, it is only because we reflect, in some sense, the love of God.

All of this take us back to the necessary task, in any endeavor of discipleship, to properly define love, to properly identify those whom we were created to love, and to properly teach the only order by which human love functions.

Conclusion: Teaching Lovers to Love Well

Christianity is not a means to an end. Loving God is not merely a means to a meaningful and moral life, to personal happiness, or to achieve fulfillment. Loving God is the *telos*, the end for which we were created, the most coherent way to be aligned to created reality.

Whether or not Gen Z will choose to embrace that vision of the Christian life is one thing. Whether or not they have the clarity to know the difference is another. They will only have the clarity they need if they understand the following points. First, who has God revealed himself to be? God's self-revelation is the only data we have to know the God we are called to love. All impressions, feelings, teachings, and wishes we hold about who God is must be evaluated in light of what he has revealed about himself, his will, his law, and his work in the world.

Second, what it means to be human is to be *imago Dei—made in God's image*. We are created beings, not self-determined. Every aspect of our humanity, from our physical bodies to the spiritual aspects of inner selves to our emotions and our relationships, were made by God *for* God. Our value and the value of every single one of our neighbors are not dependent on cultural trends or ideas.

Third, they must know what love is and what it is not. Love is not a feeling or fluidly defined concept dependent on cultural shifts. Love is defined by God's character and nature, and the truth about love does not change. Contrasting what is true about love with the falsehoods of our culture is essential to knowing the difference.

Fourth, our loves must be properly ordered. God has gifted his image bearers with the capacity to love him, others, and his world. These loves function properly only when properly ordered.

Finally, our loves shape us in profound ways. Humans are, at root, more than consumers, creators, sinners, or complainers. We are, at root, made to love. What we love and how we love shape our lives and, collectively, entire societies.

CHAPTER 6

BEING HOLY AND THE NATURE OF THE SPIRITUAL DISCIPLINES

Kyle Strobel

Shifting Generational Values and Having "Eyes to See"

Every generation faces the difficulty of assuming a set of values taken to be obvious, and then reading Scripture through those values. We all struggle to see how Scripture may attack and undermine our preferred values rather than affirm them, and we may have difficulty seeing how our cultural values are antithetical to biblical claims. Each generation, furthermore, is tempted to think of itself as particularly suited to hear the Gospel, and to see other generations as hopelessly blind. It is cliché for older Christians to look on younger Christians with disdain in this regard. In reality, no generation is particularly open to the Gospel: "There is no one righteous, not even one, there is no one who understands, there is no one seeks God. All have turned away; together they have become worthless; there is no one who shows kindness, not even one." (Rom. 3:10–12)

In the Gen Z study conducted by the Barna Group and Impact 360 Institute, the mosaic that emerges reveals a generation defining "success" in terms of career achievement and using church as a place to further one's self.[1] "A plurality of Gen Z considers personal achievement (43 percent) and hobbies (42 percent) most important to their sense of self," both of which are substantial shifts from previous generations.[2] Along with this, there is a clear focus on what we might call a "self-enclosed self," meaning someone seeking to self-define, using education, experiences, and actions as a way to determine one's identity. In this sense, a "self-enclosed self" believes that one's identity is self-determined; life is a buffet line to construct who you are. Low on the list of identities and life goals are things such as spirituality, and "few teens overall see spiritual maturity as a worthy ambition."[3] Family, furthermore, is substantially lower in value for Gen Z, another sign of how a "self-enclosed self" rejects traditional notions of human flourishing.[4]

In light of this, the goal of this chapter is to consider the nature of the Christian life and the nature of growth. In particular, this chapter will identify some key difficulties Gen Z experiences, based on their unique worldview. As just noted, this does not mean that Gen Z is somehow further from the Gospel than Boomers or Gen X. Rather, it is to say that their difficulties will be different. Boomers, Gen X, and Gen Z all require a supernatural work of God to give them eyes to see. All require holding their lives open to God before Scripture and asking the question: Am I willing to put my faith here?

Faithfulness Beyond Cliché

We are often persuaded by what many call the Pharisaic temptation: to think that because you are disciplined, biblically conservative (the Pharisees were, after all, the Biblicists of their day), and devoted to God, then you are a mature Christian. When Jesus confronted the Pharisees, his critique moved beyond actions to a deeper truth; namely, that they were "like whitewashed tombs that look beautiful on the outside but inside are full of bones of the dead and of everything unclean" (Matt. 23:27). Their hearts were sick, regardless of what their life seemed to suggest. When it comes to Gen Z, the Pharisaic temptation will likely not be their primary one. For the most part, Gen Z has not absorbed a worldview that values discipline, self-sacrifice for the greater good, or a clear sense of an external virtue that might lead them down this path. Rather than looking for an external rule that weighs their life, their primary instinct is to look within themselves for guidance on whether something is "good" or "bad." This is why the cultural axiom has become: "Be true to yourself." When we look within ourselves and see our good intentions, we can see that we intend to be faithful, biblical, devoted, and worshipful; then, when we are confronted with our lack of embodied spirituality, we deem it irrelevant to judge our faithfulness. "I am spiritual," we insist. Or perhaps we declare in defense, "It is not about a religion; it is a relationship." We often hide behind such clichés to avoid the truth that we don't have any vision for training and formation in the Christian life.

Gen Z will struggle to believe the following truths:

- To be true to oneself is to lose one's life to find it in Christ (Matt. 16:25).
- Trying to self-define is to embrace a way of being human that ultimately dehumanizes oneself and others.
- Trying to "choose" what God is like rather than submitting to a God whose ways are not our ways is to choose an idol rather than God.

Although Gen Z prefers to determine their own lives and identities, the Christian life is submitting to an authority (God) to be a part of a people (his church). Naturally, Gen Z finds these truths difficult to embrace. They require what the Bible always requires of God's people— an exodus. One of the central themes of Scripture is that God's people are called to exodus—to leave behind the rhythms and worldview of Egypt, also known as Babylon, to set their hearts and minds on the "Jerusalem above" (see Gal. 4:21–31).

The Training of the Exodus

Israel's exodus from Egypt was a training of mind, heart, and body. Deuteronomy 8:2 tells us that God led his people into the wilderness to reveal what was in their hearts. In Stephen's speech before his martyrdom, he narrated the exodus and declared that Israel turned back to Egypt in their hearts (Acts 7:39). God revealed to his people that they didn't really want him; they wanted life on their own terms. When Moses ascended into the fire on the mountain and did not come down, the people of God turned back to Egypt, wielding Egyptian worship technology in an attempt to control God. Worshipping golden calves was not an attempt to reject the God who delivered them, but to control him using pagan ritual (see Ex. 32:1–6). God had other plans. The exodus was a training to teach the people of God two major things: (1) God is in your midst and must be the center of your lives, and (2) the only truly human way to live is having your life—your days, time, holidays, work, family—all revolve around God and his call.

The exodus pattern continued into the New Testament, as the primary story of God's people was fulfilled by Jesus. Jesus was baptized (he journeyed through the water) and was immediately sent out to the wilderness to wander for forty days of testing (evoking Israel's forty years of wandering) to reveal what was in his heart: faithfulness. Then as Matthew narrated it, he journeyed to a mountain, ascended, and delivered the new law of the Lord—the Beatitudes. But even that wasn't Jesus's final exodus. Later, Jesus referred to his death as his upcoming "exodus" (too often translated unhelpfully as "departure") and called us to follow him through the water of his death (see Luke 9:31). This formed the church, which is why Paul said that we are called through the waters of Christ's death (baptism), worshipping God in singing (as Israel did when they walked onto dry land), to journey toward the promised land by partaking in the spiritual food and spiritual drink (the Lord's Supper, as the manna of the wilderness and water from the rock), to hear the word of the Lord declared (sermon) (see 1 Cor. 10). Notice that every church service is a rehearsal of the exodus—a call to remember that God has delivered us from the land of slavery into a place of freedom, to love God and love our neighbor as ourselves.[5]

Fundamental to this story—governing its logic—is the fact that God was in the midst of his people. Even more so, for Christians, God is not only in our midst but has now descended into our souls. We have God at the center of our hearts and lives; we are called to live all of life centered on God. This is why the Christian life is never merely about developing habits and virtue, tempting us to moralism and self-help; nor is it just affirming the truth and moving on in narcissism and self-centered living. Rather, the Christian life is one that finds its discipline, mission, and rhythm of life around God, for God, and to God. In other words, while Aristotle called people to develop habits that construct a virtuous character, God calls us to habits and rhythms that lead us to abide in him. The end is entirely different. The goal is God and life in the presence of God.

We may be tempted to believe that God's grace means we no longer have to shape our lives around Christ, as if obedience is somehow negated by grace. This is known as the antinomian temptation. Or we might be tempted to follow Aristotle's view rather than Christ's. But our call is not to develop a disciplined life in our own strength, but to embrace Christ. This is a way of life that bears the fruit of virtue, rather than seeking to construct it by our own power.

A Sanctified Life

Israel's training in the wilderness was not for mere goodness; Israel was being trained for *holiness*. In the same way, we tend to understand the Christian life as the life of sanctification. Unfortunately, we can easily get sanctification backwards. For instance, it is not unusual to hear someone say something such as, "We have been justified by faith alone through grace alone, and that work is complete. Now we have to do the work of sanctification, which is progressive: we have to work to grow in goodness." Few might put it in these exact terms, but most evangelicals I meet assume something like this. But notice how sanctification is addressed in the following biblical passages:

- 1 Corinthians 1:30: "He [the Father] is the reason you have a relationship with Christ Jesus, who became for us wisdom from God, and righteousness and sanctification and redemption."
- 1 Corinthians 6:11: "But you were washed, you were sanctified, you were justified in the name of the Lord Jesus Christ and by the Spirit of our God."

○ Hebrews 10:10: "...we have been made holy through the offering of the body of Jesus Christ once for all."

These passages subvert our presuppositions. Not only is sanctification *not* progressive in these passages, but it is, in some sense, complete. Christ is our sanctification (see 1 Cor. 1:30).

Two things become clear when reflecting on the biblical material about sanctification. First, in New Testament terms, sanctification is a finalized reality that gives rise to a life that progresses, culminating in knowing the full presence of God in eternity. In other words, while there is a sense that sanctification has a continuing reality, that continuing reality is built upon its finality.[6] In the preceding passages, Christ became sanctification for us, and as we are in Christ Jesus, we are sanctified. This is called "definitive sanctification," and it is the primary way the New Testament talks about salvation.[7]

Second, sanctification is primarily about presence, not morality. What makes this difficult to see in Scripture is that sanctification functions in differing registers, and it does so in varying ways. In Scripture, objects (such as those used in the temple), time (the Sabbath), and even unbelievers (interestingly, in 1 Cor. 7:14) can be sanctified and made holy. God makes his people holy, in varying degrees, but more often, we find *space* being made holy—as a way to name God's presence among his people. The concept of goodness functions in the same way. We can talk about a good sandwich, a good friend, and a good dog, using "good" in various registers with varying emphases. Nonetheless, we have no problem with each being called "good." Similarly, the meaning of sanctification varies when referring to an object, an unbeliever, and a Christian—and yet they are all aspects of what it means to be sanctified. Each of these things, in their unique ways, is sanctified according to God's action and presence.

In Scripture, first and foremost, God is holy, and his personal presence and action are what sanctify.[8] This is why, most commonly, Scripture speaks of sanctified *space*. Sanctification, in this sense, has to do with God's personal presence and what it means to be present to a Holy God. God's holy presence *makes* holy for the sake of sharing in and reciprocating his self-giving. We are called into his presence to be shaped by his presence for the sake of his presence. As Gordan Wenham notes, in his commentary on Leviticus, "The whole of man's life must be lived out in the presence of God. The recurring refrain in the later chapters, 'I am the Lord your God' (e.g., 18:2ff.; 19:3–4, 10; 20:7), reminds the people of Israel that every aspect of their life—religion (chs. 21—24), sex (chs. 18 and 20), relations with neighbors (chs. 19, 25)—is of concern to their covenant redeemer."[9] As God gives himself to his people in grace, so too are his people called to give themselves, in whole, to God.

This clarifies a problem that arises concerning sanctification in Scripture. As put by one commentator, "The Holy One cannot have communion with the unholy. Sinful humans can only approach him if they are sanctified, i.e. made to correspond to his holiness (Lev. 19:2)."[10] In other words, to be with God, we must be sanctified for his presence. Furthermore, David Peterson, claims, "The root meaning of the Hebrew noun 'holiness' (*qodes*) and the adjective 'holy' (*qados*) is separation. The Greek Bible uses *hagios* and some of its derivatives as the equivalent of the Hebrew. The terminology refers to the distinctiveness or otherness of God's character, activities and words."[11] Furthermore, "Separation was to be expressed in time and space and ritual. Sanctification was primarily a technical term of the cult, connoting both cleansing and consecration. It was also to be demonstrated in the moral and social sphere and in breaking with every form of idolatry and false religion."[12] Note that sanctification itself is not primarily moral, even though it presses into the moral sphere.[13] This is key.

The primary issues in sanctification are not moral, even though morality should flow from them. In the Old Testament, if something wasn't holy, it was considered common; the opposite of holiness wasn't sin, but a status of not being sanctified for God's presence and action. The average Israelite was, in a sense, holy, as they were a part of a holy nation. Nonetheless, their holiness was not enough to allow them to march into the sanctuary into the immediate personal presence of God. That action required special rituals that included sanctified status (High Priest), space (Holy of Holies), and time (Day of Atonement).[14]

What this picture of sanctification helps us to see is that God has called us into his presence—to be from him, and not from the world (see John 17:14–18). We are still, no doubt, called to virtue; God's presence is supposed to form our life according to his will. But virtue is not something that can be habituated merely through our action, as if Jesus's life, death, resurrection, and ascension (not to mention his continuing ministry and sending of the Spirit), have ultimately achieved nothing more than confirming Aristotle's presuppositions. Rather, Christ is our sanctification, and as we abide in him, we bear fruit. Our action must always be in, for, and by Christ, so that our formation happens only in relationship to him, because spiritual formation only happens as we abide in Christ by the Spirit.[15] Being united to Christ in faith, hope, and love is the nature of the Christian life, where the direction of our action is always to God, in Christ, by the Spirit, and never merely the formation of virtue.

Scripture employs the image of a tree bearing fruit to depict the Christian life. A good tree bears good fruit, and a bad tree bears bad fruit (see Matt. 7:17). The problem is that when Christians see sick fruit in their life, their response often runs contrary to Scripture. Scripture calls us to become a good tree, to abide in Christ, and to walk in the Spirit, so that we can bear the fruit of God. But instead, seeing diseased apples on the tree of one's life, we may simply try to replace the sick apples with new ones. We might go to the store, buy the best apples we can find, and then string them up on our sick tree. When we move on, then, we are surprised to discover that, while we have new habits, new rhythms, or new actions, we didn't experience transformation of the heart. Enacting new habits does not change the heart on its own. We are not called to "fake it till you make it" or to try hard to act like good Christians, since formation is not found in raw effort. God calls us to a new foundation of life—the Spirit's presence in the soul and among his people, transforming the deepest parts of our hearts by reorienting all of us in him and to him, so that we can bear the fruit of the kingdom.

Centered on Christ

This instinct to only habituate virtue stems, in recent decades, from a recovery of a certain kind of virtue ethic, often stemming from Aristotle, but supposedly linked to Thomas Aquinas. Unfortunately, rather than following Thomas's ultimate rejection of Aristotelean ethics as "true virtue," many have simply followed Aristotle.[16] Rather than talking about our formation in, by, and for God, our spiritual practices and rhythms of life become tools for "flourishing," as if flourishing could be habituated. In this sense, the "Christian" discussion of formation differed little from its secular counterpart, also seeking flourishing apart from Christ. Spiritual formation, in many circles, became little more than developing habits of self-help. Christ calls us to something more.

The tradition stemming from Augustine to Thomas Aquinas and through the Protestant Reformation recognized that, while Aristotle's ethics could lead to a well-ordered secular life, for the Christian, they are equivalent to what Paul named as "self-imposed worship" that has "no true value" and "in reality result in fleshly indulgence." (Col. 2:23) This form of habituation has nothing to do with holiness, any more than stringing new apples on a sick tree has brought health to the tree. In Colossians 2, Paul rejected various forms of spiritual discipline (asceticism) that stem from the flesh and warned against a philosophy that seeks the formation of human personhood that is not centered on Christ.

Paul then proclaimed the necessary orientation for our formation: "Therefore, if you have been raised with Christ, keep seeking the things above, where Christ is, seated at the right hand of God. Keep thinking about things above, not things on the earth, for you have died and your life is hidden with Christ in God" (Col. 3:1–3). The training of the new exodus in Christ is a training for Christ, to Christ, and ordered around Christ. Or in the words of Dallas Willard, "Christian spiritual formation is focused entirely on Jesus. Its goal is an obedience or conformity to Christ that arises out of an inner transformation accomplished through purposive interaction with the grace of God in Christ."[17] Like all evangelical accounts of moral action, it is formation by the grace of God.

Gen Z will be tempted to use discipline, church, and spirituality, if they show interest in them at all, for a kind of self-formation. This self-formation is not that of the Boomers, who were more likely to accept cultural norms of goodness and virtue, but is the self-formation of a person who thinks they can determine what is good for themselves. For Gen Z, perhaps the hardest part of the biblical message is trusting that their lives are "hidden with Christ in God," and therefore they are not self-defining creatures. They cannot choose who to be, what is good, or what is true.

The Training of Grace

The difficulty that all generations have with what Christ declares to us—to abide in him to bear the fruit of the Spirit, and not the fruit of the flesh—is to understand that our formation both comes from God and depends on our action. The mistake, continually made by Christians through the ages, is to reduce this down to one or the other. We have focused on the mistake of following Aristotle, thinking that our formation is entirely according to our action—what the tradition often calls *acquired virtue*—whereas Christian virtue was through *infusion*, which is another way of saying "virtue by grace alone."

The problem with ignoring virtue through infusion, or God's action, is not simply the problem of considering works without faith. Rather, the trouble with acquired virtue is that it isn't holiness. When Christians embrace the habituation of virtue as holiness, they reduce holiness down to acts of goodness, which is a category fallacy. To embrace holiness and the way of sanctification requires that one seeks the God who is holy and shares in the holiness by which God is holy: the Holy Spirit (in other words, the Spirit of God's holiness). This is why even self-control is not a fruit of the disciplined self, but a fruit of the Spirit (see Gal. 5:23).

On the other end of the spectrum, there is a different kind of mistake. That mistake is assuming that because of what Christ has done, and because our formation is from him, our action is somehow meaningless for our formation. Instead, let me suggest we follow our theological forebears who helped establish evangelicalism—Jonathan Edwards and John Wesley—who both articulated a view of formation that held together grace and action, without diminishing either of them. Using both Wesley and Edwards is interesting because it shows that the evangelical view of the means of grace did not derive from theological divergences between Calvinism and Arminianism, but from a shared understanding that grace is the proper theological mooring to understand human formation and action.

One reason why the language of spiritual discipline wasn't employed by our Protestant forebears is that they would have seen it as leaning toward self-made religion. Nonetheless, it has become the common language of our day, often without the kind of nuance the tradition provides in discussions of spiritual practices. Spiritual formation needs to be ordered around God's presence to us in Christ by the Spirit, such that Christ is our focus and our goal. Recall, Christ is our sanctification (see 1 Cor. 1:30). Our union and communion with Christ order all notions of Christian formation. Willard notes, "Well-informed human effort certainly is indispensable, for spiritual formation is no passive process. But Christlikeness of the inner being is not a human attainment. It is, finally, a gift of grace."[18] Willard upholds the evangelical desire to recognize that our "conformation to Christ" is not based on our ability to form our lives, but on Christ's grace. It is transformation through "union with God, not apart from him—not independently, on our own."[19] Like his evangelical forebears, Willard recognized that grace does not undermine human action, but provides the proper context to understand it.

Willard wrote from within a Wesleyan strand of evangelicalism, but others, employing the Reformed strand, can do the same.[20] For both Wesleyan and Reformed evangelicals, the proper source of spiritual discipline is grace, which is why these were called "means of grace." This language aims to uphold God as the ultimate source of formation, and it orients our action to God by way of a response to his self-giving. What this language can help lead us to, furthermore, is that our spiritual discipline, our spiritual rhythms of life, and the various actions we employ in the Christian life are all part of our continuing exodus, and therefore are training for life in the presence of God—life in the kingdom. As Willard noted, "Grace is opposed to earning, not to effort."[21] This is certainly right. But a further question is necessary—one that concerns the nature of the effort grace calls us into. This question helps orient us to a proper understanding of spiritual discipline and the rhythms of Christian living. Every spiritual practice, whether it is fasting, praying, Bible reading, singing, listening to a sermon, or anything else needs to be grounded in Christ, oriented to Christ, and intended to be a sharing in the grace of Christ for life in Christ. Willard is certainly right, "Christian spiritual formation is focused entirely on Jesus."[22]

CHAPTER 7

TOWARD AUTHENTIC KINGDOM DIVERSITY

Melissa Pellew

Although I'm a parent to a seven-year-old, my everyday life is an adventure of regular interactions with teens and college students. As chapter directors with Ratio Christi at a secular university, my husband and I equip college students to defend the historic Christian faith and regularly engage unbelieving and skeptical students with the truth of Christianity. In addition to our work on campus, for the last several years, we have worked with 13- to 18-year-olds through the Ratio Christi College Prep program, preparing teens for the various ideas and challenges to the faith that they will face at the university.

While we address the typical apologetics issues—such as God's existence, the reliability of the Bible, and the problem of evil—we've been spending more time delving into how to think critically and biblically regarding social issues. At the forefront of these social issues is the subject of race and racial tensions. It is no secret that we are living in a highly racialized culture. As a black woman with an interracial family dynamic, I often feel my life is saturated with these. Racial tension related to inequality is one of the primary lenses through which many interpret socioeconomics and current events in the media headlines. Why are race relations such a critical issue to the Gen Z crowd? How do these issues give us insight into connecting with those in Gen Z? Let's investigate!

Some Key Statistics

Gen Z represents the most racially and ethnically diverse group in American history. According to Pew Research's March 2020 survey, "Generation Z represents the leading edge of the country's changing racial and ethnic makeup. A bare majority (52 percent) are non-Hispanic white—significantly smaller than the share of Millennials who were non-Hispanic white in 2002 (61 percent). One in four Gen Zers are Hispanic, 14 percent are black, 6 percent are Asian, and 5 percent are some other race or two or more races."[1] The average Gen Zer also has close friendships that span across racial and ethnic groups. For these reasons alone, it is no surprise that Gen Z has a great awareness of issues surrounding race relations.

Research has established that Gen Z is also the most highly relational of all the generations. Gen Z's awareness of cultures, traditions, and the challenges of others is made more real due to their up-close-and-personal relationships and interactions. Gen Zers tend to be more intimately connected and empathetic to the daily struggles of those in their immediate circles and in society in general.

With respect to marriage and family, interracial marriage was legalized in 1967. Back then, only 3 percent of marriages were between interracial couples. In contrast, 17 percent of new marriages today are between partners of different races. Put differently, 11 million men and women have entered into marriage with someone outside of their race.[2]

Gen Zers are growing up in a radically different environment than their parents and grandparents as they are seeing and regularly doing life outside of racial bubbles.

Social Media and Race

Another factor in Gen Z's awareness of race issues is the impact of social media. A 2018 Pew Research Center survey of nearly 750 thirteen- to seventeen-year-olds found that 45 percent are online almost constantly and 97 percent use at least one social media platform, such as YouTube, Facebook, Instagram, or Snapchat.[3] Social media virtually connects Gen

Zers to individuals they have never met in person. In the same way, social media—and the internet as a whole—virtually connect Gen Zers to a variety of social issues and commentary about those issues. In short, their overabundant use of social media and technology makes them much more aware of social justice issues than previous generations have been.

Social media has been a game changer in how Gen Z both shares and receives information on specific incidents. It was a seventeen-year-old who took the incriminatory video of the brutal killing of George Floyd by police in Minneapolis, Minnesota. By recording that incident from her vantage point and sharing it to social media, this young lady played a key role in the arrest of the four police officers involved in Mr. Floyd's death—and in starting a worldwide movement that spotlighted police brutality. Today's technology and handy access to information bring people face-to-face with century-old problems in living color.

Gen Z's awareness of societal ills often brings acknowledgement of the issue and then the passion to speak out about it and to look for practical and systemic solutions. Social media, where they likely first received the information, is also the most immediate and practical tool for speaking out.

Gen Z Is Movement Oriented

In addition to being a racially diverse, highly relational, always-connected generation, Gen Z is also extremely movement oriented. Everyone wants to be a part of something bigger than themselves. For Gen Z, grappling with issues of identity, purpose, happiness, and image, this bigger-than-themselves mentality becomes an immediate motivation to get involved and do something about this larger-than-life enemy of racial injustice. The problem is that, even with a sincere heart and desire to love one's neighbor, fighting a larger-than-life enemy can lead a person to believe he or she is solely responsible for defeating that enemy.

As stories of racial injustice become increasingly mainstream and dominate news coverage and social media outlets, Gen Zers often feel highly motivated to take up this cause and mantle of ending racism through actions of social justice. Many members of this generation view their parents' and grandparents' passivity as indifference and even culpability in the problem; thus, they have an even greater motivation to distinguish themselves in the frontlines of this fight.

It *is* a worthy cause to fight for the oppressed and the marginalized—to speak up for others' rights and to demand equal treatment of fellow citizens. It is always commendable to fight for truth and justice. That passion is one of the traits that is so admirable in Gen Z. We can and should encourage this thinking that looks out for the good of others and for opportunities to promote goodness and truth. However, we must help ensure that Gen Z combines their passion with the necessary maturity, critical thinking, and biblical worldview to accurately assess, interpret, and respond to racial issues and incidents. There is a combination of factors at work here.

First, the relational nature of Gen Z makes it more difficult for them to think objectively when those close to them are emotionally involved with an issue. Relationships are a blessing from God. In the beginning of creation, God determined that it was not good for man to be alone. After all, God exists in a perfect triune Godhead, where perfect relationship and unity exists among the Father, Son, and Holy Spirit. Human relationships, however, are not the arbiter of truth. The standard lies in the perfect nature of the One who created us. What I have witnessed all too often among the Gen Z crowd is an inability to objectively seek truth, regardless of the opinions of peers, experiences of friends, and perspective of culture at large. As I've pointed out, we are dealing with a highly relational generation that is simultaneously ethnically diverse on an interpersonal level. This absolutely factors into how racial incidences and statistical socioeconomic gaps are interpreted.

Second, the overwhelming amount of data and incidences that spread through social media can make it hard to validate what is real. It is a positive that with smartphones and social media, stories of racial injustice are unable to be as easily hidden, covered up, and swept under the rug as in previous generations. However, it is way too easy—and is even becoming common—for cell phone recordings to lack important context or even to frame a racial injustice narrative where there is none. When people post videos of negative interactions between minorities and white people or tweet personal experiences, labeling them as racism, Gen Zers are typically ready to immediately affirm them as real and as demonstrating the validity of the ongoing social justice movement against racial injustice.

Without the necessary tools to think critically about viral information, videos, or personal experiences, it is all too common for Gen Zers to immediately become outraged and hit "share." They many times fail to ask the "who, what, when, where, why" questions, to investigate further, or to seek clarity and understanding of a situation before reacting. Some months back, I ran across a bumper sticker on a vehicle that read: "If you're not outraged, you're not paying attention." It's a pretty accurate depiction how this generation interprets information coming its way.

The CRT Indoctrination?

Is there a presupposition of interpreting racial incidents in a certain light among Gen Z? I would answer with a resounding "Yes." Today, Critical Race Theory (CRT) is the epistemological approach that Gen Zers often employ on the topic of racial issues. Chris Demaske, associate professor of communication at the University of Washington at Tacoma, defines CRT as "a movement that challenges the ability of conventional legal strategies to deliver social and economic justice and specifically calls for legal approaches that take into consideration race as a nexus of American life."[4] In the 1970s, as previous civil-rights-era victories seemed to wane, legal scholars and activists came together in an effort to understand why more progress was not being made and why some areas of progress were gradually deteriorating. Out of this discussion, CRT was born.[5]

Most CRT theorists hold to the same general tenets. First, racism is not an anomaly or an irregularity but an ordinary way in which society operates. Second, there is a self-interest of the majority who possess power that plays out in society through a system of "white-over-color." This phenomenon was first called "interest convergence" by the late law professor Derrick Bell, one of the original theorists of CRT. The third tenet of CRT is social construction. In *Critical Race Theory: An*

Introduction, Richard Delgado and Jean Stefancic said: "Social construction holds that race and races are products of social thought and relations. Not objective, inherent, or fixed, they correspond to no biological or genetic reality; rather, races are categories that society invents, manipulates, or retires when convenient." This racialization of society is detrimental for people of color. Fourth, "no person has a single, easily stated, unitary identity." Instead, there are *intersectional* identities around race, gender, and sexual orientation, for example, that produce potentially conflicting or overlapping identities, loyalties, and allegiances. Last is the idea of storytelling or the notion that people of color have their own perspectives and experiences that are crucial for others to understand in all areas of society and disciplines. This voice of color is unique and is embedded with the impact of racism that is needed to inform the whole of society.[6]

Since its formalized version in the mid-1970s, CRT has come to dominate social theory in academia across disciplines as it relates to analyzing and interpreting racial issues. Gen Z has unknowingly been immersed in this on a societal level their entire lives. This is a critical point in understanding Gen Z's relationship to racial issues, as well as their approach to understanding racial injustice. For such an ethnically diverse generation—so aware of racial tensions, yet without many tools to think objectively through the information—the tenets of CRT are a seemingly pragmatic approach for interpretation and understanding. Although Gen Zers are generally unaware of the formalized tenets and theory, CRT still has incredible influence on them through the media and how news is presented. The idea that racism is an all-encompassing pervasive reality woven into every aspect of society and life seems to be an easy approach and explanation for perceived racial injustice. This also fits well with the desire of Gen Z to change the world in pursuit of purpose, identity, and meaning, and to take up causes bigger than oneself. If the CRT version of racism is accurate, then upsetting and overturning institutional systems that perpetuate racism becomes a worthy, admirable, practical, and immediate cause.

At this point you may be wondering what the problem is with CRT for Bible-believing Christ-followers. Though challenging racism is a worthy cause, one of the critical issues with CRT is the way it places subjective identifiers on people in groups. CRT advocates claim that there are only two groups of people: (1) the group who represent or benefit from a powerful, oppressive, racial majority that systematically oppresses others, and (2) the marginalized minority, who are the unwilling and powerless subjects in an oppressive system. On the CRT view, rather than racism being the problem, an entire people group is the problem—whether they have actually engaged in oppressive behavior or only benefited from it. This, then, is the problem from a biblical worldview perspective—more division between image-bearers is the net result. CRT creates enemy lines by providing the framework to view racial disunity from a finger-pointing posture, identifying an underdog and a larger-than-life enemy to be defeated. Though racism is alive and exists, viewing individuals through this oppressor/oppressed relationship dynamic can deceive Gen Zers to be disillusioned to the genuine love across racial lines that exists among true followers of Christ, who pattern their lives after Galatians 3:27–29: "For all of you who were baptized into Christ have clothed yourselves with Christ. There is neither Jew nor Greek, there is neither slave nor free, there is neither male nor female—for all of you are one in Christ Jesus. And if you belong to Christ, then you are Abraham's descendants, heirs according to the promise."

In his book *Beyond Racial Gridlock: Embracing Mutual Responsibility*, Baylor University sociologist Dr. George Yancey discusses how CRT is insufficient in our epistemological approach and Christian worldview responses to racism. He demonstrates how it leads to a "White Responsibility" model in which both the problem and the solutions of racism lie at the feet of white people. Because on the CRT view, people of color by definition fall into an oppressed class, they are exempt and even incapable of being or acting racist. People of color, therefore, have no responsibility in the matter, but they can educate and inform white brothers and sisters of their own racism and guilt. Through a scriptural framework, however, we are informed that all people are sinful because of the condition of our hearts. There is no special class of humans that is exempt from any sin based on subjective socioeconomic categories. Dr. Yancey goes on to show how white people who are not guilty of the sin of racism will undoubtedly and within reason feel defensive and alienated from the cause of racial unity because of the assumptions on which CRT is based.[7]

It is true that unity cannot be achieved from a starting point of division, finger-pointing, and labeling. However, such is often the case when it comes to secular social theories. Are these the answers that we ultimately want to leave our young people with when they ask, "How do I make friends with others who are not like me? And, "Who is my neighbor?" Does the Church of Jesus Christ have nothing more to offer to this relevant issue that is already present in the social media feeds of our young people and in their interactions and discussions with their peers?

Answers?

As I have shown, Gen Z is a dynamic generation that values ethnically diverse relationships. They find purpose in being a voice for the unheard and marginalized. We who have the opportunity to be a part of the lives of this generation are incredibly blessed to come alongside them in this purpose, yet real challenges remain. How do we help them navigate through the racial issues and the reality of racism that exist among people of all ethnicities? With so many voices from mainstream news, social media, peers, educators, entertainers, and athletes, how do we help them to decipher and make sense of it all? My answer is rather simple—we must continue to raise up thinking, discerning young disciples of Jesus!

One of the key issues I brought up previously was the difficulty of Gen Zers to think objectively and independently of interpersonal relationships. Let me provide a common example of how I see this playing out. Suppose a negative encounter between a black man and a white woman is caught on video, hits the news media, and soon goes viral. In the short video, it appears that the black man was indeed disrespected and mistreated. Through the lens and worldview of CRT, however, all that matters is that this is an instance of an oppressor asserting power over a member of an oppressed class of people. Everything boils down to who has power in the situation. From a CRT perspective, this is a clear incident of white supremacy and white privilege in action, and those who see the video should simply assume that the woman's outrage was racially motivated. That is not the end of it, however. Those who have witnessed this injustice online are expected to share the video on social media so that the woman can be identified and potentially fired from her employer, ostracized, and more. This is a way to show the world that you are truly invested in solving racial injustice. This is the heart of CRT. It is the secular world's empty solution to the real problems of racism.

Based on this example above, what would the response of a thinking, discerning young disciple of Jesus be? First, amidst the highly emotional circumstances surrounding this hypothetical viral video and the peer pressure to hit share and voice immediate outrage, choose not to share it. Resist the urge to assume or assign racial motives based on the skin color of the parties involved. Rather, watch again and ask the who, what, when, where, why, and how questions. What is the context of the encounter? Is this a clear incident of racism? Asking these questions is not to excuse a person from racist actions but rather to evaluate our own ways of thinking and to ensure that we are approaching a situation objectively in judging people as people first and foremost, with no presuppositions regarding their skin color (not to be confused with a colorblind approach).

The Bible informs our minds and hearts that all men and women are created in God's likeness and image, and if that is the starting point for assessing actions and attitudes, it prevents one from the temptation to view all through the lens of skin color. It also helps our Gen Zers to make proper judgments and to identify and address legitimate acts of racism. As followers of Christ, we want to be people of truth—not of assumption or slander. That does not change with having relationships across ethnicities with those who may have been on the receiving end of racism. That does not change with peer pressure to be automatically outraged without proper investigation and examination of a situation.

If we are honest, the Church has not done the greatest job of helping Gen Z to think well. Fideism, an epistemological view of religious belief that holds that faith and reason are incompatible, remains prevalent in many youth ministries and churches today. Proponents believe that genuine faith is to be held without the tools of reason. Christian philosopher Alvin Plantinga describe a *fideist* as "someone who urges reliance on faith rather than reason, in matters philosophical and religious" and who "may go on to disparage and denigrate reason."[8] Students are many times discouraged from asking difficult questions and are often only told what to believe but not why to believe or how to think. When this happens, we cripple our young people from having a wholly biblical worldview that helps them see reality for what it is, and that they can confidently and practically apply to real-world problems. While it is impossible to cover every societal issue that exists with our Gen Zers, by helping them to develop good reasoning and thinking skills along with a robust biblical worldview, they will have the tools to think through these issues as they encounter them.

Back to the Beginning

I have mentioned in several places the biblical view of humanity—that we are made in the image of God, the *imago Dei*. According to Christianity.com, the "image of God" is defined as the metaphysical expression, associated uniquely to humans, which signifies the symbolical connection between God and humanity.[9] We see this first referenced in Scripture in Genesis 1: 26–27:

> Then God said, "Let us make humankind in our image, after our likeness, so they may rule over the fish of the sea and the birds of the air, over the cattle, and over all the earth, and over all the creatures that move on the earth." God created humankind in his own image, in the image of God he created them, male and female he created them.

We only see this language applied to humanity in Scripture, distinguishing humans from animals, plants, and the rest of God's creation. This is not an insignificant passage in Scripture but is one of the most important truths that shapes how we view ourselves, our fellow person, and our relationships with others. If only this passage and other supporting verses throughout the Bible regarding the image of God in humanity were understood and internalized, so many of our earthly societal problems and tensions would be no more.

The doctrine of the sanctity of human life is what is missing most from these racial discussions, amid the focusing on CRT and social theories of whiteness, white fragility, and more. We must encourage and equip our young people to recognize and appreciate the image of God in others from the point of conception to natural death, with no regard for race, gender, abilities, disabilities, or socioeconomic status. It is a foundational missing piece in the life of Gen Z on a personal level as they are struggling so much with questions about identity, purpose, and significance.

In discovering significance as God's image-bearer, there remains no need to look to the world, peers, or social justice activism as the source of purpose and identity. This simple yet profound truth is how we can help Gen Zers to resolve the restlessness of feeling the need to fulfill the savior role—understanding that mere humans are not capable of ultimately solving racial tensions through their works of social justice apart from God. Simultaneously, understanding how sacred the image of God is provides the objective standard in standing up against legitimate racial injustice. It becomes less about public image and the need for outrage, but about true justice and about people. It becomes not about peer pressure or conformity to secular social theories, but a deep-seated conviction based on God's truth and nature.

As Gen Zers conform their lives to this truth, they become witnesses and examples to their peers as they love like Christ does. Viewing their friends and neighbors in this way also enables Gen Zers to be examples of forgiveness and grace in this generation—something CRT has no resources to provide. As cancel culture intensifies, and understanding and dialogue decrease, there is an opportunity for our young people to extend grace in lieu of immediately assuming racial motives. Even in the cases of legitimate racism, the gift of forgiveness and the extension of grace and prayer for changed hearts and minds is a profound countercultural statement amidst our racially charged and divided society.

Worldview, Worldview, Worldview

With so many worldly, secular approaches and emotional attachments over objectivity and critical thinking, there is nothing that helps young people to navigate emotional and spiritual traps more than having a robust Christian worldview. Racial division is profitable to some. It is advantageous to politicians. It is profitable to mainstream media outlets. It is advantageous to race-baiters. It is advantageous to opportunists who play off the emotions of others. It is profitable to social media empires. The endless task of interpreting truth from fiction and discerning ideas leads to confusion in a relational generation that can result in sympathies for bad ideas. Helping our Gen Zers establish the confidence of holding a cohesive, biblical, and reliable worldview is a part of discipleship that must not be neglected. This also counters the tendency of cultural groupthink.

When those who are disciplers of younger Christians know that the Christian worldview is trustworthy, consistent, logical, and personally fulfilling, that knowledge in turn empowers our Gen Zers with the confidence to walk in God's truth and to spread it to others in their sphere of influence. There is no area of morality where the biblical worldview does not inform us. Racial issues are no different. As we encourage our young people to think critically and biblically, the need to look elsewhere for answers to this real-life problem disappears. While many are discouraged as it relates to many of the statistics related to Gen Z, I remain hopeful because I already see the Lord doing some great things in the lives of these young people. Above all, we look forward to the new heavens and new earth, where racial tensions and strife will be no more. In that day, those in Christ will be fully restored to him and to one another. This anticipation in the blessed hope is why we continue to invest in this generation so that many may ultimately come to see Christ face to face.

CHAPTER 8

SEXUAL PURITY FOR A NEW GENERATION

Sean McDowell

The Current State and the Overwhelming Need

Recently I showed a Carl's Junior commercial to a group of Christian high school students. Don't worry, it wasn't *that* commercial with Paris Hilton. But it did feature Hugh Hefner, the late founder of *Playboy*, in his infamous red robe. The commercial starts with Hefner saying, "I wake up every day and go to bed every night knowing I am the luckiest guy in the world." And then the camera pans to a blonde, a brunette, and a redhead, before focusing on Hefner, who says, "There's not a guy in the world who wouldn't welcome a little variety," as he enjoys a bite of a juicy burger. The commercial closes with these words: "Some guys don't like the same thing night after night."

After some discussion, the students picked up the clear message of the commercial—just as the same nightly food would be boring, so would having sex with the same person night after night. Simply put, *variety* is the spice of life. They also observed another message of the commercial—namely, that happiness is found in following your plea-sures. In other words, if it *feels good*, do it. This message has powerful appeal because food and sex are two of the greatest gifts God has given us to enjoy.

For contrast, I then had them open their Bibles to the temptation of Adam and Eve in Genesis 3. After describing the subtle deception of the serpent, the author of Genesis described how Eve "saw that the tree produced fruit that was good for food, was attractive to the eye, and was desirable for making one wise" (3:6a). The fruit appealed to her appetite ("good for food"), her eyes ("attractive to the eye"), and her mind ("making one wise"). Like the Carl's Junior burger, it looked very tasty. I pointed out to them that many temptations today, especially in the area of sexuality, are similar to the first temptation in the Garden of Eden.

Then I asked the students a final question: "Why would God give *this* commandment in the garden?" Why put a tree in the middle of the garden, with fruit that looked tasty and was meant to be eaten, and command them not to partake? Why not give Adam a simpler command such as, don't murder Eve? Why such a counterintuitive commandment? My friend Rachel Gilson explained:

> This would have been self-evident—I expect all of us would have nodded in approval. After all, taking human life is gruesome and unjust. We feel naturally the sinfulness of killing. We would have looked on this statute and, using our reason and intuition, called it just. But we don't need to know God to make that judgment, and the vast majority of society can obey at least its outward form without relation to him at all. Its very obviousness renders God seemingly unnecessary.[1]

And then Rachel sums up why someone *should* obey this commandment: "Why the motivation to obey a law that seems nonsensical? It can only be deep trust in the one who asks."[2] Exactly! God is the Creator, and we are the creature. God is infinite, and we are finite. If we are going to be in relationship with such a God, we must be willing to trust him when things don't make sense.

This brings me to the reason I started with this story:

> Any sexual ethic we teach to young people must be rooted in the motivation to trust God because he is good, and because his commands are meant for our flourishing.

King David said, "Give thanks to the LORD, for he is good, and his loyal love endures!" (Ps. 107:1). God doesn't merely do good; he *is* good.

God's commandments are not arbitrary, but an extension of his good character. The biblical writers understood this point, even though they often failed to live it. King David said, "The law of the LORD is perfect, and preserves one's life. The rules set down by the LORD are reliable and impart wisdom to the inexperienced" (Ps. 19:7). In his final speech before the Israelites entered the Promised Land, Moses told the Israelites that God desired they walk in obedience to his commands, which he said were for their own good (see Deut. 10:12–13).

Unfortunately, many abstinence campaigns have tried to motivate students with a different message. According to some critics, evangelical purity campaigns were motivated by fear[3] and shamed a generation of young people.[4] In her book *Making Chastity Sexy*, Christine J. Gardner argues that evangelical abstinence campaigns often co-opt a secular view of sex. Rather than asking students to be abstinent out of obedience to God, students were told not to engage in sexual behavior to avoid consequences and experience the best sex. According to Gardner, the argument went like this:

> A life of purity, including sexual abstinence until marriage, is God's plan, and God's plan is the best plan for young people, resulting in great marital sex in the future and the absence of unintended consequences such as pregnancy or STDs in the present. God's plan is best not just because it is God's plan, but because it has great benefits for the individual.[5]

Studies, in fact, reveal that married religious couples report having more and better sex than their secular counterparts.[6] And there are good reasons for this. After all, since God designed sex, we tend to flourish when we follow his pattern.[7] However, the key point here is that proper motivation for sexual purity should not be personal gain or avoiding potential harm, but out of a desire to honor God and love other people. We should be holy because God is holy (see 1 Pet. 1:16).

This is not an easy lesson for young people to learn because, as the Barna Group's Gen Z research reveals, most have uncritically accepted *consent* as the ultimate sexual ethic.[8] As long as you don't hurt anyone and the relationship is consensual, virtually any sexual behavior is considered permissible. Through social media, streaming video services, music, and an endless array of other mediums, they are daily barraged with a secular message about love and sex that makes biblical teaching seem counter-intuitive. Thus, like the command not to eat fruit in the garden, God's design for sex and marriage is not self-evident to them. This is just as true for many young Christians.

Gen Zers are the most liberal generation yet on issues of sexuality. According to the Barna Group's study, half of today's teens believe one's sex at birth defines one's gender. One in five Christian teens even believe gender is how one feels.[9] Compared to older generations, Gen Z is least likely to consider abortion wrong or to have moral objections to same-sex relationships.[10] Quite obviously, our task is great. Let's consider three types of cultural confusion that tend to shape the worldview of young Christians and contrast them with a biblical view.

Cultural Confusion 1: Love Equals Affirmation

One of the most common questions I receive from young Christians is how they can love their LGBTQ friends. They want to follow the teachings of Jesus, and they also want their friends to be happy, and yet they know that *not* affirming their LGBTQ friends will likely end up driving a wedge in their friendship. One of the reasons this dilemma is so difficult is that many young Christians have adopted a *cultural* view of love rather than a *biblical* view. Cultural love often means affirming however someone chooses to live or identify. If you don't affirm same-sex marriage, you are a considered hateful. Refuse to use a preferred pronoun, and you are labeled "transphobic." On this view, love means "I support you and affirm your self-understanding," regardless of how someone chooses to identify.

The Bible, however, offers a better definition of love. In John 13:34, Jesus said, "Just as I have loved you, you also are to love one another." How did Jesus love us? 1 John 4:10 says, "In this is love: not that we have loved God, but that he loved us and sent his Son to be the atoning sacrifice for our sins." Jesus wasn't looking out for his personal interest when he entered our world to die for us. He was focused on us and what we needed. Love is outward focused on the best of another. In light of biblical teaching, here is how I define love:

> **Love is making the security, happiness, and welfare of another person as important as your own.**[11]

Love is not a feeling, but a commitment to the best of another, *even if* the other does not recognize or accept the reality of the good. In other words, love does not necessarily imply the person recognizes that we are truly acting in a way that protects and provides for them. In fact, many may even confuse loving actions for hateful ones. After all, people jeered at Jesus on the cross. Love involves being committed to the objective good of another, regardless of how they feel.

As the designer and creator of sex, God knows what is best for all of us. He knows what is best for you, what is best for me, and what is best for our neighbors. A girl may feel like sleeping with her boyfriend, but it is not best for her to do so. A boy might enjoy looking at porn, but it is not truly good for him. A young person may feel like acting on their same-sex attraction, but despite what our culture proclaims, doing so is not for his or her own good. This understanding of love actually resonates deeply with Gen Zers, if we can help them see it. In the climax of the Avengers movie *Endgame*, Iron Man willingly laid down his life in order to defeat Thanos. Young people instinctively recognize this as a heroic and loving act. In summary, we must help this generation see through the lie that love involves affirming however someone chooses to live or identify and grasp real love which seeks the best for another regardless of how they feel.

Cultural Confusion 2: Freedom Means Doing Whatever We Want Without Restraint

Recently I asked a group of high school students to define freedom. After some discussion, they agreed on the following definition: "Freedom is being able to do what you want without restraint." They told me that the truly free person would be alone on an island to do whatever he or she wants without any person or law restricting them. Is this really freedom? I would suggest *no*. In response to their answer, I shared a story with the students about a man I met in college while we worked together at a T-shirt stand. He was an alcoholic and couldn't make it through a day without multiple drinks. Although we never discussed religion, he knew I was a Christian, and thus said to me out of the blue, "You know, I can drink if I want." I simply replied, "I agree you are free to drink if you want. But I have a question for you. Are you free not to drink?" My point was simple—he was only free if he could choose not to drink. In reality, he was a slave to his "passions and desires" as Paul described in Titus 3:3. The free person is the one who can say no to the bottle. The free person is the one who is able to say no to looking at porn. The free person is the one who says yes to loving God and loving other people as they were meant to be loved. Thus, freedom is not doing whatever we want, but cultivating the right wants that allow us to properly love God and other people.

What about the second part of the definition? Is freedom doing what we want *without restraint*? Again, I am not sure that it is. Think about it— are we freer if we bang on piano keys without restraint, or if we follow the guidance of an instructor who disciplines and guides us? The answer is obvious. The instructor helps restrain our actions so we can use a piano as it was meant to be used—as it was *designed* to be used. Discipline and restraint are necessary for producing beautiful music. Paradoxically, freedom comes not from resisting restraint, but from submitting to the right restraint. This is why boundaries are necessary for true freedom. Psalm 119:9–10 asks, "How can a young person maintain a pure life? By guarding it according to your instructions. With all my heart I seek you. Do not allow me to stray from your commands." In other words, seeking

God and following his commandments are the best ways a young man (or young woman) can stay pure. The psalm also discusses how living without boundaries enslaves us to the hunger of greed. Paradoxically, throwing off God's commandments actually restrains our freedom. To summarize, true freedom is not a matter of doing what we want without restraint but of cultivating the right desires and living in obedience to God. In other words, freedom results when we orient our lives according to God's design.

This raises the question of what God designed us *for*. Just like a car has been designed by its creator to operate in a certain fashion, and is only free when used accordingly, humans have been created for a greater purpose and experience freedom only when they discover and live that purpose. Scripture reveals that God has made us for relationship with him and with others (see Gen. 1–2). Jesus said the greatest commandments are to love God and love others (see Mark 12). Thus, ironically, the person alone on an island is one of the least free people on earth, being unable to live out our relational purpose. As we have all learned during the COVID-19 pandemic, we only flourish in healthy, intimate relationships with other people. If we want young people to begin to understand why God has given us certain commandments regarding sex and love, we need to reframe how they understand freedom.

Cultural Confusion 3: Sex Means Everything—or Nothing

It's natural for young people today to buy the lie that sex means everything. After all, from music, video streaming services, and social media, sex is everywhere. Given our culture's obsession with sex, it is easy for young Christians to think sex is the key to happiness. But this is a lie. I know many happy, single people who are not having sex. And I know many unhappy people who are sexually active. Sex is neither necessary nor sufficient for happiness. The Bible teaches that sex is a good gift from God. It's a blessing (see Gen. 1:27–28). And it's meant to be *enjoyed* between a husband and wife in marriage (see Song of Solomon). But sex is not the key to happiness; relationships are.

Young people can also be tempted to buy the lie that sex means nothing. One of the goals of the sexual revolution was to demystify sex through making the claim that it is no different than any other physical activity. I remember hearing one activist say that sex is similar to having a drink of water (I'm not sure what water he's drinking, but I digress!). We intuitively know this is false. In an interview for his role in the movie *Passengers*, Chris Pratt was asked how he cared for his co-star Jennifer Lawrence during the sex scene they filmed for the movie.[12] If sex means nothing, why was he asked about this scene? Why not ask about the scene when they shared a drink? The answer is simple—we all know that having a drink and having sex are not the same. Jennifer Lawrence had to get herself drunk for the filming of one scene of that movie. Guess which one? The sex scene. Lawrence even told *The Hollywood Reporter*, "I knew it was my job, but I couldn't tell my stomach that. So, I called my mom, and I was like, 'Will you just tell me it's okay?' It was just very vulnerable. That was the most vulnerable I've ever been.'"[13] Why was she so vulnerable? Because she knows sex means something.

Sex matters to God. On the positive side, he gave us sex as both a blessing and pattern for multiplying and filling the Earth (see Gen 1–2). On the negative side, avoiding sexual immorality (*porneia*) is found in every vice list in the New Testament.[14] Specifically, Paul said to glorify God by avoiding sexual immorality because it is the one sin we commit against our bodies, which is a temple of the Holy Spirit (see 1 Cor. 6:12–20). And yet, we must also remember that sexual immorality is not the ultimate sin—idolatry is (see Rom. 1:18–32). We must help young people see that sex is not everything, but it's certainly not nothing.

Teaching Sexual Purity to Gen Z

In my experience and research on Gen Z, I have found three important steps for helping them cultivate a biblical worldview on sex, love, and relationships.

Teach the "Why" Behind the "What"

Not long ago, my father and I partnered together to lead a weekend seminar on Christian sexual ethics. After one of my sessions on the dangers of pornography, a young teen came up to me with his mother and said, "Thanks for explaining to me why pornography is wrong. I have always been told that it's bad and that I shouldn't do it, but I never knew why." In learning why pornography is wrong, he moved from having beliefs he accepted to having convictions he owned. This is why my friend J. Warner Wallace has an approach he calls, "Two Whys for Every What."[15] Rather than merely explaining to a young person what the Bible says on a particular topic, we need to give two whys. First, explain why the claim we are making is true. It's tempting to default to "because the Bible says so" when we are asked to defend a claim, but it is also important to make connections beyond the Bible, so students can see why biblical teaching is true.

For example, why is the biblical pattern for sex objectively good for society? Recently I asked a group of high school students to imagine what the world would be like if everyone followed the sexual ethic of Jesus. After some reflection, they realized there would be no sexually transmitted diseases, no crude sexual humor, no divorce, no pornography, and no victims of sexual abuse. The world would objectively be a better place. This simple exercise helped them connect the why behind biblical teaching.

The second why, according to J. Warner, involves offering an explanation of why this should matter to them in the first place. How does it change the way they view the world or treat those around them? Why should they care? I recently led a discussion with a group of high school students about how certain bodily actions—a kiss, slap, or hug—carry inherent cross-cultural meanings. We discussed how a kiss on the forehand means something different than a French kiss. And we discussed what sex communicates, including commitment, trust, permanency, and exclusivity. They all agreed that we communicate with our bodies. Then I asked them a few final questions to relate this practically to their lives (the second why): If we communicate with our bodies, and we are called to honor God and love others, then how should we dress? What kinds of pictures should we post, and not post, on social media? If we want students to embrace the sexual ethic of Jesus, we have to show them why this teaching is important for their daily lives.

Focus on God's Design

Have you ever noticed the first attribute Scripture explicitly reveals about God's character? Genesis 1:1 says, "In the beginning God created ...." We are told that God is a creator, before we are told that God is holy, loving, or just. Why? One reason is that Scripture wants us to know that the world is purposeful. The world is not accidental, and God has designed it according to a plan, which is revealed both in Scripture and nature (see Rom. 1:18–27). As the first few chapters of Genesis reveal, there is a purpose for nations, language, families, plants, marriage, and sex.

Specifically, Genesis 1:27–28 and 2:24 indicate that God designed sex to be experienced between one man and one woman in marriage. While many biblical figures fail to live this pattern, the creation narrative serves as the standard for how God intends humans to relate sexually to one another.

In his book *Flame of Yahweh: Sexuality in the Old Testament*, Richard Davidson demonstrates that God's original design for human sexuality in Genesis is the basis for a biblical theology of sexuality.[16] For instance, Leviticus 18:22 says, "You must not have sexual relations with a male as one has sexual relations with a woman; it is a detestable act." For a range of reasons, including the use of *male* and *woman*, this passage prohibits same-sex sexual behavior because it violates the creation narrative of human beings in Genesis 1:26–27.[17] Similarly, Jesus pointed back to both Genesis 1 and 2 when discussing the permissibility of divorce (see Matt 19:3–6). And the apostle Paul condemned same-sex sexual behavior because it violates God's design in nature, which he says all people should know by observing creation (see Rom. 1:18–27).

I recently had the opportunity to write a book for students on sex, love, and relationships. It's part of the *True Love Waits* campaign, which began in 1993.[18] After much research and reflection, I decided to divide it into three main parts. In part one, my goal is to rewire the secular thinking of our students through addressing their faulty views of love, freedom, and the character of God. The second part is dedicated to God's positive design for sex, singleness, and marriage. And then in the final part of the book, I discuss pornography, cohabitation, the LGBTQ conversation, and other thorny issues of today. Simply put, the approach begins by stripping away secular thinking, building a positive case for God's design, and then tackling difficult issues individually. You may come up with a different approach for teaching Christian sexual ethics, but just be sure to follow the lead of Jesus by pointing students back to God's original design for sex and marriage.

Third, Create a Safe Place for Conversation

There is a lot of talk about creating "safe spaces" today. Sometimes this can mean affirming whatever someone believes and never making people feel uncomfortable. This is *not* what I mean. The best teaching environments incorporate tension and debate. Young Christians need to be pushed out of their comfort zones. And yet this has to be done in a thoughtful manner. According to the Barna Group's Gen Z study, "Many teens are deeply reluctant to make declarative statements about anything that could cause offense, and thus they struggle with anxiety and indecision when it's time to give an answer."[19] Thus, kids need the space to wrestle with honest doubts and ask difficult questions while knowing they will be loved.

One helpful approach is to listen empathetically. Trying to genuinely understand where a young person is coming from is helpful for building relational bridges and trust (see Prov. 24:3). Another key is asking good questions. Jesus was the master at this. Even though he knew the answers, he asked hundreds of questions either to teach a lesson or to prompt faith. People shared with him because they knew he loved them. In my experience, asking good questions is one of the most effective ways to help young people develop a biblical worldview on sex, love, and relationships.

Finally, in your conversations with young people, share stories. Along with asking questions, Jesus told a ton of stories, such as the parables of the prodigal son, the good Samaritan, and the sower and the seed. We love and remember stories. In order to develop biblical convictions on sex, young people need to hear stories of older married couples who have remained faithful to each other. They need stories of singles who follow the ethic of Jesus and live meaningful lives. They need to hear stories of people with same-sex attraction who are resisting the narrative of our culture. They need to hear the stories of de-transitioners who regret their sex change and transition back to living in congruence with their biological sex. They need to hear stories of people who have failed sexually and been restored by God's grace. And they need to hear *your* story. Whether you are married or single, you have a story and life experience young people need to hear.

Because of the ubiquity of smartphones, this generation of young people are often referred to as "screenagers."[20] They have more voices speaking into their lives than any previous generation. As a result, they desperately need caring adults who will help them see through the lies of our secular culture and cultivate a biblical sexual ethic. My prayer is that this might be *you*.

CHAPTER 9

WHO AM I? GEN Z, IDENTITY, AND THE *IMAGO DEI*

Jacob Shatzer

Identity as a Moving Target

"Who am I?" What a question! We start exploring it as children through the eyes of others and based on static characteristics. Tim Flach's *Who Am I? A Peek-Through-Pages Book of Endangered Animals* reminds us of this: "I have a black furry mask, and I'm naturally shy. I spend nearly fourteen hours a day eating and can weigh up to three hundred pounds! Who am I?"[1] (A giant panda, by the way.)

We don't graduate from this question when we finish children's board books, however. It just keeps coming at us from different sources, and different people propose different ways to answer it. Pop psychology encourages us to somehow negotiate the balance between self-direction (You can be whomever you want to be!) and self-discovery (Find the true you on the inside!) all while skirting the boundary of self-deception. Movies and novels draw us in with stories of lost memory and reconstructed identity—whether that's Jackie Chan's 1998 *Who Am I?* action film ("The one thing he didn't forget was how to fight!") or a novel by Sam Tschida, *Siri, Who Am I?* (a millennial with amnesia pieces together her life through her Instagram account).[2]

Christians certainly toss our answers in, as well. Books and sermons abound on finding our identity in Christ, as a child of God, in the image of God, as a servant of God, as an alien in this world, as a priest, as a friend of God, and on and on. While attempting to provide some strong sense of identity, even the Christian answers can sometimes provide more confusion and diversity than certainty!

If we're honest, this question of identity has probably been with us as long as there has been an us. I'm almost certain that, right before Adam heard God ask in the Garden, "Where are you?" Adam was thinking to himself, "Who am I?" Especially after his sin. Yet we see this question taking a new, powerful, and often painful twist in our world today.

This is true because of a number of factors. For one, there seem to be so many options available to us to choose who we want to be and how we want to live. And as an aside, we often struggle to distinguish between who we are and what we do in a performance-oriented society. We can become overwhelmed by our choices, not sure if we can make the right one, or whether we should stick with the path we've chosen. But there's more to it than that. We also are constantly bombarded by messages that intentionally or unintentionally make us feel inadequate and in need of change. The intentional messages are called ads. The unintentional messages are the ones we pick up on social media as we see how awesome everyone else is and how much fun they're having. This is hard enough to navigate as adults; it is far more difficult in the formative years of youth and young adulthood.

Research on Gen Z demonstrates many of these difficulties.[3] For instance, Gen Z considers their sexuality or gender to be central to their identity, in a much higher degree than previous generations. As we'll see in the following, this topic is related closely to our understanding of what it means to be human and whether we entirely construct who we are or not. They also are growing up in a much more diverse society, which has benefits as well as challenges. Gen Zers have a greater appreciation for diversity, but they also have an increasing belief in religious and moral relativism. The goals that Gen Zers set for themselves also show this challenge of finding an identity in what we do. The drive to accomplish a lot before the age of thirty—finish education, start a career, become financially independent, and follow their dreams—is stronger in comparison even to Millennials. Gen Z recognizes and appreciates how different people can be, which, in turn, expands their sense of what might be right and wrong and drives them to make their particular mark early in life. And as they wrestle with what it means to be an adult, financial independence ranks highest, even in a time when such independence is more and more of an economic challenge because of rising student loans, fewer entry-level jobs, and general job insecurity in a rapidly changing economy that has been ravaged from the effects of the COVID-19 pandemic. In short, the very elements of life that Gen Zers think might allow them to chart their identity are uncertain and changing. The target is moving, and it's getting smaller. And some don't think there is a target at all. In short, the issue of identity looms large in all of these challenges, but the potential answers scatter attention and increase confusion.

Our Culture's Answers

Our culture is ready to provide a plethora of possible answers to questions of identity. But underneath this variety of answers are a few basic commitments and assumptions. Coming to understand the answers at these levels provides us with an understanding not only of particular approaches but of the undergirding logic that makes sense of and fuels them all. In what follows, we'll focus on two basic commitments or assumptions, with a few connections to particular issues. As you read, consider what elements of identity you're aware of that also connect to these underlying issues.

Constructivism

First, in our culture, we tend to see the self primarily as something we create. This is *constructivism*, and we are too often blindly committed to it. We build who we are. On the philosophical level, this is based on the idea that there really isn't anything solid that determines us as human. Rooted in a rejection of essences, this philosophical mood flips the way many people think. There is not some stable humanity by which we know when we see a human, or whether we are humans. Instead, *human* is just a term we use, age by age, to refer to the commonalities that we happen to have. Those commonalities might change, and we certainly can't use them to limit anyone's freedom or sense of identity. While this is rooted in ancient debates going back at least as far as Plato and Aristotle—and flaring up in the modern period around the advent and development of nominalism—it regularly pops up in our popular culture as well.

One place where this line of thinking is making the most headway is in the area of sexuality. An increasing number of people are moving from the idea that there are social aspects to expressions of sex roles to the idea that gender itself is a completely social construct, and thus fully malleable. Rather than seeing any sort of essence at the root of discussions of sexuality, these thinkers argue that everything about being human—and especially sexuality—is not biologically determined but instead a social performance.[4] These perspectives are becoming much more prominent in Gen Z, with one-third saying that "gender is 'what a person feels like.' "[5] This idea reflects not only philosophically-based social constructivism, but it also seeps into, reinforces, and is reinforced by elements in our popular culture.

On a popular level, we recognize this assumption in a variety of stock phrases that we tend to take for granted. "You can be whatever you want to be" used to be a phrase meant to encourage children to try hard in school or in sports or in art or in whatever field they wanted to pursue. Without many of us noticing, it has taken on new meaning as it has been expanded to include other sorts of self-making. It has seeped into our collective consciousness and made us think that who we are is more rooted in the way we answer that call—be whoever you want to be—than it is by who we were made to be, or who we are called to be, as it would have been in earlier eras.

Another popular phrase pushes us in the opposite direction, demonstrating the way our modern sensibilities tear us apart. You can be whatever you want to be, but you also should "be true to yourself." While the first phrase emphasizes that you can set out to decide what you want to be, the second implies that there is something inside you that you need to seek out, excavate, and then honor. Or at the very least, as you build yourself into whomever you want to be, make sure you check that you are authentic to who you already are. But can you be who you want to be if you don't find it authentic with what you discover when you look into your depths? In other words, how are these two orienting questions related? We often simply live with the tension caused by this drive to constructivism.

Techno-Optimism

A second basic commitment or assumption of our culture, in addition to constructivism, is a strong sense of *techno-optimism*. This optimism is related to a much deeper assumption about progress. Again, a classic modern idea has gained renewed momentum. Just as with new social attitudes and technological possibilities, phrases such as, "You can be whatever you want to be," take on new meaning, so, too, does the classic idea of progress morph into something new. The modern idea of progress was related to specific goals, such as decreasing violence, increasing human rights and political participation, and alleviating poverty. In our world, however, the idea of progress has become more closely linked to our insatiable appetites for increasingly faster, more interesting devices. The modern idea of progress also had a much clearer moral component as well; it was linked to becoming better humans—measured in morality, not simply life expectancy and quality of life. While this desire for moral progress still exists in some circles, it is largely absent from the assumptions behind technological pushes for progress.

What makes our techno-optimism different than the modern belief in progress is the location of the improvement. By and large, we all believe that technology can and will solve any problem to which we apply it. In some cases it might take more time or money than we expect, but deep down, we think technology will eventually solve it. Even though new technology inevitably creates new problems, we expect technology to fix those too. Where does this hope come from? It stems from an optimistic outlook on the ongoing march of technological solutions.

Toward the extreme end of the continuum are transhumanists and posthumanists who argue that since what we currently call human is simply the product of the evolutionary process, we can (and should) take control of that process to make ourselves into whatever *human* is going to be next, rather than just waiting the millions of years for evolution to take care of it by natural means. Choices may include making possible radical life extension, creating human-machine hybrids, and departing the biological body entirely to live eternally in some digital environment.

These transhumanist visions are beginning to entice the popular imagination. Such television shows as *Black Mirror* explore some of the more shadowy corners of these possibilities, while such movies as *Downsizing* approach possible changes with more humor. Famed sci-fi novelist Neal Stephenson's *Fall: Or, Dodge in Hell* (William Morrow, 2019) teases out the complexities and uncertainties of digital consciousness, as he weaves a story tracing the sudden death of a billionaire with his family's attempt to navigate the strange world of cryo-preservation and digital immortality. The book also wrestles with what it might be like for a person to be "reborn" in a digital world, with limited if any memories from their first life. This leads to multiple questions of identity: Who am I? What makes me who I am? How am "I" related to my body? My mind? My memories? Such cultural products help us grasp the difficulties of these questions, even if they don't provide compelling answers.

Constructivism and techno-optimism provide what we might call two values or directions that characterize a cornucopia of cultural answers to questions of identity. We think that our identities are primarily ours to build and shape, and we're very optimistic about our ability to use things like technological advance to make our lives and identities better. These ideas underlie all sorts of ways we process and talk about identity. And, as you're probably thinking, both can be good things! But they're only good when subordinated to other values and trimmed of their idolatrous edges. But what might these bigger values be? And how do we avoid idolatry in our understanding of identity?

The Bible's Framework

The Bible teaches that humans were created in the image of God. This topic can, and has, taken up entire books. It isn't that the Bible speaks of this idea over and over again, but that the idea serves so foundationally for the biblical story and for Christian reflection on what it means to be human.

Who We Are

The idea that we are created in the image of God is introduced in the earliest chapters of Genesis. Genesis 1:27 says simply, "God created humankind in his own image, in the image of God he created them; male and female he created them." Some of what is going on here, as argued by many Old Testament scholars, relates to the actions of rulers in the ancient Near East. It was common for rulers to set up images of themselves in far off lands to represent their rule—to stand in for them and point to them. That is part of what God communicates here about humans, the high point of God's creation, given a gift and a task by God. We see later that being created in the image of God serves as a reason for the significance of human beings. For instance, in Genesis 9:6, the death penalty for murder is based on the fact of the victim of murder being created in God's image.

Christians have circled around three main ways of explaining just what this image of God in humanity is. We'll look at them briefly, in no particular order. First, the *substantial* or *substantive* view holds that there is some unique quality that humans possess, such as moral freedom or intellectual abilities or the human will. To be in the image of God, then, is to be able to think, to be moral, or to exercise a will. Second, the *relational* view sees the image of God as the ability and need to establish and maintain relationships. According to this view, to be in God's image is to be in relationship with God and with others, just as God is a relational Trinity, always in relationship as the Father, the Son, and the Holy Spirit. Third, the *functional* view of the image of God centers on the idea that the image is more about a task or role humans are given by God. The image is seen in what humans do.

Problems emerge when we seek to isolate one of these. If we only emphasize the substantive view, we might think of some humans as more human than others, simply because they more clearly demonstrate the particular quality, such as intellect. The relational view on its own cannot adequately distinguish humans from other creatures because other creatures exist in degrees of relationship and dependence as well. The functional view seems incomplete when focused only on what humans do because it relies on certain qualities, as in the substantive view, in order to carry out particular tasks.

Fortunately, we do not have to pick only one of these three perspectives. In fact, we can connect them in a way that balances some of the tensions we have observed in our cultural answers about identity. The substantive aspect of the image of God reminds us that God has created human beings with unique capabilities and qualities that define us as human beings. While some display these to a greater degree than others, we do not earn our humanity by demonstrating them. The relational view reminds us that we cannot think of ourselves independently; to be a person is to be in relationship. The functional view reminds us that we are not left on our own to determine our direction. Rather, when God created humans, he gave us a task and the capabilities and relational qualities needed to accomplish it, by his grace.

Did you catch how these views help cut through the current tension? We noted before that modern culture pulls us in two directions: pick who you want to be, whatever that might be, and look deep inside to find who you really are. We see with the image of God, that God has created us as humans with certain qualities and abilities, things that define who we are as humans. He has put us in relationships that bind us in and limit us and define us. He has also given Christians a task to do—to steward his creation and to work as members of the body of Christ. These truths help balance the ways in which we seek to live into the unique human beings God has called us each to be, while rooting ourselves deeply in God's creation and call.

Reflecting on the image of God helps us in another way too. Theologians have explained that the image of God is not something we can lose. It was marred by the fall into sin, and we fail to be faithful to God's image when we choose to sin, but we don't lose God's image. To be human is to be in the image of God. Similarly, humans who suffer with disability, pain, illness, and injury do not become less human because of these problems.

If we cannot lose the image of God because of disability, we also cannot create it on our own—nor do we need to. It is given to all by God. We receive. Further, just as disability does not diminish the image, no form of human enhancement can increase that image. If the image of God was only about our intellect, then we might think someone with a brain-computer interface that increases intelligence is *more* in the image of God. But we can't enhance God's image by increasing capabilities. The only path to true identity is through receiving our identities as given by God, redeemed by Christ, and sanctified by the Holy Spirit.

Now, there are all sorts of modern advances that can help overcome evil and pain and suffering, and we should embrace them as signs of God's grace and coming kingdom. Christians do not need to be against biomedical advancements that save lives and alleviate suffering or improvements in consumer technology that make it possible to communicate meaningfully with family and friends who are far away. But we can't use these things to make humanity, or remake humanity, in aggregate or in the mirror. That's not where those things fit theologically. We don't make humans; we don't make ourselves more human; and we don't create who we are.

Where We Are Going

As noted, the only path to true identity is through accepting our identities as given by God, redeemed by Christ, and sanctified by the Holy Spirit. In other words, where we are going is toward the image of Christ. God has decided that his people will be made into the image of his Son (see Rom. 8:29). That means, when we wonder what we should look like in the future, the dominant image should be that of the Firstborn Son, Jesus Christ. We should not imagine a self that is constructed upon our own desires, goals, and preferences, but one formed into the image of Jesus. Later we'll talk about the balance between the created aspects of our identity and the transformational, Christ-constructed aspects of our identity.

How We Get to Where We Are Going

Before we explore that, however, we need one more element when considering our identities. If we are created in the image of God, and we're headed to being made into images of Christ, how do we get there? The foundation of our hope in becoming like Christ is not our own personal intellectual or moral effort. God has not set a standard and then left us alone to figure out how to get there. Instead, he has promised to send the Holy Spirit, who helps us remember the teachings of Jesus (see John 14:26) and works out our salvation within us (see Phil. 2:12). There is obviously much more that can be said about the work of the Holy Spirit, but when it comes to our growth into our mature identities, we must remember that the primary answer to "How do we get there?" is the work of the Holy Spirit—by God's grace—not our ingenuity, effort, or desires. Granted, the Holy Spirit can and does work through all of those things, but we must line them up under the work of the Holy Spirit into the image of Christ for the glory of God, and not elevate our abilities on their own or orient them to our own choice of ends or goals.

We know that being shaped into the image of Christ, while determining our identities, doesn't actually mean we will all look like a first-century carpenter-turned-prophet-and-teacher. Yes, there is something that is the same about all humans who have been created by God and all Christians who are being made into the image of Christ. But there are also individual elements that are genuinely different and truly developing through life. How can we balance both the stable and the changeable aspects of our identity?

The answer is locating the stability in God and the changeability in his work in his people. Theologian Ryan Peterson provides helpful thinking here, as he argues "the imago Dei is given stability by the life of God, and therefore human identity as God's image has a stable frame of reference." God provides that stability, and we can't change that. However, we are in the process of being conformed "to God through vision and love," which "necessitates that humans become what they are through time. Therefore, while the [goal] is stable, the process of human 'becoming' is fluid and flexible."[6] In other words, we do not have to pretend that our identities do not grow and change. We can see that in connection with God's work in us, constructing us into younger siblings of Jesus Christ.

We must, however, remember who sets the rules for this construction. When we think carefully about the Bible's presentation, it follows that "constructed identities are self-characterizing interpretations of (1) one's particular existence within creation as an individual human being, (2) one's connection to other particular human beings, and (3) the roles and responsibilities one has or ought to pursue." In other words, God himself constructs us as individuals with our particular gifts, in our particular communities, and for his glory. For "as creatures of God, humans interpret their existence socially and individually before God. This interpretive enterprise is logically posterior to one's created identity."[7]

Anderson helps us understand that *identity* must be used in two ways: (1) God's determination to create human beings with a unique nature, and also (2) God's calling, formation, and sanctification of individuals as individuals. As Anderson argues, "Therefore, God's determination of human identity and the fulfillment of that identity in Christ, as these are communicated in Scripture, should guide the self-characterizing interpretations of God's people as we continue to construct personal and social identities."[8] This combination—of created and constructed identities—helps us hold together the way that we see identities and selves develop and change, especially in relation to life stage and particular callings and desires. But it does so in a way that is not in conflict with our created identities. God's work to construct us into the image of Christ builds identities that are created by God and serve as mirrors of Christ in their own beautiful, individual ways. By doing that, we live into the new covenant that Christ established on the cross. It isn't that our identities are static and unchanging; rather, it is God who stabilizes our identity as humans and constructs our identities as individuals, in accordance with his Word and by the power of his Spirit.

Conclusion

Our identity is not built but continually received, as we live life *coram Deo*, before the face of God, as those invited into covenant with God. To be human is to be one who covenants with God. Our human covenantal relationships prepare for and point to this. Self-actualization occurs, then, in Christ, as we're continually formed into his image. Seeking our identity elsewhere will fail, but centering identity in—and growing into—Christ underdetermines diverse aspects of identity. In other words, it determines some things—our redemption, status as children of God, and growth in holiness, but it doesn't determine everything. There are many ways to live a faithful Christian life. Our identity in Christ opens up and fuels development of godly personalities, interests, and more.[9]

Perhaps if we consider our identities as developing properly within the context of covenant with God, we can see growing to be like Christ as the center of gravity, with worshipping idols marking the out of bounds. This sort of thinking keeps us focused on Christ and the hard "working out your salvation with awe and reverence" (Phil. 2:12), while also protecting us from some of the extreme versions of transhumanism and other forms of remaking humanity in other ways. It protects us from worshipping the idols that humans have continually grown adept at creating and promoting. We can't allow our identities to become idols or to be swept up in the worship of anyone or anything but God.

Gen Z's pursuit of an identity is best seen as our answer to a very important question. It is the question that the Gospel writers wanted to place before us, the one on the lips of Jesus himself when he asked his disciples, "But who do you say that I am?" (Matt 16:15). The Gospel writers presented us with Jesus Christ in order to confront us with the question, "Who is this man?" Our identities are formed as we answer that question with the stories that are our lives. *Homo sapiens* become *homo narrans* (humans as storytellers) and *homo confessionis* (humans giving confession), constructing and living into our stories, as we confess the answer, "Jesus is Lord" and "Here I am" (Isa. 6:8).[10] Such a response is the only way to creatively and faithfully receive our identities from God, as he has created us and continues to construct us into the image of his Son, Jesus Christ.

PART THREE
LIVE

Live a Life of Kingdom Influence

Live a life of Spirit-empowered Kingdom influence as you cultivate a servant's heart.

CHAPTER 10

GEN Z'S OVERPROTECTIVE, UNDERPROTECTIVE PARENTS

Stephanie Shackelford

From Helicopters to Drones

About a decade ago, I founded a coaching company to help students and recent graduates live into their purpose. During this time, I've interacted with hundreds of clients, gaining an up-close understanding of Gen Z and their parents. One summer I coached a rising high school senior who always arrived late to our meetings. Her mom would check an app on her phone to see how far away her daughter was, then call to inform me of her estimated arrival time. Although this scenario sounds like helicopter parenting 2.0, it resembles a new parenting style adapted for this digital age: drone parenting. Rather than physically hovering over their child's every move like a helicopter, drone parents rely on today's technology, apps, and devices to monitor from a distance.[1] Not wanting to be perceived as helicopter parents, the parents of Gen Z keep a close, but distanced watch.

Drone parents can track their children like one does an Amazon package, knowing their kids' every move throughout the day. Parents with a radar-like presence can quickly become overprotective and over-involved, leaving their kids with no freedom to explore and develop on their own. With continuous parental oversight, children risk losing their creativity, emotional awareness, and ability to connect with others.[2]

At the same time, parents can now give more freedom to their children while remaining loosely aware of what's happening in their kids' lives. The risk of this hands-off, app-on approach is underprotective parenting at a very vulnerable time in their kids' lives. Parents think that because they're monitoring their children, they are safe. Meanwhile, kids need greater support in learning to navigate the world of social media, cyberbullying, and inappropriate and harmful online content.

Are Gen Z's parents overprotective or underprotective? Both. They are what the apostle James calls "double-minded" (James 1:8). This chapter explores the dichotomy of Gen Z's parents, who are simultaneously overinvolved and too detached. It also offers a middle ground for providing engaged and appropriately connected support to Gen Z.

Who Are Gen Z's Parents?

The parents of Gen Z are a part of Generation X, born 1965 to 1983 and known as the Latchkey Generation.[3] Generally left alone by their parents to fare for themselves, how they were—and were not—parented now affects their own parenting style. Neil Howe, a leading historian, states that Gen Xers are "overcompensating for their neglected childhoods," viewing their own childhood as "the blueprint of 'what not to do' when it comes to their kids."[4] Gen Xers desire to create home and school environments that allow their kids to develop social and emotional awareness—something they feel they lacked in having to fend for themselves as children.[5]

Whereas a typical Gen Xer may have returned home from school to an empty house, Gen X parents tend to be very involved in their children's schools and extracurricular activities. Since Gen Xers grew up in an era of Watergate, the Challenger tragedy, antiwar protests, and other crises, they distrust established organizations and authorities.[6] As a result, they aim to be the ultimate authority on what's best for their child. As Howe explains, Gen X "parents are about complete control. They often have an extreme distrust of institutions—really, of anyone and everything outside of their inner circle of family and friends. Combine that with the tight bonds they have with their children, and you get parents who demand control, options, transparency and oversight."[7]

Some ways this control plays out is ensuring kids' safety—whether keeping bottles free from harmful BPA or developing Owlet, a smart sock for a baby to wear so his or her vitals can be monitored via a smartphone at any time of day or night. Yet, Gen X parents are also aware of what they can't control. They present their children with a realistic view of what's necessary for a successful career—hard work and self-discipline—and that everyone does *not* get a trophy.[8] While Gen X parents are heavily involved in their kids' lives, they are also pragmatic and value independence. For instance, one large-scale study surveyed Americans across the generations and found that only a quarter (26 percent) of Gen Z receives homework help from their parents. To compare, 40 percent of the Millennial and Gen X responders agreed that they received parental help on their homework.[9]

As the ultimate authority of their children, Gen X parents also question traditions and values placed on them by others. They are open-minded toward different family structures and cultural perspectives, and they are raising their children to value diversity and inclusivity. Not only is Gen Z the most racially diverse generation in U.S. history, but their friendships also reflect diverse backgrounds, race, and sexual orientations.[10]

Gen X parents are in a complicated situation, raising the first generation of complete digital natives. There is a tension for Gen X parents to be present with their children and protect them from harm, while also placing a high value on independence and self-direction. This double-mindedness can create situations where parents are too protective in some areas of their children's lives and overly detached in others. This chapter will examine each side of the spectrum and its implications for Gen Z's development.

Overprotective Parenting

Safety is a priority for Gen X parents. They define good parenting as keeping their children protected, well-behaved, and happy.[11] These ideals are meant to provide safety, but as research is now revealing, overprotective parenting can have negative implications on adolescents' mental, emotional, physical, and spiritual well-being—the very things that parents desire to protect.

Consider Leo, who was part of my college admissions preparation program. Though typically the program is between the student and me, Leo's mom found a way to engage in every session. When it was time to work on college essays, she was particularly concerned about portraying Leo as service-oriented, though he had a very minimal number of volunteer hours. She had a lot of reasons for why he hadn't been able to volunteer throughout high school, and yet she felt he needed to stretch the truth to ensure that he came across as a well-rounded applicant. She wanted to protect him from potential college rejections, rather than highlighting his other involvements, interests, and strengths.

Leo's mom is not alone in stepping in to protect her child from perceived emotional danger—whether of a college rejection or other scenarios. Gen Z is so accustomed to their parents' involvement in every area of their lives that they lack motivation to separate from their parents.[12] They are comfortable with their parents being ever-present, including on hangouts with friends or on dates. Seven large, national surveys found that today's twelfth-grade students go out with friends less often than eighth-grade students did in the early 1990s.[13] Today's twelfth graders are also going on dates as often as tenth graders did in the early 1990s. These findings, along with a decline in adolescents working for pay, driving, and participating in other adult activities, show that adolescents' development has slowed down. Researcher Jean Twenge writes, "They are simply taking longer to grow up."[14]

The comprehensive study of the worldview of Gen Z by the Barna Group and Impact 360 Institute found that only half (52 percent) of Gen Z are *somewhat* excited about becoming an adult.[15] One in four (28 percent) are *not* looking forward to adulthood, and only one in four (22 percent) Gen Z teenagers are most looking forward to freedoms of adulthood. Experts agree that this apathy toward growing up reveals a growing lack of purpose and meaning among this generation. Without their parents' presence, Gen Z feels vulnerable and unsure of themselves. By failing to separate from their parents, however, Gen Z is losing a sense of identity. Having been monitored and managed by their parents their entire childhood, they fear growing up and thinking for themselves.[16]

It makes sense that Gen Z would be hesitant to separate from their parents because they've very rarely been apart from them. Several studies show the decline in children's freedom to roam, explore, and play unattended by adults as compared to a generation ago. One large survey found that children in the 1970s (Gen X) were allowed to go to the playground alone and walk one to five miles by themselves by second or third grade.[17] Now that Gen Xers are becoming parents, they hold a tighter leash. Their children (largely Gen Z) must wait until fourth or fifth grade until they can play outside by themselves. Walking one to five miles alone isn't allowed until middle school. Even when Gen Z has the opportunity for free play, they are not alone. Their parents follow them around via smartphones and tracking apps.

When asked why they are overly protective, parents will often state that the world is more dangerous than when they were kids. But data shows this isn't the case; we are simply more aware of what's going on thanks to social media and 24-7 news channels.[18] As one survey respondent, who was born in 1972, told *Slate*, "Sadly, I find myself parenting from a newspaper headline point of view. If something bad happened after a parenting choice I made, how would it sound when reported in the papers? It makes me more conservative than I'd like to be and my kids miss out on the independence of open-ended play, like I had."[19]

Instead of the freedom to play and imagine unaccompanied, children are monitored every hour of the day, causing what psychologist Peter Gray calls a "play deficit."[20] When they are constantly watched, children lose the autonomy to "explore in their own chosen way." In an article titled "The Overprotected Kid," Hanna Rosen explains it this way, "Ask any of my parenting peers to chronicle a typical week in their child's life and they will likely mention school, homework, after-school classes, organized playdates, sports teams coached by a fellow parent, and very little free, unsupervised time. Failure to supervise has become, in fact, synonymous with failure to parent."[21]

A case could be made for the opposite. Failure to give healthy, appropriate amounts of freedom and space to a child is a failure to allow children to learn how to navigate risks, think creatively, and build relationships on their own. Parents cannot shield their children from all potential perils, and trying to do so prevents children from learning how to handle the physical, emotional, social, and financial risks that they will face in the future. Kids are wired for risk and adventure, and freedom to play can help facilitate growth and development. As Rosen further explains:

> [C]hildren used to gradually take on responsibilities, year by year .... Their pride was wrapped up in competence and independence, which grew as they tried and mastered activities they hadn't known how to do the previous year. But these days, middle-class children, at least, skip these milestones. They spend a lot of time in the company of adults, so they can talk and think like them, but they never build up the confidence to be truly independent and self-reliant.

As parents aim to protect their children and manage their day-to-day schedule, children begin to overly rely on this protection, making it difficult to grow into their own person. Childhood mental health disorders, particularly anxiety and depression, are on the rise.[22] There is also a trend toward a decline in empathy and a rise in narcissism among college students.[23] A researcher of creativity, Kyung Hee Kim, has found that "over the last 20 years, children have become less emotionally expressive, less energetic, less talkative and verbally expressive, less humorous, less imaginative, less unconventional, less lively and passionate, less perceptive, less apt to connect seemingly irrelevant things, less synthesizing, and less likely to see things from a different angle."[24] Much of this he attributes to the reduced amount of free play for children and overscheduling structured academic and extracurricular activities, alongside increasing amount of time interacting with electronics. When children don't have the freedom to play, make decisions, and make mistakes, they turn to electronics to entertain them, and they rely on their phones to connect with others. When children are happily occupied by technology, parents then tend to swing toward underprotective parenting.

Underprotective Parenting

Though much of this news about parenting styles is negative, consider how Gen X was largely raised with minimal parental involvement. Many Gen X parents indicate that they now desire to give their children the protection that a loving, attentive parent can offer.[25] These are worthy aims, and the Barna Group's Gen Z study found that half of Gen Z says that parents are their primary role model. However, only one-third state that family is core to their identity. All other generations rank family and religion as most important to their sense of self. In contrast, a majority of Gen Z rates personal achievement (43 percent) and hobbies (42 percent) as central to their identity.

It appears that Gen Z feels the suffocation from their overprotective parents. And they are using technology and devices to fuel their identities. Social media "likes" can feed their feeling of achievement, and video games can become a serious hobby. Overprotective parents struggle to let go of the handholding and allow their children to make decisions on their own—always knowing their parents will be ready to offer love and support as needed. The exception to this is in the world of electronics, social media, phones, and technology. Parents need to hold these hand-held devices alongside their children. Here, however, parents are largely underprotective.

The Barna Group's Gen Z study found that only two out of five (41 percent) engaged Christian parents have talked to their teenager about healthy media usage. One-quarter (24 percent) feel unprepared to have a conversation about it. Other chapters in this volume have already covered the data around digital technology and mobile devices. Kids and teens are spending *a lot* of time online. The problem is that parents oftentimes don't know how to monitor all of the devices and how to appropriately limit screen time. The Barna Group's Guiding Children study found that engaged Christian parents rank peer influence (35 percent), digital content (31 percent), video games (30 percent), busyness (25 percent), social media (23 percent), family struggles (20 percent), and internet searches for inappropriate material (17 percent) as among their top three struggles in guiding their children's spiritual formation.[26] One-third (34 percent) of engaged Christian parents are media-stressed, meaning they ranked at least two media-related issues among their top three struggles. "Distraction, pornography, bullying and information addiction are all ancient problems. But when the world can fit in your pocket, they become all but inescapable."[27] With youth anxiety, depression, and suicide on the rise, children are certainly feeling these pressures—as are their parents.

One study out of Michigan State University found that adolescents consider themselves experts in IT, believing they surpass their parents' technological abilities.[28] This gap leaves room for teens to use their knowledge of technology to create alternative worlds in which they choose to participate, using IT as a means to explore their autonomy and identity apart from their family. Adolescents have almost constant access to numerous types of communication technology, relying on them to interact with others and develop their own identities. Another study found that communication technology exacerbates the levels of anxiety and distress that often accompany the identity development process.[29] When adolescents prefer to use technology for interpersonal communication, it corresponds to higher levels of peer aggression, relationship anxiety, and existential anxiety. Furthermore, it is related to a decrease in the quality of peer relationships.

All one needs to do is observe a group of teenagers who have free time. For instance, during one of my weeklong college preparation programs, students jumped on their phones as soon as I released them for lunch. Even during five-minute breaks throughout the day, they did not know how to engage or interact with one another, avoiding eye contact and concentrating on their phones instead—escaping into the perceived safety of their curated, crafted online world. One teen spent the entire forty-five-minute lunch break neglecting to eat his sandwich in favor of choosing the best Snapchat filter.

Kids are certainly addicted to technology. "However, it may be valuable to reflect more on *how* kids spend their screen time than on *how much* time they spend—whether active or passive, social or isolated, creating or merely consuming," explains the Barna Group's Guiding Children study.[30] "Media issues are not only about the scope or scale of screen time; among other things, they also relate to the issue of peer influence—because, thanks to their mobile devices, kids (especially older ones) bring peers with them everywhere."[31]

Though many parents have time limits for their children's media consumption, they don't know *how* that time is being spent. When there is little supervision and parental engagement, it leaves space for children and adolescents to find answers to hard questions online. Peers, as well as YouTube influencers and TikTok stars, become kids' primary mentors and guides. At a time when adolescents are still maturing, learning to discern truth, and understanding how to make wise decisions, they need a parent as a guide alongside them. Over half (52 percent) of Protestant youth pastors say that a defining factor of Gen Z is how technology and social media have shaped the way they think and interact with others.[32] Almost half (46 percent) of pastors also indicate that spiritual and moral relativism is a defining trait of Gen Z. Media and technology have a huge influence on Gen Z's worldview. Without a parent's presence to help navigate the myriad voices and perspectives, charismatic YouTube channels, curated photos on social media, and peer "likes" fill in the gap to define Gen Z's life for them.

For concerned and overprotective Gen X parents, screens can be a break from always needing to be present. As the research makes clear, however, being uninvolved in kids' online lives can have detrimental effects. Gen Z needs parents who strike a balance, being neither overprotective of their children's freedom to play, develop friendships, and learn from mistakes while also being more engaged digitally, helping their kids through the tricky world of technology.

The Way Forward: From Double-Mindedness to Single Focus

Parents desire the best for their children. They want to invest in them, develop them, and keep them safe. When combined with the available technology to schedule each minute and track every movement, these good desires can lead to overprotective parenting. Though parents may be on their phones managing their kids' lives and keeping track of their whereabouts, they aren't always aware of what their kids are doing on their own devices. Being ever-present is tiring, and keeping up on the latest technology is exhausting, so it's easy to see how parents become underprotective in monitoring their kids' online lives. However, as the apostle James warns, this kind of "double-minded" person is "blown and tossed around by the wind" (1:6). What Gen Z needs is a secure place from which to navigate the bumpy waters of growing up.

As this chapter illustrates, the emotional, social, and mental implications of double-minded parenting can be dire. Yet, also consider the effects on children's spiritual development. When overprotective parents constantly tell their kids what to do and how to act, it leaves little space for children and adolescents to learn to wrestle with challenging spiritual questions. Instead, hard questions are either avoided or answered for them. When they enter adulthood and leave home, young adults are ill-equipped to practice their faith on their own. For kids who don't settle for the answers that adults in their life give, they seek out answers online. When kids turn to their devices, online media becomes their source of authority. If adults are not present in these spaces, they are unable to have meaningful dialogue around what kids see and learn online.

What is needed to move past double-minded parenting? A single mind, one focused on the ultimate authority found in Christ. Much of overprotective parenting stems from fear. Paul reminds us in Philippians: "in every situation, through prayer and petition with thanksgiving, tell your requests to God" (Phil. 4:6). If the desire is to make Gen Z disciples for Jesus, then parents must let go of control. Disciples learn through instruction and modeling, but they also learn by doing.

One children's pastor cautioned, "Children need boredom and nonscheduled time . . . our kids *need* downtime—time left to just play . . . we haven't allowed them the practice a child needs to become imaginative."[33] Scheduled activities certainly have many benefits and are encouraged for children's development. But parents also need to create margin and resist the temptation to sign their children up for every afterschool opportunity. If kids only engage in activities that are structured and initiated by an adult, they can struggle to grow in their own leadership and problem-solving. Children need space to practice resolving conflict with peers, playing imaginatively, and discovering new interests and strengths.

Along these same lines, children need the freedom to create, imagine, play, and explore. Parents can consider ways they can provide age-appropriate freedom for their kids and allow them to flex their muscles of responsibility. Mistakes will happen and kids will make poor decisions. They will also discover strengths they didn't know they had, and their confidence in figuring things out on their own will increase. These experiences provide fertile ground for discipleship and processing through triumphs and failures.

If fear drives overprotective parents to control, it may be that information-overload causes parents to withdraw. Parents can easily be overwhelmed by today's world, and it can feel hopeless to learn how to navigate all the new technology. To create disciples, however, parents need to come alongside of their children as they engage with media and technology. Particularly for adolescents, tech is a big part of their world. Though learning the latest app may not be parents' idea of fun, it's important to understand where kids spend their time. Without understanding the various opportunities an adolescent has to engage online, it is difficult to make wise decisions on what is appropriate.

Research shows that a helpful way to mitigate potentially negative effects of media is to dialogue with kids about what they're seeing.[34] Parents need to be engaged, asking questions and initiating open dialogue about difficult topics seen in media such as violence, bullying, and sexual behavior. Watching movies together can be one way to engage on tough topics, asking what their kids think about the choices characters make and other themes portrayed.

Lastly, it's important to be present together as a family offline. As one children's church director reminds us, "The research into kids retaining their faith as they grow points toward the need for family warmth. The families that have a high 'stickiness' factor aren't just those who read the Bible every night, but those who simply enjoy each other's company and have fun together."[35] Put the phones away and make time for regular connection as a family, such as going for walk around the neighborhood after dinner, playing a board game, or cranking up the music for a dance party in the living room. Simply providing time and space for unprompted conversation, connection, and experiences can be opportunities for discipleship.

Though this chapter focuses on parenting, the same principles apply to any adult leading Gen Z students. To help grow disciples who are resilient in their faith requires letting go of the tendency to grasp for control and overprotection. When children know they have a secure foundation, the opportunity to flex new muscles on their own is a healthy part of development. Part of providing this secure base, however, is helping kids navigate and process all the media bombarding their lives. Essential interpersonal skills, communication, and problem-solving are best learned in real relationships, not through a device. Let us resist the doublemindedness of over- or underprotectiveness by setting our minds on things above, guarding our hearts and our minds in Christ Jesus (see Col. 3:2; Phil. 4:7).

CHAPTER 11

DISCERNING, DEVELOPING, AND DIRECTING VOCATION

John D. Basie

"So what are you going to do when you graduate?" Undoubtedly this is the most common question college students hear from friends and family as they work their way toward commencement. The question is usually well intended, and yet the way it is phrased assumes that *doing* is paramount—namely, getting a job that can pay the bills and hopefully be somewhat rewarding personally. Recent data show that Gen Zers certainly care about their career success. What I hope to demonstrate in this chapter, however, is that Gen Zers do well to keep the biblical understanding of vocation in mind as they pursue their careers. Toward this end, I will introduce a model that can be helpful in aligning Gen Z's career aspirations with who God designed them to be as his image-bearers. Aligning our gifts with his purposes for us is what discerning, developing, and directing vocation is all about.

A Case Study in Vocational Mistaken Identity

A few years ago I had a phone call with one of my former students (we'll call him James), who was asking for advice on his next career steps. He had been out of college for three years. This young man had a ton of potential and skill but had bounced around from job to job since graduating and

didn't really seem to have much focus. After catching up and exchanging
pleasantries, the substance of the call went something like this:

Basie: So I understand you've been thinking about your next
steps, right?

James: Yeah, I've been thinking a lot about that lately, and I want to
get your thoughts.

Basie: Great, fire away.

James: Well, I was talking with our mutual friend, Rick, the other
day, and he and I are on the same page on this. We *really* want
to make a difference in what we do in this life.

Basie: Absolutely! I'm thrilled to hear you still have this conviction.

James: No, I don't think I'm being clear enough. What I mean is we
want to make a difference through being major influencers in
what we do.

Basie: Super. I hear you. We discussed that kind of thing a lot in
class a couple years ago—and also how influence and God's
call are tied together in whatever station he places you.

James: (Reluctantly) Right ...well, let me put it this way. I don't want
to have influence just through being a "great guy" or a good
Christian working at a fast-food joint—or even some decent-
paying office job. I believe God is leading me to something
bigger—probably much bigger. I'm thinking I'm going to run
for office in my congressional district. And if not, I want to be
CEO of an influential, well-respected company.

Basie: Wow, James—you have some pretty big hopes and dreams
there. It's good to dream big. Many people don't dream
enough. I've got a question for you though.

James: Okay, shoot.

Basie: What indicators tell you these two possibilities are the best
ones for you?

James: Probably the best indicator for me personally is how I thrived
as president of my college's chapter for Students in Free
Enterprise. That was such a great fit and I loved it, and I was
good at it.

The conversation continued, but ultimately, I discovered that James had seized onto the idea that his calling was to be a visible, out-in-front leader of some sort. He was sure it would happen soon, probably just a few short years down the road, and he was *determined* to make it happen. He believed his passion and energy would get him there, and he even gave a tip of the hat to God's power in all of it.

A few years came and went, and James and I kept in touch. While he didn't land that top spot, he eventually landed in a good place. It was only through some trying experiences and hard lessons that he discovered that when he dreamed of his larger-than-life future, he had not been envisioning true vocation. What he realized only much later was that he had been dreaming of the accolades and significance that such a "bigger" vocation would bring.

James's understanding of vocation was a case of mistaken identity. Put differently, he had mistakenly linked his worth—even his very dignity—with achievement and status. In so doing, he had assigned ultimate worth to something fleeting, temporary, and fragile. He was suffering the consequences of idolatry.

James had not understood that true vocation is found only through a heart of service to others. In what follows, I'd like to outline a few of the challenges related to this as well as other common versions of mistaken identity with Gen Z.

My Self Is on a Search—But I'm Coming Up Empty

Like James in the preceding dialogue, all of us are searching for meaning and purpose. To the degree that I am living according to my divine design, my soul—or self—finds meaning and purpose. Put differently, when I live in a way that is consistent with how God designed me, my search leads to true vocation and a flourishing life. Mistaken identity is much less likely for me because I am living with my chief end in mind, which is to glorify God in every aspect of my being, including my work.[1] If I live with this end in mind, I will not be satisfied with cheap substitutes. Many successful professionals, however, never achieve fullness in this sense. Many are on an ongoing frenetic search for meaning through their careers, but all they come up with is perpetual emptiness. They are, in a very real sense, "empty selves." It is no different for Gen Z.

Defining the Empty Self

The notion of the empty self became a topic of scholarly study in the '80s and '90s, with historian and psychologist Philip Cushman providing groundbreaking thought leadership on the subject.[2] In his book *Love Your God with All Your Mind*, Christian philosopher J.P. Moreland, a long-time Impact 360 Institute guest professor as well as a contributor to this volume, takes Cushman's notion of the empty self and unpacks its characteristics.[3] These include the following: inordinate individualism, infantilism, narcissism, passivity, sensate culture, no interior life, and busyness. Although I can easily argue that Gen Z struggles with each of these, let's take four of the most obvious ones.

- *Inordinate individualism:* McKinsey & Co. found in 2018 that expressing individual truth, or "undefined ID," is very important to Gen Z.[4] The key here is that they do not want to be defined by stereotypes. Rather, they want to experiment with various ways of "being myself" and thus shape identity over time.

- *Passivity:* This goes hand-in-hand with apathy toward growing up, which could be evidence for "a creeping lack of purpose and meaning." Moreland points out television as a chief culprit. The Barna Group's and Impact 360 Institute's research on Gen Z is consistent with this claim, noting that Gen Z members are "screenagers" who have never known a world without the internet or personal handheld smart devices, and who spend hours and hours each day on their devices.[5]

- *No interior life:* Spirituality is a low priority; only 16 percent said that becoming spiritually mature is a future goal.[6]

- *Busyness:* Exploring "deep" identity isn't a priority for most; only 31 percent said they desire to discover who they really are. "Doing" is the primary focus of their attention. Finishing their education, starting a career, and success in that career are the highest priorities.[7]

What are we to make of the fact that for Gen Z, career success is the highest priority, but spirituality and discovering their core identity are the lowest priorities? Might it be that Gen Zers, like others who have gone before, are not sufficiently aware of their deepest motivations for choosing a career path? By what means do they discern the way to move forward and avoid the problem of mistaken identity in their search for true vocation? Is it reasonable for an empty self to expect God to grant such discernment in the absence of authentic, biblically-centered spiritual formation?

The Inadequacy of the Empty Self in Vocational Understanding

The real-life vignette with which I began this chapter shows how an ambitious young man, James, put his need for affirmation ahead of serving others. He also lacked humility, which blinded him to the real needs of others and prevented him from achieving the vocational clarity he so desperately wanted. His anxiousness to secure a successful outcome was masked as prideful ambition, and it was quickly taking control over his soul. He had deceived himself into believing he could guarantee the outcome. His soul was an anxious soul.

The anxious and empty self cannot see or discern authentic vocation as service to others, nor can the empty self truly desire it. This is because an anxious self or soul is driven primarily by its baser appetites, a dynamic resulting from living in a fallen world marred by sin. As it pertains to authentic vocation, the empty self just can't get there. All it can see are ways to satisfy its instinctual desires through socially acceptable career rewards, including money, prestige, and power.

The unchecked empty self will never be satisfied. It is insatiable. Because the believer suffering from *empty-self syndrome* demands that his or her own needs be met constantly, this kind of person inverts God's design for vocation and puts the self and all its infantile needs above service to others. In its most extreme form, the desire for career rewards becomes its own form of unchecked sensuality. As Dallas Willard once said, "Sensuality cannot be satisfied. It is not self-limiting."[8] Willard went on to show how the apostle Paul understood this quite well when he wrote, "their god is the belly" (Phil. 3:19), "the feeling center of the self." In other words, they are willing slaves of their feelings or appetites (see Rom. 16:18).[9]

This is not to say that experiencing a few jitters related to one's vocational journey is inherently sinful. Certainly not. Especially with the changing job landscape due to the global COVID-19 pandemic, it is understandable that some Gen Zers are experiencing more anxiety than might otherwise be the case.[10] Gen Z has a deep interest in their future. Specifically, they want to know the future in terms of career. The Barna Group/Impact 360 Institute study on Gen Z referenced throughout this volume makes this clear. Additional statistical nuancing shows that Gen Z members who are self-professed, engaged Christians are even more invested in professional and educational achievement than their Gen Z counterparts who do not consider themselves to be engaged Christians.[11] But this doesn't necessarily mean they have the mindset needed to discern God's will in terms of authentic vocation that lays the Great Commandment—a love of God and love of neighbor—as the foundation of their career edifice.

To be clear, I am not using the terms *vocation* and *career* synonymously, although I am using *vocation* and *calling* interchangeably. One can have a career without authentic vocation, and often that is what we see. A *vocation* is a station of service to others—which may or may not be a paid one, such as being a parent, a caregiver, or other role—whereas *career* refers to what one does in a paid profession to keep bread on the table. A career position can also be a vocation if the primary intention is to serve others. But very often Christ-followers, led by their baser appetites, are enticed by the rewards of a career, and as a result, are blinded to the needs of others. Moreover, they often assume that because they have a full-time paying job, or are preparing for one through pursuing a college education, that the culture says is meaningful that they, therefore, have a vocation also. This isn't necessarily the case.

Disciplines that Lead to Discernment of Vocation

Proverbs 9:10 says, "The beginning of wisdom is to fear the LORD, and acknowledging the Holy One is understanding." Discerning the ways in which we can best serve others requires tremendous awareness. More specifically it requires self- or soul awareness. The conundrum is this: we will not have the kind of soul awareness we need if we rely only upon our own resources to look inward. We need someone outside of us, namely, the One who designed us, to help us see ourselves clearly. To do that, we must admit we cannot do it on our own—an admission that requires tremendous humility of spirit. Once again, Willard has a helpful reminder from the Bible, specifically 1 Peter 5:6: "And God will exalt you in due time, if you humble yourselves under his mighty hand." Humility, says Willard, entails a loss of self-sufficiency.[12] To the extent that this is true, it could have some uncomfortable implications for us, including the possibility that we must admit we are not fully in control of our future.

Combining Passion with Humility

Much of the conversation in the Christian community on finding a vocation revolves around following our passions. There is certainly a place for this. But how discerning are we as Christians with respect to the advice we heed? How would we know if our method of finding vocation is of the Lord? When someone says he or she "feels led by the Lord" to do something, how would we know whether it was, in fact, prompted by the Lord? Rather, what if what the person felt was an impulse grounded in subjective egocentricity? As one writer recently stated, "The follow-your-passion model is egocentric." Furthermore, "it gives the initiative to each person's self-appraisal."[13]

In other words, in our "you-do-you" culture, we are all expected to validate and not question or even evaluate another person's passion-driven decision on vocation. Each person's own conclusion is unassailable since the only method of discernment recognized as valid is an internal sense of call. Yet this formula leaves out the external call—the validation of one's internal call by trusted individuals. This validation ought to occur in robust Christian community, where brothers and sisters in Christ have permission to speak into one another's lives both with encouragement and challenge. Theologian Dan Doriani points out that a person must have both internal and external validation to be certain of a true calling. In the absence of the latter, he or she may be following mere aspiration.[14] This is not to say that passion is irrelevant. Rather, it's to counter to what our increasingly secularized culture tells Gen Z: passion—apart from humble submission to external validation—cannot count for everything.

Jesus's Example of Humility

Left to our own devices, our fallen souls cannot be trusted to discern God's call on our lives. We must have help, and we must be willing to put ourselves in a posture of receiving that help. In the Gospels, Jesus, the second person of the Trinity, continually humbled himself. The first instance of this was in his willingness to take on human flesh and dwell among us. In other instances, when he could have chosen to build a fan base by wowing the people with his miracles, he pulled away from the crowds to be with his Father in silence and solitude. Put differently, silence and solitude were spiritual disciplines that Jesus practiced to humble himself, commune with God the Father, and properly discern his good and perfect will.

My former student James was anxious to quickly secure a position and career accolades. As a young professional, mostly driven by an unhealthy appetite for positional leadership, he unconsciously believed that, in achieving those rewards, he would find rest. But his soul was not at rest in the pursuit of those rewards. Consequently, he had been unsuccessful in the process of discovering, at a deep level, how God had designed him. What was James missing? At a fundamental level, he lacked humility.

Peace as Evidence of Humility

One way to spot authentic humility in someone else is the degree to which they exude a deep sense of peace, especially when others in the same set of circumstances are telegraphing anxiety to everyone else around them.

Humble people take to heart the apostle Paul's instructions, "Do not be anxious about anything. Instead, in every situation, through prayer and petition with thanksgiving, tell your requests to God. And the peace of God that surpasses all understanding will guard your hearts and minds in Christ Jesus" (Phil. 4:6–7).

Those who have found the blessing of this kind of humility are less likely to become anxious about the future. As Willard points out, "Humility is a great rest of soul because it does not presume to secure outcomes."[15]

Gen Z's Lack of Preparedness for Discerning Vocation

As I mentioned previously, Gen Z places little importance on understanding their spiritual depths. Instead, career success is the highest priority, while spirituality and discovering their core identity are the lowest priorities. Based on this data, along with many real-life examples at Impact 360 Institute that corroborate the data, few Gen Zers are sufficiently aware of their deepest motivations for choosing a career path. They tend to assume, instead, that an exciting career equals a God-given calling or vocation.

The reason I have spent this much time discussing the deeper challenges of discernment is that so many Gen Zers lack the kind of interior life and spiritual depth required to be able to discern what God wants to tell them about how they could best serve others through various vocations. What would it take for the Church to help them discern the way forward and avoid the problem of mistaken identity in their search for a true vocation? What if we were to discover that the best vocational discernment process includes practicing the spiritual disciplines of solitude and silence, as Jesus did? How willing would we be to engage more often in these disciplines and then walk alongside Gen Z disciples in doing the same?

The Role of Gifts

Discovering our gifts is fundamental. This is related to the idea of discerning vocation, and certainly these concepts—discernment and discovery—go hand-in-hand. I have had the joy and privilege over the years of walking alongside many young Christ-followers in discovering their various gifts and strengths. What does this look like practically? One way is to take planned, dedicated time to talk—to debrief— what they are learning in their work. This involves asking good, open-ended questions about what is working, what isn't working, and where they can improve. It also involves asking thoughtful questions that help them to pay attention to where they sense God's pleasure in various aspects of their work, as well as where they are encountering obstacles—what pastor Tim Keller calls "thorns and thistles"—in their work. This is a key piece of discipleship that has been sorely lacking in most Bible-believing churches today.

Many Jesus-loving people in the church pews may not fully understand how their faith connects with their work because, among other reasons, their church has most likely emphasized that they are citizens of heaven only. On this view, "ordinary" work such as construction, nursing, or running a small business doesn't really have any inherent eternal value. Sadly, these churches have forgotten that a more biblical view is one that affirms our dual citizenship both in heaven *and* here on earth— the *already* and the *not yet* aspects of God's kingdom. Helping members of Christ's church understand how the Great Commission mandate in Matthew 28:19 ("go and make disciples of all nations") is connected to the cultural mandate in Genesis 1:28 ("fill the earth and subdue it") is one of the most important things we as members of the Church universal can do.

Career Coaching as a Feature of Vocational Discipleship

The discovery of personal strengths and gifts can be facilitated through assessments and professional career coaching. There is something to be said for investing the resources of time and money into exploring one's design with the assistance of personality and career assessments. Although there are many free options available on the internet, I strongly recommend finding a certified professional career coach who holds to a biblical worldview. The main reason for hiring a credentialed coach is that quality coaching—contrary to popular belief—isn't done consistently well when one just wings it.

Coaching is different from mentoring. There are best practices that trained leadership coaches and career coaches have taken considerable time to master. Several of us at Impact 360 Institute, as well as my colleague contributor to this volume, Stephanie Shackelford, have taken time to learn these best practices and have become certified in some key assessments in order to be at the top of our coaching game as we help young Christ-followers learn about how their gifts connect with God's call on their lives. At the Institute, we have made great strides in helping our undergraduate and graduate students understand at much deeper levels their God-given design through credible assessments that measure career interests, personal strengths and weaknesses, and emotional intelligence. Many of our students, alumni, and staff members have also benefited from a formalized, biblical-ly-grounded, life-purpose planning process that has helped them to discern, develop, and direct their various vocations.

Strengthening the Sense of Call through Intentional Development

Discernment as it relates to hearing God's call is essential to discovering our various vocations. In the last section, I noted a few challenges partic-ularly for Gen Z in this regard. Zooming out and seeing the big picture from another perspective, this chapter is about how to engage our call-ings as apprentices of Jesus Christ.

Vocational Discipleship

The endeavor to engage others on how to think about vocation and then live it out is what authors David Kinnaman and Mark Matlock call "vocational discipleship."[16] Pastor Tim Keller and Katherine Leary Alsdorf also offer insightful consideration of this concept in their work.[17] Specifically, "vocational discipleship means knowing and living God's calling—understanding what we are made to do (especially in the arena of work)—and right-sizing our ambitions to God's purposes."[18]

This is at the core of our work with Gen Z disciples at Impact 360 Institute. Our mission is to cultivate leaders who follow Jesus. A signifi-cant part of that cultivation effort includes vocational discipleship. Gen

Zers often experience that the fun part of vocational discipleship is the discovery part—increasing awareness of what they are made to do— through coaching, discipleship groups, personality assessment tools, and more. The not-so-fun aspect is the latter part of Kinnaman's definition—"right-sizing our ambitions to God's purposes." Energetic, ambitious Christ-followers are often much more aware of their capabilities than their limitations. How can we help them find balance? Here are a few ideas:

Clarifying Our Calling through Identifying and Cultivating God-Given Gifts. As we develop our gifts, we stand a greater chance of clarifying our purpose. As that happens, we develop a clearer sense of calling as well. How does this work? As an example, think for a minute about a young person for whom you've provided some kind of instruction or mentoring. You probably noticed gifts possessed by her or him that couldn't be reduced to a practiced skill. Put differently, you probably saw in this young person some ability that could be explained only in terms of *gifting*, something God put in this young person, such as a talent for art that cannot be explained only by skill development or practice. If they have invested time into practicing their gift, then they have also participated in *gift cultivation*. The point here is to say that gift identification and cultivation can give us helpful clues as to our calling.

Valuing Good Work. Developing our calling also means putting effort into desiring it. How does such a thing happen? Is it simply a matter of praying more frequently or more fervently? Certainly, a fuller prayer life is better than less; however, God expects us to steward well the time we've been given, which means choosing a certain sort of mentality about the work God is asking us to do right now. Namely, we choose to see the value and dignity of the work itself instead of obsessing over how the work makes us feel. This isn't about playing mind-games. Rather, it is literally choosing to identify the inherent value and dignity of the work that exists in reality. Put differently, if God has asked us to put our hands to a task for a season, then there is objective value and dignity in the work itself, whether or not we choose to see that reality.

Right-Sizing Ambitions. Strength of calling is related to a healthy desire for the work. I've had the joy and privilege of helping many people discern, develop, and direct their various God-given vocations. Some of those individuals are Christ-followers who have sought to discern whether they had a call to full-time ministry, specifically church-planting. In a few cases, the interview and assessment process revealed that they did not have enough personal desire to do the work. They were not energized about this avenue of service. Their stories often revealed that they were being encouraged by others who saw some gifts that could be used in church planting. But the candidates themselves were not sufficiently invested emotionally and spiritually to be able to say, "I have a strong internal call to this work." That is to say, the external call by far exceeded the internal call.

Challenges for Gen Z in Developing Vocation

One struggle Gen Zers face with respect to developing their vocation pertains to screen time and the use of social media. In volume 2 of the research on Gen Z by the Barna Group and Impact 360 Institute, the data supports the claim that excessive screen time and social media consumption have a deleterious effect on a young person's healthy psychological and spiritual development. For example, "the higher a teen or young adult's screen time, the more likely he or she is to report feelings of isolation, insecurity, and self-criticism."[19] Social media encourages unhealthy comparisons, and as millennial experts Brian and Gabrielle Bosché have pointed out, "comparison kills purpose." Additionally, "social media accounts can be manipulated to make you appear more successful, more happy, and more connected than you really are, yet we give social media and its influencers more power than they deserve."[20] If the ubiquity of screens and social media weren't already challenging enough, COVID-19 has only amplified those challenges to a significant degree.[21]

Another potential struggle is in the area of discipline. Discipline is a key foundational element of developing self and vocation. My experience with Gen Z and younger millennials is that many of them struggle with disciplined habits and follow-through. Although this struggle is common to all generations to some degree, it seems to afflict Gen Z disproportionately, in part due to the amount of social media they consume (on average, seven-and-a-half hours per day, not including school or work-related screen time[22]). What Gen X and Boomers consider to be the basic building blocks of a solid work ethic—punctuality, timely communication, and the ability to look someone else in the eye with confidence as handshakes are exchanged—are uncomfortable and less practiced concepts for many Gen Zers. These are important, but even more important is grit—the discipline to stick with a task when it gets difficult.[23] Gen Zers need to see that long-term discipline goes hand-in-hand with experiencing joy.

The Need to Develop Deep Awareness of Strengths and Challenges

This builds on *discovery* of strengths and challenges. A global study conducted by Gallup in the early 2000s showed that most people, regardless of nationality, believe that the key to success is identifying weaknesses and fixing them. This typically doesn't work. The reason we seek to fix weaknesses is to prevent perpetual, career-wrecking failure.[24] A college student who struggles with slow reading speed and comprehension can certainly benefit from a speed-reading course. This strategy is an example of fortifying a weakness in order to prevent failure, but the student should not be discouraged if she never breaks any speed-reading records. Her natural strengths are elsewhere.

Developing Strengths through Disciplined Practice

I've established that weakness-fixing is necessary in order to prevent failure, but this isn't enough to claim success. Success has to be more than merely not failing. A proven way to drive long-term success is to identify key strengths and seek to build on those. Back to the speed-reading example, participants who were already above-average speed readers prior to a speed-reading course improved exponentially, compared to the below-average reading group. This is a clear example of taking a natural talent, cultivating it through practice, and turning into a strength.

Directing Vocation through Saying Yes and No Intentionally

Although the process of discerning, developing, and directing vocation does not often happen in a neat, linear progression, these elements are present in a process that God uses to form us into the disciples we need to be to carry out the work he calls us to do. That said, to direct or aim one's vocation in a way that produces consistently healthy fruit for the kingdom, one must first have committed himself or herself to discerning and developing that vocation.

Jesus is the best example of this in the Bible. Only after he had taken three decades to discern and develop his sense of calling, as he grew in favor with God and man (Luke 2:52), did he begin to direct his vocation in the fullest sense at the age of thirty. Like Jesus did, we want to say yes to opportunities for service when those opportunities are well-aligned with our sense of God's calling and purpose for our lives.

In his three-year ministry, Jesus said yes to many opportunities for kingdom influence. He stuck with the main plan—the redemption of the world through his crucifixion, death, and resurrection—while also taking (from a merely human perspective) unplanned opportunities to display the grace and power of his Father through performing miraculous healings, feeding hungry crowds, and teaching valuable lessons to his disciples.

Every serious Christ-follower I know wants to bring their best efforts to the work of building Christ's kingdom. As my colleagues in this volume have noted, the culture in which we find ourselves living is increasingly hostile to our faith. Indeed, as others have noted, it is like we are living in a present-day version of Babylon. Bringing one's best to the work means, at least in part, (1) having a deep self-awareness of one's own unique gifts, (2) knowing how he or she can most effectively leverage those gifts long-term for the sake of faithful kingdom-building, and (3) having the fortitude and confidence to push forward, no matter what the challenges might be along the way.

To do this, we must learn which opportunities to accept and which to decline. Simply put, we consider saying yes to opportunities that match up well with our calling and graciously decline those that are outside the bullseye. In my experience as a leadership coach, this kind of discernment is undervalued to a considerable degree, particularly in the Christian community. It seems very few Christ-followers make these decisions with true intentionality. Many say yes to opportunities for service for the wrong reasons, and many say no for the wrong reasons as well. Too often the decision to say yes or no to an opportunity is decided entirely on the mere accident of how much time the person happens to have left in an already crowded schedule.

Another unfortunate dynamic that can interfere with making good decisions about the direction of our calling is an imbalance in our *locus of control*—the degree to which we make decisions based on external factors, including unhealthy pressure from others, versus internal ones, including a healthy sense of self and calling. In my experience, Gen Z Christ-followers tend to lean toward an external locus of control. They may say yes to an opportunity only because they fear harming a relationship if they say no. In some cases, an extreme bent towards an external locus of control goes back to one's childhood and a fear-based pattern of needing to please his or her parents. I have seen many young people choose college majors and even career paths based solely on a desire to please their parents. This is fear-based decision-making. It is a lack of understanding and confidence in how God has uniquely designed us. One of the greatest gifts we can give a Gen Zer is to encourage them to examine their unique design as God's image bearers and to walk with them as they seek to honor him in their various vocations.

Conclusion

Jesus demonstrated perfectly what it means to discover, develop, and direct vocation. Although he was tempted by Satan himself to focus on temporal rewards, he continued to look outside himself to his Father. Jesus did not allow accidents of circumstance to control his decisions to say yes or no to opportunities for kingdom service. A significant key to unlocking a deep understanding of what it means to direct your vocation intentionally is the fact that the resource of time, once it has been used for a certain task, is a resource we can never recover. Fundamentally, this points to a stewardship issue. As Psalm 90:12 says, "So teach us to consider our mortality, so that we might live wisely." May we be faithful in passing this wisdom on to Gen Z, that they may know what it is to flourish as they live out their various God-given vocations.

CHAPTER 12

GEN Z AND SERVANT LEADERSHIP

Phil Alsup

Shifting the Spotlight
from Millennials to Gen Z

Every generational shift brings change. Although advertising dollars always signal the first pivot to a new generation, due to the amount of disposable income teenagers possess, the true cultural changes—and collisions—manifest themselves once the new generation emerges in the workplace. This is where the true clash of both ideas and ideals begins. New thinking pushes against traditional ideas—though often what is deemed traditional is simply what another generation brought with them a decade or so before. Gen Z is no different, and it is clear that they are entering into the workplace in unprecedented times.

In many ways, the marketplace is still adapting to Millennials, a diverse and very different group from the formerly dominant Boomers. The Millenial footprint has been disrupted and delayed by two great upheavals: the 2008 recession and the 2020 COVID-19 pandemic. The 2008 recession eroded Boomer retirement savings, causing them to stay in the marketplace and positions of authority years longer than they anticipated. Just as many Millennials began to progress in their careers, the pandemic hit, affecting and wiping out many industries. With the shift toward remote meetings and touchless services, Gen Z is entering a rebooted marketplace and work culture. In other words, this new marketplace is rife with change. They bring with them many preconceived notions and biases that will sometimes push against norms and other times fill vacuums of the undefined categories produced by the post-pandemic workplace. These uncertainties give Gen Z the chance to have immediate influence as a generation. The question comes to those who now lead: how do we best influence the influencers of the immediate future? The command-and-control models of leadership are all but gone. My hope in this chapter is to demonstrate that servant leadership, among the many theories of influence, is uniquely positioned to be a key strategy in helping emerging leaders of Generation Z to flourish.

Definition and Origin of Servant Leadership

In the history of leadership thought and culture, servant leadership is a relatively new paradigm. Throughout time, the prevailing assumption regarding what qualified someone to lead effectively was centered on the Great Man theory of leadership. In other words, only those born for it could lead others. This was dominant in times of low literacy, when wealth was concentrated in the ruling party. It was difficult to lead kingdoms when one did not have avenues to break into the circles of power.

The Age of Enlightenment began to create some philosophical room for the concept that people did not have to be kings to influence their communities, though this idea remained largely aspirational until the Industrial Revolution. The new era ushered in a middle class and, in turn, created new layers of influence. Still, the assumption that influence was directly tied to positional authority continued through the mid-1900s, especially in the business world. Although pieces of the servant leader model began to show up in leadership writings in the mid-twentieth century, it was not until the 1970s, when Robert K. Greenleaf began to write about specific practices regarding servant leadership, that the concept became formalized as a leadership philosophy that could be studied and strategically implemented. As we will see, however, the practice of leadership as service to others is far older than Greenleaf's thinking; it is the model that Jesus himself demonstrated in his earthly ministry.

The short definition of a servant leader, according to Greenleaf, is someone who seeks to be a "servant first." It "begins with the natural feeling that one wants to serve, to serve first."[1] What Greenleaf was trying to identify is a central motivation, namely a motivation that isn't grounded in an unhealthy desire for position, power, or control. It doesn't even begin with a desire to see change in a current organizational reality. Rather, it springs internally from a desire to serve others. Although not necessarily intended by Greenleaf, this serves as a practical observation of how Jesus sought to influence others and how he taught others to think of themselves. We see this in how Jesus, in the gospel of Matthew, instructed his followers to build their leadership dispositions:

> But Jesus called them and said, "You know that the rulers of the Gentiles lord it over them, and those in high positions use their authority over them. It must not be this way among you! Instead whoever wants to be great among you must be your servant, and whoever wants to be first among you must be your slave, just as the Son of Man did not come to be served but to serve, and to give his life as a ransom for many." (Matt. 20:25–28)

In this passage, Jesus got at the root of how servant leaders function. Their orientation is not toward power and positions of authority; rather it is toward humility. Jesus instructed that, just as he came to serve, his followers must seek to do the same in their efforts to influence others.

Pastor and author Gene Wilkes summed it up this way: "service, not status" should be the goal of the servant leader.[2] In Wilkes's thinking, true servants of Christ do not have a controlling need for success and are perfectly content in *not* seeking the stage. Instead, they seek to serve others—to encourage and coach those around them. By extension, it is through this attitude of servanthood that true influence is created, leaving to God whether he would choose to exalt them rather than seeking self-elevation. The mature Christian is positioned to do this both because they are already serving others and because they have trusted

God to exercise control in their live. This approach actually multiplies leadership influence by empowering others to lead.

Servant Leadership and Gen Z

Anyone who wants to influence a group must first know how group members think. They must be willing and able to work within the group's particular orientations to reach the target group. With this in mind, let's look at some next steps for Gen Z equippers. What follows are insights I've gleaned from other experts as well as my experience in serving this generation at Impact 360 Institute.

Gen Zers Are "Screenagers"

According to the Barna Group/Impact 360 Institute study, 57 percent of Gen Z surveyed are on screens for more than four hours a day.[3] Often referred to as *digital natives*, Gen Z is the first generation to never know a time without smartphones. Their screen time, however, includes more than social media and texting. They are also dedicated consumers of media through outlets such as YouTube and TikTok, among others. Their 24-hour, on-demand access to friends, influencers, and media creates a near-symbiotic relationship between Gen Z and their devices, according to social scientist Dr. Jean Twenge.[4]

The one-way-at-a-time discourse encouraged by social media— either sharing information or consuming it while rarely engaging in true dialogue—has undoubtedly inhibited the socialization skills that traditionally accompanied the growing freedoms of the teenage years. Since their emergence as a recognized group in the 1950s, teenagers have tended to group together in-person for activities or just to hang out. Today's digital natives, however, tend to communicate by shooting electronic messages back and forth. This has caused them to develop differently in several ways.

Whereas in the past, teens were separated from their parents when they were with friends—a natural part of adolescent development— now students are actually *less* mobile and mostly engage with their social circles from home through social media rather than in person. While this means a significant drop in many risky behaviors, such as reckless driving, drinking, and pregnancies, it has worsened social issues as bullying, isolation, and suicide. In other words, according to Twenge, Gen Z may be physically safer, in many ways, but they are more at risk psychologically and emotionally.[5] So how can those who seek to minister to and equip Gen Z work with their "digital native" nature?

Perhaps most important, we must be willing to adapt to new methods of communication. Members of Gen Z have grown up on electronic communication, using a keyboard to talk. The reluctance or refusal of Gen Z to pick up the phone can be frustrating for Boomers and Gen Xers, but we need to understand that they are not at all accustomed to communicating that way. Email is also usually a dead end for contacting Gen Zers. Even texting is not an absolutely reliable; they will usually get around to it, but not always in a timely manner. For many Gen Zers, their primary forms of communication are social media apps, such as Snapchat and Instagram. The familiarity and ease with which they consume social media, even more so than Millennials, means they desire to digest info—including communications—quickly and move on.

For those of us seeking to reach and invest in Gen Z, we have to understand their desire to communicate via social media, while also looking for ways to move beyond it and engage more personally. In many cases, it may not be as difficult as you might think. There seems to be growing tension for many Gen Zers between wanting to be on social media and wanting to break free of its influences. As Twenge writes, "many understand social media is controlling their life but don't feel like they can break free because they would have no life without it."[6] They know that, even if they do actually get together with friends in person, much of that time will be spent looking at screens anyway. This tension represents an opportunity for those who are patient enough to invest in Gen Z. We have the opportunity to *become* the break from screens they know they need but do not quite know how to make it happen in real life.

Those who desire to build influence with Gen Z have to be willing to find ways to meet with them in person, encourage them to put their phones down, and engage in real conversation. By participating in this simple act, we can help them begin to build the basic social development skills many Gen Zers are lacking, which they need to lead and influence others.

The concepts and practice of servant leadership may be a refreshing change from the me-first self-promotion they are likely accustomed to through social media. Success on social media is being seen by as many of your audience as possible. By its very nature, this is an exhausting activity, much like trying to keep a roaring fire burning all hours of the day and night; it has to be continually fueled or it goes out. Imagine how radically different servant leadership appears from the culture of social media. While social media promotes self—or worse yet, an unreal idealized picture of self—servant leadership promotes others. It is based on humility and does not reduce the relationship to how useful a friend is in getting more likes.

Consider this within the context of Wilkes's earlier insight on servant leadership, namely the wisdom that we must first humble ourselves and wait for God to exalt us. In order to influence Gen Zers to be servant leaders, we must first help them break down their cultural orientation that presents an idealized life and prioritizes likes. Jesus understood this as a teacher within the context of his own time. He did not come as a king or a military ruler with the natural authority those positions bring. He intentionally avoided gaining influence by presenting a glamorized view of who he was. Jesus, a teacher from a humble background, sought to connect with people from all walks of life. He was a day laborer just like most of them. Because of his posture of humility, they followed him.

This understanding of leadership and our worth as image-bearers of God can bring tremendous relief to the Gen Zer who has been inundated with messages comparing themselves with the idealized images of others. Again, this was why people connected with Jesus. He was not a powerful, worldly ruler or even a well-off religious leader. He was someone who knew hard days of labor. He went to bed tired only to get up and labor again the next day. He may have even sometimes wondered where his next meal might come from. They saw him, in many ways, as one of them.

This is the inherent message of servant leadership. Not "I get to influence you because of what I achieved," but "I hope to influence you because God believes your life matters." The student does not have to achieve thousands of views or hundreds of likes to merit an investment in them; they get it simply because they are recognized as a child of God—as his image-bearer.

Gen Z's Worldview Is Post-Christian

The Barna Group/Impact 360 Institute research clearly demonstrates that Gen Z's worldview is squarely post-Christian.[7] Even more troubling is that the percentage of those expressing a biblical worldview, according to the Barna Group's criteria, drops with each succeeding generation (Boomers, 10 percent; Gen X, 7 percent; Millennials, 6 percent; Gen Z, 4 percent). While this is indeed concerning, there is simultaneously an amazing opportunity. The same research indicates that Gen Zers, rather than being antagonistic, are often more of a blank slate on spirituality. They are very much a part of a culture that is post-Christian, but they are still drawn to the spiritual. Many of them may not carry the baggage that has caused previous generations to leave the faith. The teachings of Jesus may even be fresh, encouraging, and inviting to them. This gives servant leadership even more of an opportunity to be deeply transformational.

Let's explore this ripe opportunity for a Christ-based influence by looking at how leadership expert Robert Clinton defines leadership. According to Clinton, the "central task of leadership is influencing God's people toward God's purposes."[8] While equipping and influencing followers of Christ is essential, modeling the same principles to those who are not Christ-followers but have a baggage-free model of Christ's love can yield tremendous opportunities for sharing the Good News.

Imagine how powerful the opportunity can be to model Christ to someone with a spiritual blank slate, especially through the practice of servant leadership. Henry Blackaby's definition of spiritual leadership has this principle inherent in its purpose. According to Blackaby, spiritual leaders should seek to lead those who are not God's people as well as those who are.[9] So, the servant leadership practitioner has two distinct opportunities for influence: (1) discipling Christ-followers and (2) sharing the Good News with others.

Servant Leadership as Discipleship

The term *discipleship* has many definitions and strategies. A singular desired outcome of discipleship, however, is to move Christians further and deeper in their journey with Christ. This involves helping them engage in activities in which they are formed spiritually through knowledge and action.

Servant leadership is a tried-and-tested method for discipling others, as demonstrated by the teaching and actions of Jesus himself. Jesus clearly demonstrated that servant leadership is not about position or skill; rather, it is an outflow of demonstrating God's heart for others.

While the ultimate demonstration of the servant leader was captured in Christ's willingness to die on the cross for the sins of humankind, it is also evident in his daily habits, captured in the Gospels, that show Jesus was intentionally modeling something different and meaningful to his disciples. Eschewing the trappings of position and power, Jesus consistently highlighted the importance of putting people ahead of agendas, taking initiative on needs, patiently debriefing teachable moments, and investing the gift of time into people. These are aspects of being a servant leader that anyone can follow. Building up and investing in a Christian brother or sister doesn't require having a title or power; it only requires being willing to take the time to share insights from life experience and distill them into applicable steps for those with less experience.

Blackaby said that, as in Clinton's definition of leadership, we as Christians should not settle for leading people to accomplish stated objectives. The Christian servant leader is only satisfied by leading people toward God's purposes. As Blackaby puts it, the primary task is to "move people from where they are to where God wants them to be."[10] This is the goal of discipleship, and servant leadership can deliver the results to accomplish this, especially when implemented through intentional, in-person time with young people. Here are some ways a Christian servant leader can invest in a younger Gen Z Christian.

Modeling Care

While it is certainly desirable to be able to teach from a position of career success and acumen, when it comes to discipleship, it is neither a prerequisite nor an excuse to keep one from seeking to invest in others. When we invest in Gen Zers, they benefit from and learn the deep value of time spent together. For a generation used to quick, offhand, social media interactions, the opportunity to experience firsthand the value of one-to-one interaction is immeasurable. Even Gen Zers who are still maturing emotionally can see the care evident in one investing their time in them. If Jesus had the time to stop, sit down, and talk with those around him about how to apply what they were learning to their lives, then we too can make it priority.

Modeling Soft Skills

A bonus of investing time in Gen Z is introducing or reinforcing soft skills such as listening, reading body language, facial expressions, tone, and having empathy and compassion for others. In fact, in most cases, one does not even have to *try* to model soft skills—it comes naturally through the interaction. Since Gen Zers are screenagers, and their phone screens are their natural habitat, most of their communication lacks the important soft skills needed for success in the adult world. These skills are often not developed in the years of adolescence as much as they have been in past. By investing face-to-face time, the servant leader is teaching important, needed aspects of emotional intelligence that can benefit Gen Zers in their ability to model Jesus for others.

Modeling "Adulting"

Multiple changes in the fabric of society over the past decades have created a void in how one generation passes knowledge to the next. Historically, a slower pace of society and slower social and career mobility, combined with more stable and larger nuclear families, produced many opportunities for parents, grandparents, aunts, uncles, older siblings, and neighbors to both model and speak into the lives of the younger generation. In a time when more people fixed their own cars and canned their own foods, many life skills—and the inherent development of resiliency—were naturally imprinted on the emerging generation from the prior one. The reality of two-income families and a society where goods are largely readily available and disposable is that many of these former opportunities for happenstance passages of knowledge now simply don't exist. This, among other factors, has played a role in emerging generations experiencing an elongated time of adolescence and a gap in their ability to "adult" in life. The intentional investment of time by one with more life experience will undoubtedly create more opportunities to bring awareness to and focus upon life decisions and how to approach them. One has the chance to model and talk about the wisdom of choosing career paths that allow one to be fully used by God; beginning marriage and parenthood on the right basis; and other foundational life experiences. While this may not be traditional, "hard core" discipleship, it is the intentional modeling and guidance that can help set a young Christian up for a kingdom view of success in life. This, in turn, may end up sowing the seeds for a future harvest.

Other Desirable Outcomes

These three examples serve as pragmatic, low-hanging-fruit types of outcomes that a servant leader can generate from a simple investment of time in a Gen Zer. There are additional desirable outcomes from investing time that can play a significant role in helping shape a Gen Zer and position them for a lifetime of greater influence. One of these is the ability for the servant leader to cultivate critical thinkers.

We live in a society awash in opinions and information. As the saying goes, everyone is entitled to his or her opinion, but the possession of said opinion does not automatically make their opinion the correct one. A servant leader has the opportunity not only to shape a person's attitudes and outlooks, but also to help shape and develop the important skill of critical thinking—helping them learn to think well on important issues.

How does this play out practically? Think back to Wilkes's goals for the Christian servant leader. One of them was to encourage and coach those around them[11] by picking up Jesus's towel of servanthood. Encouragement and coaching are hallmarks of the servant leader because in these relationships, the direction of the value brought to the relationship is reversed. Positional leadership asks, "What can this subordinate bring that is of value to me?" In contrast, the servant leader asks, "What value can I bring to this person to enhance their potential influence?"

The servant leader should be equally invested in developing a good thinker as they are in developing a good leader. In the days before so much information was at our disposal, it was important for leaders to be smart. The leader had to know what to do in every situation and gained that knowledge largely through business case studies and other formal learning. Today the main value of a leader is not as much in the information they possess—since most information is readily accessible through the internet—as how a leader responds to what they learn. This is where good critical thinking skills come in.

By building relational equity with their followers, the servant leader has an opportunity to shape how their followers think about important issues, as well as how they act. This is critical when we consider how Dallas Willard defined *acting faith* simply as "acting as if something were true."[12] Actions come from intention, and intention is framed by critical thinking. As a Christian servant leader, this involves both modeling and offering intentional instruction about how modern culture teaches on issues and what an informed biblical worldview looks like.

Servant leadership is also uniquely positioned to help Gen Z develop good critical thinking skills about their own future lives. The Barna Group/Impact 360 research clearly demonstrates that personal achievement, whether educational or professional, is most central to Gen Z's identity.[13] This should not be surprising, given our understanding of how the false ideas about life are constantly streamed to them on social media. Naturally, this creates a desire to compete, to attain the seemingly perfect lives they see flashing before them on their personal screens. According to the research, Gen Zers live in a constant paradox of having "safe spaces" available to them, while seeing cancel culture demonstrate that real safety is a myth if one steps out of culturally accepted lines. Servant leaders who have earned the opportunity can speak the truth into their lives in this area. Gen Zers, even more so than Millennials, have a highly developed (and rightfully cynical) radar for inauthenticity.

This skill is honed from becoming the generation that has been the most marketed to in history. However, servant leadership develops personal relationships that will inherently communicate authenticity, which is highly valued but rarely seen by Gen Z.

Ultimately, all of this ties together with the mandate for all Christians, regardless of birth demographic, to follow, namely, the Great Commission. As Christians, we are commanded to make disciples. The Gen Z research clearly demonstrates a generation who want success and influence. They are also a generation with a historically low level of spirituality but a higher openness to it. To top it off, it is a generation who long for authentic community. We cannot ignore the power of servant leadership to work within this gap.

As we seek to influence Gen Zers and model Jesus to them, a powerful first step is to serve them and grow our influence with them. The opportunity to demonstrate and teach more of Jesus and less of self is more than a leadership model; it is a life orientation that can be applied to work, social circles, community, church, and family.

As the world becomes more antagonistic toward the hard truths of Christianity, the words of Jesus, as shared in the gospel of John, ring true: they will know we are Jesus's disciples by our "love for one another" (John 13:35). The essence of servant leadership is authentic care and investment in another—and by seeking to do so toward Gen Zers, we help to place the cause of Christ deeply in the hearts of those with whom we interact.

CHAPTER 13

WINNING THE LOST IN A POLITICALLY CHARGED CULTURE

Hunter Baker

A Gen X Testimony

I graduated from high school in the spring of 1988 as a Gen Xer before the name became a popular label for my cohorts. Our generation was the unheralded, less numerous successors to the Baby Boomers. The Cold War was still presented as an existential danger. "Forever Young," a popular graduation anthem by Alphaville, wondered "Are you gonna drop the bomb or not?" Punk rock music featured pierced, mohawked, neon, and leather-clad bodies portraying existence in a post-apocalyptic world.

While many people looked at Christianity and saw Pope John Paul II standing bravely against Soviet atheism and communism, others, like me, saw scandals enveloping televangelists such as Jim Bakker and Jimmy Swaggart and began to think of public professors of faith as conmen. Having little sophistication or discernment, I lumped all TV preachers in with those two as Elmer-Gantry-type disgraces. I imagined all of them yelling out the name of "GEEEZUSSSS" and walking around in old-fashioned three-piece suits with blow-dried, sprayed hair.

As I read through the 2018 Gen Z research by the Barna Group and Impact 360 Institute, I know I should have experienced shock at what appears to have been lost. But it is hard for me to feel that way having grown up in the American South with extremely little affinity for the faith and a minimal sense of what it meant or why it matters. Who I was then and who I have become affect my reception of this research.

My parents were not atheists. One parent attended Catholic school; the other grew up in the hardcore segment of the Church of Christ. They both promoted respect for God and sometimes took me and my siblings to church. There were even periods when we attended regularly. The door was open to seek a deeper relationship with God, but I felt no desire to walk through it. I definitely believed in God's existence, but not the biblical God. My god was a cosmic genie who generally approved of you unless you were truly an awful person. In other words, he was a lot more like Santa Claus, for whom I'd been a playground apologist as a little boy.

I prayed sometimes, hoping this god would grant my wishes and give me good grades, money, and girls. I had no desire, however, to serve this god, to save my soul, or to learn how to love him or other people. What I wanted was a giant, wealthy, and powerful superforce who would make everything go my way. In other words, I was like a lot of Americans of my time. I was like a lot of American Millennials and Gen Zers today with their moral therapeutic deism.[1] In response to the narrative of religious decline, I argue that some of the taken-for-granted beliefs have changed, but the real situation is not so different.

In 1988, my parents dropped me off at Florida State University. Although I had graduated from one of the big, bustling Florida high schools (there were 2,000 of us), I was completely overwhelmed by the size and scope of FSU. Having quickly set up the small room I shared with a roommate, my folks left me a USA *Today* newspaper and a roll of quarters for the laundry. While my mother put up a good front, I saw a tear glistening in my father's eye as they departed. That devastated me, and for a long time that afternoon, I just sat on my bed and felt desolate. Like many of today's kids, accustomed to helicopter parents, I was not ready to live an independent life. After a while, I walked out to the dorm lobby and fed my quarters into the Asteroids arcade machine. Sure, the money was for the laundry machines, but I had no idea how to wash and dry clothes. Forget the needs of the next few weeks; more urgent was figuring out how to get through the next few hours.

In a lot of ways, I was a *tabula rasa*. My strongest opinions had to do with sports rivalries, especially football. Also, like many, I dreaded the possibility of nuclear war with the Soviets. My friends and I would discuss questions such as, would you try to drive away from an atomic explosion, or would you drive toward it? Outside of sports and nuclear war, my mind was wide open—and I had entered a wide-open sort of place at FSU.

One of my first courses at Florida State was called something like "Male and Female Roles in Modern Literature." The first book we read was *Lolita*, a well-written but morally-depraved story of a middle-aged man who lusted after a girl in her early teens. Everything seemed up for grabs, and we spent little time on the moral problem inherent in the story. Rather, the wild nature of the plot captured our attention. Whatever bourgeois morality I was supposed to have didn't assert itself much. Other than the book, I remember there was a considerable amount of discussion about white males. I kept thinking in my naïve way, "My dad's a really good guy." But the things that came to dominate my first year were the big, personal questions of life and how to live it. The academic questions stayed in the background, while the spiritual ones stormed to the fore.

Although I was frightened and overwhelmed at the beginning of the school year, I quickly made friends in the dorm (especially with girls). While I had not been popular in high school, the change of social contexts somehow allowed me to become a totally new person, the kind who got invited to parties with liquor and pornographic films. The new guy wasn't going to mess things up by raising moral questions or being critical. I still remember the first time I sat with a drink in hand to watch a pornographic movie. At first, it took my breath away in an uncomfortable way—kind of like stepping into a bath that is too hot. After a moment, you get past the resistance and slip into the water. I felt cool, sophisticated, and accepted by people who otherwise might have made fun of me for my lack of experience.

At one such gathering, after having been in the apartment complex swimming pool drunk with my clothes on, I passed out on the floor. Later I learned that two girls at the party had been taken advantage of while they were intoxicated. Based on what I was told, one of those incidents likely took place a few feet from where I was unconscious in my wet clothing. A deep, moral discomfort grew inside me as I thought about what had happened that night. The thrill of transgression (the underage drinking and pornography) gave way to a sense of shame.

It took another lost evening, however, to push me in a different direction. A friend of mine and I bought a jug of vodka from a girl in the dorm. We spent that evening in a drinking duel, as though from a scene in a movie. My recollection is that I had something like fourteen vodka shots that night. By that time, my drunkenness was so severe that I impulsively slammed my head into the table—and felt no pain, just a massive impact. When I tried to go to sleep, the ceiling spun lazily above me, leaving me nauseated on top of what was probably a severe concussion. I retreated to the lower bunk trying to escape it.

The next day was one of the worst in my life. Suffice it to say that I spent twelve or so hours feeling as though I were being involuntarily wrung out with violent force. Toward the end of the ordeal, I began to fear for my life and prayed one of my transactional prayers. "God, if you allow me to live, I will attend a religious meeting of some kind." Not exactly a profound or inspiring prayer, but that was what I offered. I began to recover almost immediately.

A good friend was involved with Intervarsity Christian Fellowship (IVCF) on our campus, so I decided to go to their next meeting. My plan was simple. I would sit in the back, discharge the promise to my transactional god, and be done with it. Plus, I'd be more careful about drinking in the future. Things didn't turn out that way.

I did go to the meeting and sat in the back. When I was invited to join the rest of the group in the first few rows, I declined the offer. Everything was going to plan. In fact, I watched with light embarrassment and amusement as the group sang songs with lyrics printed on transparencies projected on a screen. The student leaders were not cool. IVCF's staff worker was an exuberant ex-hippie type.[2] None of it was really geared to a person like me who aspired to be sardonic, hip, and worldly.

In many ways, I was much like the Gen Z young people described in the Barna Group's report. I defined success largely in terms of material and social outcomes. In other words, I wanted to be well liked and financially secure. These were my top priorities. This IVCF group at Florida State wasn't committed to those things at all. They were constantly talking about Jesus. To me, people who did that were strange and off-putting. In my mind, even saying the name *Jesus* was embarrassing. It was the equivalent of ripping your pants or tossing a fork into the disposal. *Jesus* was discordant.

But something strange happened. During that meeting, I observed at a distance like some kind of visiting sociologist engaged in qualitative research. When it was over, the deal with my transactional, genie-god was done. My obligation was dispensed. But I kept going to the Tuesday night meetings. In addition, I stopped attending drinking parties and started hanging out with the IVCF Bible study and fellowship crowd. I had not yet become a Christian. In fact, I remember trying to talk with a couple of girls in the dorm, one a Christian and one not, about Jesus and found myself just totally at sea. Truly, I had no idea what I was talking about and madly tried to get my brain around this Jesus person and why I was supposed to be so excited about him.

Just a few months earlier, I remember walking past an early morning meeting of B.A.S.I.C. (Brothers and Sisters in Christ) at my public high school. I looked through the pane of glass in the door and saw them praying together. They were alien to me—truly weird—because they were openly religious! Yet here I was—just months later—with this Christian fellowship group looming ever larger among my priorities. The most honest reason I can give why this happened is that something inside me responded to the IVCF students and the staff worker. They seemed different than other people I'd known.

Yes, it was strange to hear them talking about their relationships with Jesus and their desire to follow him. When I'd first arrived at Florida State, a couple of students with Campus Crusade stopped me outside the cafeteria and asked if I had a personal relationship with Jesus Christ;

I walked quickly past them. But then I began spending time with the students in IVCF and acclimating myself to their "God talk." It struck me that they seemed to be some of the most honest, sincerely friendly, and admirable people I'd ever met.

My experience with this group was somewhat like the plot of the Kevin Costner film *Dances with Wolves*. Costner's character, a Union soldier, encountered Native Americans out on the Western frontier. While they were strange to him at first, he found himself admiring them, and ultimately, he wanted to be part of their community. My conversion to Christianity was similar to that. I evaluated the IVCF students at a comfortable distance, but I appreciated what I saw and felt. Over time, it became clear to me how a relationship with Christ filled people with strength, endurance, sincerity, and love.

My admiration for Christians didn't make me a believer right away. Rather, I became something of an envious fellow traveler. I wanted to be part of their community. The problem was that I couldn't seem to access whatever was working in their hearts and minds. This is one reason why I relate to Gen Zers with respect to the Christian faith. They desire community but for various reasons, many do not accept Christianity's truth claims. At the time, I didn't really believe what those Christians believed and couldn't even talk about it in a coherent way. Like a man staring through a window at a family enjoying a delightful and joyous feast, I only knew I wanted what they had and didn't know how to get it. Though I had this hazy idea that I could say a prayer and it would take care of everything, that wasn't the way forward for me. It would have been insincere because I didn't believe, much less understand. I wanted the fruits of belief but didn't know how to get there.

A year or more went by this way. I fully identified with the members of the group and even ended up doing some jobs inside the chapter, but I did not have their faith. Finally, something happened. It was the fulfill-ment of a dream I'd had, shortly after my first IVCF meeting, in which I perceived God traversing a moonlit desert landscape with his massive presence not seen, but rather felt. We forget most of our dreams, but that one is with me more than thirty years later. The shadow of God's presence was overwhelming and desirable—like I was made for it.

In those days, IVCF meetings always featured a book table. I picked up one titled *Between Heaven and Hell* by Peter Kreeft. For a lover of politics such as myself, it had an irresistible premise. Kreeft imagines that C.S. Lewis, John F. Kennedy, and Aldous Huxley—three influential men who died within 24 hours of one another—had a conversation somewhere between heaven and hell, with each of their fates open, at least for a time.[3] *Between Heaven and Hell* had a lasting influence my spiritual and intellectual development. To begin with, it introduced me to the personality and thinking of C.S. Lewis. More important, by the time I finished it, I found that I believed in the resurrection of Jesus Christ. My amorphous desire to belong among the believers finally found a focus point. I knew I could be a Christian because Jesus Christ really is the son of God, as evidenced by his victory over death. The massive figure in my dream had arrived. Now I could see his face.

Up to that point, while I loved Christians and wanted to be one, I couldn't see how any of it was different from following Buddha, Muhammad, Moses, or any other enlightened figure. It seemed almost like an aesthetic choice. But when I read Kreeft's book, I connected with the same reality Paul urged upon the men of the Areopagus (Acts 17:31). The resurrection is the key to moving past the unknown god to Christ the King.

Reflecting Upon the Testimony with Gen Z in View

I offer my testimony in a volume like this for a few reasons. The first is the most important. While wisdom dictates that we should try to understand where people are and how we can reach them, the simple fact is that God moves in people's lives. He moved in mine. In a sense, I'm unable to unravel it decisively. From one angle, I see the whole thing as a set of choices I made in response to a series of events. But if I turn the kaleidoscope, it looks like choreography, with me as the dancer in a planned performance. So first, in light of the realities discussed in this book, I counsel against both despair and the conservative Christian's characteristic temptation toward grim satisfaction at the forecasted decline and fall of society as we know it.

Second, though my story takes place in the late 1980s and the beginning of the 1990s, I see myself back then very much like the Gen Zers described in the Barna Group/Impact 360 Institute research. I was unreflectively pro-choice, instinctively disapproved of anyone I perceived as dogmatically religious, fully embraced pop culture, and just wanted to live a fun life with plenty of money. Christianity couldn't really market itself to me. I would have chosen Madison Avenue every time. My favorite part of Christmas was the big guy with the red suit, no question. Santa *was* Christmas for me. The religious part was a sideshow. I had to have an encounter with something deeper than my own autonomy drenched in modern consumerism, materialism, and hedonism. Because of my similarity to the cohort in question, I think my experience is relevant. So, too, is my insight as a scholar of religion and politics who is also an adult Christian convert.

It is true that the culture has tilted even further away from the church, but when I converted, I instantly grasped that I was moving out of the normal, the reasonable, and the mainstream. It was more than clear to me that I was moving away from the accepted and into the marginal and strange. My high school best friend's reaction when I told him about my conversion confirmed that reality. For him, I was essentially joining a cult. He instantly brought up the name of a televangelist and asked, "So, you're like him?" We like to tell ourselves that Christianity has occupied a high place in American culture and that it is only recently that the position has been threatened. The reality is that the exalted place of Christianity only held when it wasn't taken too seriously.

Steven D. Smith's recent book *Pagans and Christians in the City: Culture Wars from the Tiber to the Potomac* explains how Christianity overcame paganism in the Roman empire and then established a central place in Western culture. But the story is not a triumphalist one. Smith argues that paganism has remained just below the surface and is actually operational in the worldviews of many, especially secular elites. They find that materialistic positivism leaves them without any grounding for human rights and seek to impart some kind of sacred glow through a performative, participative, social religion.[4]

I suspect that the major change that has come about is simply that, in a previous age, elites were uneasy about attacking Christianity for a couple of reasons. First, they feared undermining the social fabric. The American founders were, at best, a mixed bag in terms of their faith commitments, but it is clear they generally found Christianity socially useful. Second, they feared repercussions from a public steeped in a faith that was still legally established to various degrees. Those concerns were far—very far—away from real belief in Jesus Christ. The story of Dwight Eisenhower joining a church at the urging of Billy Graham to set a good example does not ring with a sense of brokenness, conviction, and repentance. Rather, it is the same old civil religion to which most Americans have usually resorted.

If anything has changed, it is simply that the civil religion has begun to demand that the church affirm things it simply cannot affirm and still be the church. That has been the central point of division between the mainline on one side and the evangelical and fundamentalist churches on the other. The mainline is willing to serve in the Niebuhrian Christ of Culture role, where it often affirms the culture's conclusions. More doctrinally strict churches end up in a place of opposition.[5] They reject the compromised position Reinhold Niebuhr criticized as holding up a counterfeit in which "a God without wrath brought men without sin into a Kingdom without judgment through the ministrations of a Christ without a Cross."[6] The price is diminished prestige and authority in the earthly sense. Some Christians are only feeling it more recently, but I felt it keenly when I joined the church in the late 1980s.

In Kreeft's book that was so important to my own conversion, he represented Jack Kennedy as the kind of American who believed that, as long as you do more good than bad, you will please God and go to heaven. In so doing, Kreeft presented Americans to themselves. I certainly saw myself in that portrait. Good and bad can be defined to the benefit of one's own interests.

What happened to me is that I saw that somehow knowing Jesus seemed to actually affect the course of people's lives and the development of their character. This was more than just stacking good and bad deeds, however flexibly defined, on a scale. This was the attractive force of authentic holiness driving Christians toward sanctification, as my colleague Kyle Strobel has clearly articulated in his chapter of this volume. It was a kind of demanding, authoritative, deep, sacrificial goodness. I could recognize that much, thus my conclusion at the time that these were the finest people I'd ever known. The reality is that they were probably not moral superheroes, as I perceived them, but that they were in touch with God in ways that far exceeded my own experience. What was required in order for me to become a Christian was to understand that Jesus, son of God and conqueror of death, was "the Way" as early Christians called him. I needed to understand that he is Lord and why he is Lord (Acts 24:14). The Acts emphasis upon Christians as witnesses to the resurrection supplied the indispensable piece of the puzzle for me.

Christ and culture are interactive, but the relationship is not malleable in terms of its ultimate reality. Jesus is Lord. Our central mission as the church is to proclaim that truth. A sinful humanity will ultimately acknowledge his kingship when "every knee will bow …and every tongue confess that Jesus Christ is lord," but until that inevitable moment arises, we will be the bearers of the news throughout history (Phil. 2:10–11). The world's temptations always apply. We will constantly face the tension of how best to express the good news to the world. How to do that and how much to adapt to the culture in which we find ourselves, geographically (as with a nation having no or few believers) or temporally (as with Millennials or Gen Z), will always be a matter of great concern. Human sexuality has become the dominant controversy facing the church. We will wrestle with how to deal with the challenge before an increasingly hostile culture. As I write this chapter, a new American president and his administration have been in office for only a few days, and already these and other issues that have potential impact on the Church's witness have come to the public policy foreground. In the end, however, the issue is the same. Jesus Christ is Lord. The central question is: "Who do you say that I am?" (Matt. 16:15).

Though I experience some of the same anxiety prompted by the survey data gathered by the Barna Group, Impact 360 Institute, and others, I can't help but feel that things have changed less than we think. Christianity has functioned more as the reigning cult of culture and less as the true arena for submission to the lordship of Christ in our society. In other words, it has performed a sociological function rather than a true discipling process for the vast majority of Americans. The change we are experiencing is probably less about a recession of true Christianity and more an exposure of the weakness and shallowness of our social religion.

Conclusion

Pre-COVID, my morning ritual involved eating breakfast at a McDonald's near campus where I would read a book or journal. One of my regular fellow diners is a dentist in town, a man perhaps a dozen years older than me. At some point, he read *The Shack* and ended up embracing a kind of universalism.[7] On one occasion, he saw me reading some conservative religious text and approached my table to talk. In his mind, he'd moved on from Christian orthodoxy and wanted to persuade me to readjust my own beliefs. "The kids aren't buying it," he informed me, seeming to feel he'd laid a trump card down on the table. "Religious truth isn't determined by taking a poll," I replied.

While the Christian faith has sometimes been successfully marketed, the truth is that the great strength of Christianity lies in its transcendence of popularity. I can't help but find myself thinking of the scriptural moment when Jesus gave an especially challenging teaching in which he urged eating his flesh and drinking his blood. Many of his followers abandoned him. He asked Peter if he would be leaving as well. Peter responded as we must, "Lord, to whom would we go? You have the words of eternal life" (John 6:67–68).

What can we do about a skeptical, materialistic, personal-autonomy-driven culture that mocks the faith? I recommend we do what my friends at IVCF at Florida State did with me. Be patient. Be winsome and kind. Be tolerant of ignorance. Be bold. But the most important thing to be is faithful. We must not trim our sails by one centimeter at the cost of truth. People deserve to hear the undiluted gospel, even if it is a scandal in the minds of modern men and women.

I've saved the most important words for last. It is critical not to make the mistake of thinking that we need to preserve Christianity as the sociological religion of the United States. Our only task is to be faithful in proclaiming the good news of the gospel and to live in such a way as to bear witness to the power of the resurrection.

KNOW—BE—LIVE

John W. White, III

We're living in a modern-day Babylon.

The book of Daniel describes the struggle one righteous man and his few close friends faced in a social and political climate ruled by government policies, self-interest, arrogance, intolerance, and a horrendously misguided sense of morality. People were told what to eat, drink, say, do, think, and believe. Politicians vied for more power and prestige, while citizens did their best to abide by the ever-changing decrees passed down from "on high." The name of God was not only mocked and ignored by the elite; it was criminalized. In today's terms, we might say the Babylonian culture tried to *cancel* God.

Today, here in twenty-first century America, it's clear that Almighty God is being canceled once again as we also face many of the other challenges Daniel struggled against. The church and the next generation of Christ-followers are facing intense political and cultural challenges. No, we're not being thrown into a pit of lions, but every day we hear about Christian voices being silenced. We're accused of hate speech for daring to believe and teach the Word of God. We're faced with the incongruity of our Christian beliefs and the new, ungodly policies being forced upon us. We're made to grapple with fundamental biblical truths contrasted with modern political redefinitions of marriage, sex, gender, and even life itself. We're told that murdering the unborn is *right* and asserting the biological differences between men and women is *wrong*. Sometimes it seems as though the world has turned upside down. Daniel, sitting in a den of lions, reminds us that it always was. The question for us, then, is how will we respond?

Christian education has never been more important than it is right now. We must equip our pastors and church leaders, and we must undergird our Christian institutions with a solid foundation of truth rooted in Scripture rather than the shifting sands of political correctness. And you—are you a member of Gen Z? If so, you must prepare yourself for life on the front lines of the battle. It falls on you to articulate and defend the faith to a culture that hates everything you believe. If you are a discipler of Christ-following Gen Zers, then it falls on you to do everything to steward the time you have in helping them become equipped to be faithful in this present-day Babylon.

This compilation of essays was written by faithful men and women who want nothing more than to help you prepare yourself and those whom you are discipling for life in our post-Christian world. Our culture, not much different than ancient Babylon, is defying God more and more each day. This puts those of us who call upon the name of the Lord in a tight spot. As Rod Dreher warns:

> A time of painful testing, even persecution, is coming. Lukewarm or shallow Christians will not come through with their faith intact. Christians today must dig deep into the Bible and church tradition and teach themselves how and why today's post-Christian world ... is a rival religion to authentic Christianity.[1]

Put another way, Dreher is saying, "You think it's bad now? Just wait until you see what comes next."

My goal here isn't to scare you but to simply warn you. Hard times aren't just coming; they're already here. We, therefore, like Daniel and his three friends, must keep our eyes fixed on the truth. As the author of Hebrews exhorts, "Therefore, since we are surrounded by such a great cloud of witnesses, we must get rid of every weight and the sin that clings so closely, and run with endurance the race set out for us, keeping our eyes fixed on Jesus, the pioneer and perfecter of our faith" (Heb. 12:1–2). Daniel and his friends ran the race, and in response to their faithfulness, "God endowed them with knowledge and skill in all sorts of literature and wisdom—and Daniel had insight into all kinds of visions and dreams" (Dan. 1:17).

But what about us? Are we truly followers of Christ, or are we merely admirers of Christ? Are we daily disciples, or are we fair-weather fans? What does faithfulness to God even look like in a world that seems so increasingly anti-God?

That's what the authors of this book have been trying to show you throughout this collection of essays. We believe the answer to the challenges of life in the modern world lies in the three pillars of spiritual development at Impact 360 Institute: God's call on us to Know, Be, and Live. You've already read what many of my friends and colleagues have to say on these topics, so I won't rehash the entire scope of this book here at the finish line. Rather, I'll just give my two cents on what I think each pillar means to us, right here, right now.

Pillar 1: Know

Knowing God and becoming transformed by him into the man or woman he has called you to be begins with a sincere reverence—called *fear* in the Old Testament—for who he is. As the psalmist reminds us, "The fear of the LORD is the beginning of wisdom ... Blessed are those who fear the LORD, who find great delight in his commands" (Ps. 111:10, 112:1 NIV). In fact, one might argue that the only way to truly know *anything* is through a biblical worldview centered on God alone. It was God who spoke the universe and everything in it into being; everything has its beginning and end in him. Knowing him, therefore, is the crucial first step toward fully understanding anything in his creation.

Daniel, to whom God granted the ability to discern the deeper meanings of dreams, found favor with King Nebuchadnezzar by interpreting his dreams when no one else in the kingdom could. This act not only ingratiated the prophet to Nebuchadnezzar; it also saved the lives of all the so-called "wise men" of Babylon, whom the king had ordered to be executed out of frustration for their inability to interpret his dream. Realizing God had given him the answer to the king's dilemma, Daniel exclaimed:

> Let the name of God be praised forever and ever, for wisdom and power belong to him. He changes times and seasons, deposing some kings and establishing others. He gives wisdom to the wise; he imparts knowledge to those with understanding; he reveals deep and hidden things. He knows what is in the darkness, and light resides with him. (Daniel 2:20–22)

He gives wisdom to the wise. He gives knowledge to the discerning. He reveals hidden things. He knows what lies in darkness. He has the answers to life's problems, and he knows the secrets of life's joys. Put simply, God knows. And he wants to impart much of that knowledge to you.

I encourage you to make a commitment to lifelong learning. While technology has created many challenges in the modern world, it has brought us even more blessings and rich opportunities—chief among them is the endless wealth of educational resources we now have at our fingertips. When I was a student, I was limited to in-person classes, workshops, and seminars. I dug through books and spent countless hours in the library trying to find that one crucial book that was essential to my studies. Of course, I was also competing with hundreds of other students searching for that same resource! Today information is practically free. Digital delivery makes the same resources available to every student in the world simultaneously in a variety of formats. You can virtually attend lectures in London from your sofa in Savannah. What a time for faithful students of God's Word to be alive!

No one can make you seek after God's truth; you must decide for yourself to continue your education for the rest of your life. Are you willing to carry this journey into the next phase of your life, taking with you all the wisdom and knowledge of our heavenly Father? Commit to reading good books. Work through the classics. Absorb the books listed in Appendix A of this volume. Go digital when necessary, and discover a century's worth of audio and video presentations from recent history's most profound teachers and preachers. God has brought the best teachers from around the world and all throughout history right to your door. Your charge is to simply open the door and let them in.

Pillar 2: Be

The second pillar of spiritual transformation is learning how to *Be*. Impact 360 Institute expresses this as a process of transformation. We are called to be transformed in our character as we discover our identity in Christ and our God-given calling. Character is key here. Your character reflects who you are; it is your self-identity. The call to *Be* is a call to be transformed as a new creation in Christ, a transformation that continues as the indwelling Holy Spirit works to create integrity between your mind, will, and emotions (see Romans 12:2).

We are truly wondrous, complex beings with a miraculous blend of physical, emotional, and spiritual elements. God wants us to experience the full potential of each aspect of ourselves as we strive to become "conformed to the image of his Son" (Romans 8:29). Dallas Willard described this process as *integration*, through which our entire being is integrated into a life in the kingdom of God. This happens, he explained, when all the essential factors of one's life are centered and effectively organized around God. Willard wrote, "Spiritual formation in Christ is the process leading to that ideal end [fully integrated], and its result is love of God with all of the heart, soul, mind and strength, and of the neighbor as oneself. The human self is then fully integrated under God."[2]

We were made in the image of God, and we were made for relationship with him and fellowship with others. Therefore, we most experience the power of *Be* when we're *becoming* more like his Son in the context of community.

Pillar 3: Live

The third pillar of spiritual development, *Live*, focuses on learning how to make our way through this modern-day Babylon. It's an odd thing, isn't it—living as children of light in a dark, ungodly world? The psalmist asks, "How can we sing a song to the LORD in a foreign land?" (Ps. 137:4). Though in Christ we are no longer slaves to sin and death and are free to live the spirit-filled life for all eternity, we're still stuck here in what too often feels like a "foreign land." How do we reconcile our life in Christ with our life in a world that doesn't seem to fit?

Though frustrating, I believe that living in this world means we will remain a work in progress until the Lord returns. We're here as apprentices of Jesus Christ, working out our salvation through continual growth and transformation. This is how we mature both spiritually and emotionally. This is where *Know. Be. Live.* comes together, as our knowledge of God and our understanding of who we are in Christ empowers us to live out our Christlikeness in a world that neither knows him nor seeks him.

The psalmist proclaims, "You lead me in the path of life. I experience absolute joy in your presence; you always give me sheer delight" (Psalm 16:11). We can live a flourishing, meaningful, and truly joyful life only in the presence of God. When we learn to live in his presence and walk in his ways, we begin to understand what it means to be "children of light in a dark, ungodly world."

Revelation 18 tells of the great fall of the mighty Babylonian empire. A once-great kingdom ultimately became a dwelling place of demons and unclean spirits and a cesspool of sexual immorality. The apostle John wrote:

> Then I heard another voice from heaven saying, "Come out of her, my people, so you will not take part in her sins and so you will not receive her plagues, because her sins have piled up all the way to heaven and God has remembered her crimes....She will experience her plagues in a single day: disease, mourning, and famine, and she will be burned down

> with fire, because the Lord God who judges her is powerful! (Revelation 18:4, 8)

Though Christ-followers will be spared this final judgment, it is an ever-present reality for the world around us. I pray it becomes both a refining fire to further hone and sharpen your faith and a motivation to live a life that attract unbelievers to the saving grace of our heavenly Father.

A Prayer for Transformation

True spiritual transformation only comes when we engage in a loving relationship with God the Father through his Son Jesus Christ and by the fullness of the indwelling Holy Spirit. I pray the essays contained in this book and their broad discussion of our *Know. Be. Live.* pillars have challenged you to engage in that relationship to the fullest by pursuing the rich, full, abundant life that God intends for his children.

Jesus declared that he is "the way, and the truth, and the life" (John 14:6). May his life call forth from us a dedication and devotion to *Know* him, *Be* conformed into the likeness of his Son, and *Live* for his kingdom. May we all be more inspired, more motivated, and more dedicated to obeying the voice of the Lord, loving him with all our hearts and walking in his ways. May we incline our eyes and hearts to his Word and commands.

Lord, make your face shine upon your people who are called by your name. Empower us to risk intentionally, daring to *Know, Be,* and *Live* as your ambassadors among a people who do not know you, a people whom you love as deeply and dearly as you love us. May we learn to see them—and ourselves—through your eyes as we go out into the world, daring to make a difference for your kingdom.

APPENDIX A

KNOW. BE. LIVE.
RESOURCE LIST

Know

Baker, Hunter. *The End of Secularism*. Wheaton, IL: Crossway, 2009.

Baker, Hunter. *Political Thought: A Student's Guide*. Wheaton, IL: Crossway, 2012.

Bartholomew, Craig G., and Michael W. Goheen. *Living at the Crossroads: An Introduction to Christian Worldview*. Grand Rapids, MI: Baker Academic, 2008.

Bartholomew, Craig G. *Christian Philosophy: A Systematic and Narrative Introduction*. Grand Rapids, MI: Baker Academic, 2013.

Bartholomew, Craig G. *Introducing Biblical Hermeneutics: A Comprehensive Framework for Hearing God in Scripture*. Grand Rapids, MI: Baker Academic, 2015

Bock, Darrell L. *Cultural Intelligence: Living for God in a Diverse, Pluralistic World*. Nashville, TN: B&H Academic, 2020.

Chesterton, Gilbert K. *Orthodoxy*. Lawrenceville, GA: CrossReach Publications, 2017.

Dockery David S., and Trevin Wax. *Christian Worldview Handbook*. Nashville, TN: Holman Reference, 2019.

Dockery, David S. *Renewing Minds: Serving Church and Society through Christian Higher Education*. Nashville, TN: B&H Academic, 2008.

Fant, Jr., Gene C. *The Liberal Arts: A Student's Guide*. Wheaton, IL: Crossway, 2012.

Finn, Nathan A. *History: A Student's Guide*. Wheaton, IL: Crossway, 2016.

Goheen, Michael W., and Craig G. Bartholomew. *The True Story of the Whole World: Finding Your Place in the Biblical Drama*. Grand Rapids, MI: Brazos, 2020.

Lewis, C.S. *The Weight of Glory*. San Francisco, CA: HarperOne, 2001.

Lewis, C.S. *The Problem of Pain*. New York: Harper Collins, 2001.

Lewis, C.S. *Mere Christianity*. San Francisco, CA: HarperOne, 2006.

Lewis, C.S. *The Abolition of Man*. San Francisco, CA: HarperOne, 2015.

Moreland, J.P. *Love Your God with All Your Mind*. Colorado Springs, CO: NavPress, 2012.

Moreland, J.P. *The Soul: How We Know It's Real and Why It Matters*. Chicago, IL: Moody, 2014.

Moreland, J.P., and William Lane Craig. *Philosophical Foundations for a Christian Worldview*. Downers Grove, IL: IVP Academic, 2017.

Morrow, Jonathan. *Questioning the Bible: 11 Major Challenges to the Bible's Authority*. Chicago, IL: Moody, 2014.

Packer, J.I. *Knowing God*. Downers Grove, IL: IVP, 1993.

Pearcey, Nancy R., and Charles B. Thaxton. *The Soul of Science: Christian Faith and Natural Philosophy*. Wheaton, IL: Crossway, 1994.

Pieper, Josef. *The Four Cardinal Cirtues: Human Agency, Intellectual Traditions, and Responsible Knowledge*. Notre Dame, IN: University of Notre Dame Press, 1966.

Plantinga, Alvin. *Knowledge and Christian Belief*. Grand Rapids, MI: Eerdmans, 2015.

Stark, Rodney. *The Rise of Christianity*. San Francisco, CA: Harper San Francisco, 1997.

Stark, Rodney. *The Victory of Reason: How Christianity Led to Freedom, Capitalism, and Western Success*. New York: Random House, 2006.

Trueman, Carl. *The Rise and Triumph of the Modern Self: Cultural Amnesia, Expressive Individualism, and the Road to Sexual Revolution*. Wheaton, IL: Crossway, 2020.

Willard, Dallas. *Knowing Christ Today: Why We Can Trust Spiritual Knowledge*. San Francisco, CA: HarperOne, 2009.

Willard, Dallas. *The Allure of Gentleness, Defending the Faith in the Manner of Jesus*. San Francisco, CA: HarperOne, 2015.

Wolters, Albert M. *Creation Regained: Biblical Basics for a Reformational Worldview*. Grand Rapids, MI: Eerdmans, 2005.

Be

Anderson, Ryan T. *When Harry Became Sally: Responding to the Transgender Moment*. Encounter Books, 2018.

Bartholomew, Craig G., and Michael Goheen. *The Drama of Scripture: Finding Our Place in the Biblical Story*. Grand Rapids, MI: Baker Academic, 2014.

Blanchard, Kenneth., Phil Hodges, and Phyllis Hendry. *Lead Like Jesus Revisited: Lessons from the Greatest Leadership Role Model of All Time*. Nashville, TN: Thomas Nelson, 2016.

Cloud, Henry. *Integrity: The Courage to Meet the Demands of Reality*. New York: HarperBusiness, 2009.

DeYoung, Kevin. *The Hole in Our Holiness: Filling the Gap between Gospel Passion and the Pursuit of Godliness*. Wheaton, IL: Crossway, 2012.

Enlow, Jr., Ralph E. *Servant of All: Reframing Greatness and Leadership through the Teaching of Jesus*. Bellingham, WA: Kirkdale Press, 2019.

Evans, Tony. *Oneness Embraced: Reconciliation, the Kingdom, and How We are Stronger Together*. Chicago, IL: Moody, 2015.

Lewis, C. S. *The Four Loves*. San Francisco, CA: HarperOne, 2017.

McDowell, Sean, and John Stonestreet. *Same-Sex Marriage: A Thoughtful Approach to God's Design for Marriage*. Grand Rapids, MI: Baker, 2014.

McPherson, Miles. *The Third Option: Hope for a Racially Divided Nation*. Nashville, TN: Howard Books, 2020.

Metaxas, Eric. *Bonhoeffer: Pastor, Martyr, Prophet, Spy*. Nashville, TN: Thomas Nelson, 2011.

Moreland, J.P. *Kingdom Triangle: Recover the Christian Mind, Renovate the Soul, Restore the Spirit's Power*. Grand Rapids, MI: Zondervan, 2007.

Nouwen, Henri. *Life of the Beloved*. Chestnut Ridge, NY: Crossroad, 2002.

Ortberg, John. *Soul Keeping: Caring for the Most Important Part of You*. Grand Rapids, MI: Zondervan, 2014.

Packer, J.I. *Rediscovering Holiness: Know the Fullness of Life with God*. Grand Rapids, MI: Baker, 2003.

Pearcey, Nancy R. *Love Thy Body: Answering Hard Questions about Life and Sexuality*. Grand Rapids, MI: Baker, 2018.

Pieper, Josef. *Josef Pieper: An Anthology*. San Francisco, CA: Ignatius Press, 1989.

Scazzero, Peter. *The Emotionally Healthy Leader: It's Impossible to be Spiritually Mature While Remaining Emotionally Immature*. Grand Rapids, MI: Zondervan, 2017.

Smith, James K.A. *You Are What You Love: The Spiritual Power of Habit*. Grand Rapids, MI: Brazos, 2016.

Sproul, R.C. *The Holiness of God*. Orlando, FL: Ligonier, 2006.

Strobel, Kyle., and John Coe. *Where Prayer Becomes Real: How Honesty with God Transforms Your Soul*. Grand Rapids, MI: Baker, 2021.

West, Christopher. *Theology of the Body for Beginners: Rediscovering the Meaning of Life, Love, Sex, and Gender*. North Palm Beach, FL: Beacon, 2018.

Willard, Dallas. *The Divine Conspiracy: Rediscovering Our Hidden Life in God*. San Francisco, CA: Harper San Francisco, 1998.

Willard, Dallas. *Renovation of the Heart: Putting on the Character of Christ*. Colorado Springs, CO: NavPress, 2002.

Willard, Dallas. *Hearing God: Developing a Conversational Relationship with God*. Downers Grove, IL: IVP, 2012.

Yuan, Christopher. *Holy Sexuality and the Gospel: Sex, Desire, and Relationships Shaped by God's Grand Story*. New York: Multnomah, 2018.

Live

Blackaby, Henry T., and Richard Blackaby. *Spiritual Leadership: Moving People onto God's Agenda*. Nashville, TN: B&H, 2001.

Bosché, Brian, and Gabrielle Bosché. *The Purpose Factor: Extreme Clarity for Why You're Here and What to Do About It*. Nashville, TN: Post Hill Press, 2020.

Childers, Alisa. (2020). *Another Gospel? A Lifelong Christian Seeks Truth in Response to Progressive Christianity*. Carol Stream, IL: Tyndale, 2020.

Cloud, Henry. *Boundaries for Leaders: Results, Relationships, and Being Ridiculously in*

Charge. New York: Harper Business, 2013.

Colson, Charles. *Born Again.* Grand Rapids, MI: Chosen Books, 2008.

Doriani, Daniel. *Work: Its Purpose, Dignity, and Transformation.* Phillipsburg, NJ: P&R, 2019.

Dreher, Rod. *Live Not by Lies: A Manual for Christian Dissidents.* New York: Sentinel, 2020.

Garber, Steven. *Visions of Vocation: Common Grace for the Common Good.* Downers Grove, IL: IVP, 2014.

Gen Z: The Culture, Beliefs and Motivations Shaping the Next Generation. Ventura, CA: Barna Group, 2018.

Gen Z: The Culture, Beliefs and Motivations Shaping the Next Generation, vol. 2. Ventura, CA: Barna Group, 2021.

Greenleaf, Robert K. *Servant Leadership: A Journey into the Nature of Legitimate Power and Greatness.* New York: Paulist, 2017.

Guinness, Os. *The Call: Finding and Fulfilling the Central Purpose of Your Life.* Nashville, TN: Thomas Nelson, 2003.

Keller, Timothy with Katherine Leary Alsdorf. *Every Good Endeavor: Connecting Your Work to God's Work.* New York: Viking, 2012.

Kinnaman, David, and Mark Matlock, M. *Faith for Exiles: 5 Ways for a New Generation to Follow Jesus in Digital Babylon.* Grand Rapids, MI: Baker, 2019.

Kruger, Michael J. *The Ten Commandments of Progressive Christianity.* Minneapolis, MN: Cruciform, 2019.

Kunkle, Brett, and John Stonestreet. *A Practical Guide to Culture.* Colorado Springs, CO: David C. Cook, 2017.

Lennox, John C. *Against the Flow: The Inspiration of Daniel in an Age of Relativism.* Grand Rapids, MI: Monarch, 2015.

Moreland, J.P. *Finding Quiet: My Story of Overcoming Anxiety and the Practices that Brought Peace.* Grand Rapids, MI: Zondervan, 2019.

Nouwen, Henri. *In the Name of Jesus: Reflections on Christian Leadership.* Chestnut Ridge, NY: Crossroad, 1992.

Palmer, Parker J. *Let Your Life Speak: Listening for the Voice of Vocation.* San Francisco, CA: Jossey-Bass, 2000.

Perman, Matt. *What's Best Next: How the Gospel Transforms the Way You Get Things Done.* Grand Rapids, MI: Zondervan, 2016.

Ryken, Leland. *Redeeming the Time: A Christian Approach to Work and Leisure.* Grand Rapids, MI: Baker, 1995.

Shackelford, Stephanie, and Bill Denzel. *You on Purpose: Discover Your Calling and Create the Life You Were Meant to Live.* Grand Rapids, MI: Baker, 2021.

Shatzer, Jacob. *Transhumanism and the Image of God: Today's Technology and the Future of Christian Discipleship.* Downers Grove, IL: IVP Academic, 2019.

Smith, Gordon T. *Courage and Calling: Embracing Your God-Given Potential.* Downers Grove, IL: IVP, 2011.

Twenge, Jean M. *iGen.* New York: Atria, 2017.

Veith, Jr., Gene Edward. *God at Work: Your Christian Vocation in All of Life.* Wheaton, IL:

Crossway, 2002.

Wilkes, C. Gene. *Jesus on Leadership*. Nashville, TN: Lifeway, 1997.

Willard, Dallas. *The Spirit of the Disciplines: Understanding How God Changes Lives*. San Francisco, CA: HarperOne, 1999.

Willard, Dallas, and Keith Meyer. *The Kingdom Life: A Practical Theology of Discipleship and Spiritual Formation*. Colorado Springs, CO: NavPress, 2016.

Williams, Thaddeus J. *Confronting Injustice without Compromising Truth: 12 Questions Christians Should Ask about Social Justice*. Grand Rapids, MI: Zondervan, 2020.

Wurmbrand, Richard. *Tortured for Christ*. Colorado Springs, CO: David C. Cook, 2017.

SCRIPTURE REFERENCES AND DEVOTIONAL INSIGHTS

Compiled by Beth Yoe

Know

"Hear, O Israel: The Lord is our God, the Lord is one! You must love the Lord your God with your whole mind, your whole being, and all your strength. These words I am commanding you today must be kept in mind, and you must teach them to your children and speak of them as you sit in your house, as you walk along the road, as you lie down, and as you get up. You should tie them as a reminder on your forearm and fasten them as symbols on your forehead. Inscribe them on the doorframes of your houses and gates." (DEUT. 6:4–9)

When Moses finished reciting all these words to all Israel he said to them, "Keep in mind all the words I am solemnly proclaiming to you today; you must command your children to observe carefully all the words of this law. For this is no idle word for you—it is your life! By this word you will live a long time in the land you are about to cross the Jordan to possess." (DEUT. 32:45–47)

Now Ezra had dedicated himself to the study of the law of the Lord, to its observance, and to teaching its statutes and judgments in Israel. (EZRA 7:10)

"The one true God acts in a faithful manner; the Lord's promise is reliable; he is a shield to all who take shelter in him. Indeed, who is God besides the Lord? Who is a protector besides our God? The one true God is my mighty refuge; he removes the obstacles in my way. He gives me the agility of a deer; he enables me to negotiate the rugged terrain." (2 Sam. 22:31–34)

How can a young person maintain a pure life? By guarding it according to your instructions. With all my heart I seek you. Do not allow me to stray from your commands. In my heart I store up your words, so I might not sin against you. You deserve praise, O Lord. Teach me your statutes. With my lips I proclaim all the regulations you have revealed. I rejoice in the lifestyle prescribed by your rules as if they were riches of all kinds. I will meditate on your precepts and focus on your behavior. I find delight in your statutes; I do not forget your instructions. (Ps. 119:9–16)

Be kind to your servant. Then I will live and keep your instructions. Open my eyes so I can truly see the marvelous things in your law. (Ps. 119:17–18)

I choose the path of faithfulness; I am committed to your regulations. I hold fast to your rules. O Lord, do not let me be ashamed. I run along the path of your commands, for you enable me to do so. (Ps. 119:30–32)

O Lord, your instructions endure; they stand secure in heaven. You demonstrate your faithfulness to all generations. You established the earth and it stood firm. Today they stand firm by your decrees, for all things are your servants. If I had not found encouragement in your law, I would have died in my sorrow. I will never forget your precepts, for by them you have revived me. (Ps. 119:89–93)

Your instructions are a doorway through which light shines. They give insight to the untrained. (Ps. 119:130)

Those who love your law are completely secure; nothing causes them to stumble. (Ps. 119:165)

Every word of God is purified; he is like a shield for those who take refuge in him. Do not add to his words, lest he reprove you, and prove you to be a liar. (PROV. 30:5–6)

"Do not think that I have come to abolish the law or the prophets. I have not come to abolish these things but to fulfill them. I tell you the truth, until heaven and earth pass away not the smallest letter or stroke of a letter will pass from the law until everything takes place. So anyone who breaks one of the least of these commands and teaches others to do so will be called least in the kingdom of heaven, but whoever obeys them and teaches others to do so will be called great in the kingdom of heaven." (MATT. 5:17–19)

These Jews were more open-minded than those in Thessalonica, for they eagerly received the message, examining the scriptures carefully every day to see if these things were so. (ACTS 17:11)

Remind people of these things and solemnly charge them before the Lord not to wrangle over words. This is of no benefit; it just brings ruin on those who listen. Make every effort to present yourself before God as a proven worker who does not need to be ashamed, teaching the message of truth accurately. (2 TIM. 2:14–15)

Every scripture is inspired by God and useful for teaching, for reproof, for correction, and for training in righteousness, that the person dedicated to God may be capable and equipped for every good work. (2 TIM. 3:16–17)

For the word of God is living and active and sharper than any double-edged sword, piercing even to the point of dividing soul from spirit, and joints from marrow; it is able to judge the desires and thoughts of the heart. And no creature is hidden from God, but everything is naked and exposed to the eyes of him to whom we must render an account. (HEB. 4:12–13)

My aim is to know him, to experience the power of his resurrection, to share in his sufferings, and to be like him in his death, and so, somehow, to attain to the resurrection from the dead. Not that I have already attained this—that is,

I have not already been perfected—but I strive to lay hold of that for which Christ Jesus also laid hold of me. Brothers and sisters, I do not consider myself to have attained this. Instead I am single-minded: Forgetting the things that are behind and reaching out for the things that are ahead, with this goal in mind, I strive toward the prize of the upward call of God in Christ Jesus. Therefore let those of us who are "perfect" embrace this point of view. If you think otherwise, God will reveal to you the error of your ways. Nevertheless, let us live up to the standard that we have already attained. (PHIL. 3:10–16)

Then Jesus said to those Judeans who had believed him, "If you continue to follow my teaching, you are really my disciples and you will know the truth, and the truth will set you free." (JOHN 8:31–32)

A Little Butter for the Bread

Our claim is that God has revealed himself by speaking; that this divine (or God-breathed) speech has been written down and preserved in Scripture; and that Scripture is, in fact, God's Word written, which therefore is true and reliable and has divine authority over men.

—JOHN STOTT

You don't truly know God unless you surrender, believe, and truly obey the Word of God.

—ANN VOSKAMP

And the only way to know the God of the Word is to know the Word of God.

—DONNA EVANS

If there were one piece of advice, one bit of encouragement, that I could give you, that would be: know God's word for yourself and have it memorized. Take those Scriptures that you read and take the time to get them deep and embedded into your heart and your mind. Because here's what happens in life: you hit a moment of crisis. Many times, it can come out of the blue. It's not something that you always get a forewarning or impression that something's coming. And what will hold you, and what held me on that darkest day, are God's word and his promises.

—CATHE LAURIE

Be

He says, "Stop your striving and recognize that I am God. I will be exalted over the nations! I will be exalted over the earth!" The Lord of Heaven's Armies is on our side! The God of Jacob is our stronghold! (Selah) (Ps. 46:10–11)

The Lord will deliver them over to you, and you will do to them according to the whole commandment I have given you. Be strong and courageous! Do not fear or tremble before them, for the Lord your God is the one who is going with you. He will not fail you or abandon you!" (Deut. 31:5–6).

"I am about to die. Be strong and become a man! Do the job the Lord your God has assigned you by following his instructions and obeying his rules, commandments, regulations, and laws as written in the law of Moses. Then you will succeed in all you do and seek to accomplish." (1 Kings 2:2–3)

"And you, Solomon my son, obey the God of your father and serve him with a submissive attitude and a willing spirit, for the Lord examines all minds and understands every motive of one's thoughts. If you seek him, he will let you find him, but if you abandon him, he will reject you permanently. Realize now that the Lord has chosen you to build a temple as his sanctuary. Be strong and do it!" (1 Chron. 28:9–10)

"Make sure you are very strong and brave! Carefully obey all the law my servant Moses charged you to keep. Do not swerve from it to the right or to the left, so that you may be successful in all you do. This law scroll must not leave your lips. You must memorize it day and night so you can carefully obey all that is written in it. Then you will prosper and be successful. I repeat, be strong and brave! Don't be afraid and don't panic, for I, the Lord your God, am with you in all you do." (Josh. 1:7–9)

"Do not work for the food that disappears, but for the food that remains to eternal life—the food which the Son of Man will give to you. For God the

Father has put his seal of approval on him." So then they said to him, "What must we do to accomplish the deeds God requires?" Jesus replied, "This is the deed God requires—to believe in the one whom he sent." (JOHN 6:27–29)

Therefore, be imitators of God as dearly loved children and live in love, just as Christ also loved us and gave himself for us, a sacrificial and fragrant offering to God. (EPH. 5:1–2)

And he himself gave some as apostles, some as prophets, some as evangelists, and some as pastors and teachers, to equip the saints for the work of ministry, that is, to build up the body of Christ, until we all attain to the unity of the faith and of the knowledge of the Son of God—a mature person, attaining to the measure of Christ's full stature. So we are no longer to be children, tossed back and forth by waves and carried about by every wind of teaching by the trickery of people who craftily carry out their deceitful schemes. But practicing the truth in love,[i] we will in all things grow up into Christ, who is the head. From him the whole body grows, fitted and held together through every supporting ligament. As each one does its part, the body builds itself up in love. (EPH. 4:11–16)

And I pray this, that your love may abound even more and more in knowledge and every kind of insight so that you can decide what is best, and thus be sincere and blameless for the day of Christ, filled with the fruit of righteousness that comes through Jesus Christ to the glory and praise of God. (PHIL. 1:9–11)

Rejoice in the Lord always. Again I say, rejoice! Let everyone see your gentleness. The Lord is near! Do not be anxious about anything. Instead, in every situation, through prayer and petition with thanksgiving, tell your requests to God. And the peace of God that surpasses all understanding will guard your hearts and minds in Christ Jesus. (PHIL. 4:4–7)

Finally, be strengthened in the Lord and in the strength of his power. Clothe yourselves with the full armor of God, so that you will be able to stand against the schemes of the devil. For our struggle is not against flesh and blood, but against the rulers, against the powers, against the world rulers of this darkness, against the spiritual forces of evil in the heavens. For this reason, take up the full armor of God so that you may be able to stand your ground on the evil day, and having done everything, to stand. Stand firm therefore, by fastening the belt of truth around your waist, by putting on the breastplate of righteousness, by fitting your feet with the preparation that comes from the good news of peace, and in all of this, by taking up the shield of faith with which you can extinguish all the flaming arrows of the evil one. And take the helmet of salvation and the sword of the Spirit (which is the word of God). With every prayer and petition, pray at all times in the Spirit, and to this end be alert, with all perseverance and petitions for all the saints. (EPH. 6:10–18)

But the fruit of the Spirit is love, joy, peace, patience, kindness, goodness, faithfulness, gentleness, and self-control. Against such things there is no law. Now those who belong to Christ have crucified the flesh with its passions and desires. If we live by the Spirit, let us also behave in accordance with the Spirit. Let us not become conceited, provoking one another, being jealous of one another. (GAL. 5:22–26)

Let no one look down on you because you are young, but set an example for the believers in your speech, conduct, love, faithfulness, and purity. Until I come, give attention to the public reading of scripture, to exhortation, to teaching. Do not neglect the spiritual gift you have, given to you and confirmed by prophetic words when the elders laid hands on you. Take pains with these things; be absorbed in them, so that everyone will see your progress. Be conscientious about how you live and what you teach. Persevere in this, because by doing so you will save both yourself and those who listen to you. (1 TIM. 4:12–16)

I solemnly charge you before God and Christ Jesus, who is going to judge the living and the dead, and by his appearing and his kingdom: Preach the message, be ready whether it is convenient or not, reprove, rebuke, exhort with complete patience and instruction. For there will be a time when people will not tolerate sound teaching. Instead, following their own desires, they will accumulate teachers for themselves, because they have an insatiable curiosity to hear new things. And they will turn away from hearing the truth, but on the other hand they will turn aside to myths. You, however, be self-controlled in *all things, endure hardship, do an evangelist's work, fulfill your ministry. (2 TIM. 4:1–5)*

Instead, be kind to one another, compassionate, forgiving one another, just as God in Christ also forgave you. (EPH. 4:32)

A Little Butter for the Bread

Allow the grace of kindness to pervade your whole nature, mellowing all that would be harsh or austere. It cost nothing to be kind, yet its benefits are priceless. And as a child of the King we are bearers of this pleasant fruit.

—BETH H. YOE

Be patient with God's patient work. The way of Abundance is always first the dying and then the rising. Be not afraid of practicing your faith everywhere— your God is practicing resurrection everywhere.

—ANN VOSKAMP

On him then reckon, to him look, on him depend: and be assured that if you walk with him, look to him and expect help from him, he will never fail you. An older brother, who has known the Lord for forty-four years, who writes this, says for your encouragement that he has never failed him. In the greatest difficulties, in the heaviest trials, in the deepest poverty and necessities, he has never failed me; but because I was enabled by his grace to trust in him, he has always appeared for my help. I delight in speaking well of his name.

—GEORGE MUELLER

We may be certain that whatever God has made prominent in his Word, he intended to be conspicuous in our lives.

—CHARLES SPURGEON

Live

Therefore consider carefully how you live—not as unwise but as wise, taking advantage of every opportunity, because the days are evil. For this reason do not be foolish, but be wise by understanding what the Lord's will is. And do not get drunk with wine, which is debauchery, but be filled by the Spirit. (EPH. 5:15–18)

So I say this, and insist in the Lord, that you no longer live as the Gentiles do, in the futility of their thinking. They are darkened in their understanding, being alienated from the life of God because of the ignorance that is in them due to the hardness of their hearts. Because they are callous, they have given themselves over to indecency for the practice of every kind of impurity with greediness. But you did not learn about Christ like this, if indeed you heard about him and were taught in him, just as the truth is in Jesus. You were taught with reference to your former way of life to lay aside the old man who is being corrupted in accordance with deceitful desires, to be renewed in the spirit of your mind, and to put on the new man who has been created in God's image—in righteousness and holiness that comes from truth. (EPH. 4:17–24)

Finally, brothers and sisters, whatever is true, whatever is worthy of respect, whatever is just, whatever is pure, whatever is lovely, whatever is commendable, if something is excellent or praiseworthy, think about these things. And what you learned and received and heard and saw in me, do these things. And the God of peace will be with you. (PHIL 4:8–9)

For this reason we also, from the day we heard about you, have not ceased praying for you and asking God to fill you with the knowledge of his will in all spiritual wisdom and understanding, so that you may live worthily of the Lord and please him in all respects—bearing fruit in every good deed, growing in the knowledge of God, being strengthened with all power according to his glorious might for the display of all patience and steadfastness, joyfully giving thanks to the Father who has qualified you to share in the saints' inheritance in the light. He delivered us from the power of darkness and transferred us to the kingdom of the Son he loves, in whom we have redemption, the forgiveness of sins. (COL. 1:9–14)

So put to death whatever in your nature belongs to the earth: sexual immorality, impurity, shameful passion, evil desire, and greed which is idolatry. Because of these things the wrath of God is coming on the sons of disobedience. You also lived your lives in this way at one time, when you used to live among them. But now, put off all such things as anger, rage, malice, slander, abusive language from your mouth. Do not lie to one another since you have put off the old man with its practices and have been clothed with the new man that is being renewed in knowledge according to the image of the one who created it. Here there is neither Greek nor Jew, circumcised or uncircumcised, barbarian, Scythian, slave or free, but Christ is all and in all. (COL. 3:5–11)

For I am not ashamed of the gospel, for it is God's power for salvation to everyone who believes, to the Jew first and also to the Greek. For the righteousness of God is revealed in the gospel from faith to faith, just as it is written, **"The righteous by faith will live."** (ROM. 1:16–17)

So do not throw away your confidence, because it has great reward. For you need endurance in order to do God's will and so receive what is promised. For **just a little longer** *and* **he who is coming will arrive and not delay. But my righteous one will live by faith, and if he shrinks back, I take no pleasure in him.** *But we are not among those who shrink back and thus perish, but are among those who have faith and preserve their souls.* (HEB. 10:35–39)

"Teacher, which commandment in the law is the greatest?" Jesus said to him, **"'Love the Lord your God with all your heart, with all your soul, and with all your mind.'** *This is the first and greatest[e]commandment. The second is like it:* **'Love your neighbor as yourself.'** *All the law and the prophets depend on these two commandments."* (MATT. 22:36–40)

Then he said to them all, "If anyone wants to become my follower, he must deny himself, take up his cross daily, and follow me. For whoever wants to save his life will lose it, but whoever loses his life because of me will save it. For what

does it benefit a person if he gains the whole world but loses or forfeits himself?
(LUKE 9:23–25)

The one who says he resides in God ought himself to walk just as Jesus walked.
(1 JOHN 2:6)

I have been crucified with Christ, and it is no longer I who live, but Christ lives
in me. So the life I now live in the body, I live because of the faithfulness of the
Son of God, who loved me and gave himself for me. (GAL. 2:20)

But the wisdom from above is first pure, then peaceable, gentle, accommo-
dating, full of mercy and good fruit, impartial, and not hypocritical. And the
fruit that consists of righteousness is planted in peace among those who make
peace. (JAMES 3:17–18)

But be sure you live out the message and do not merely listen to it and so
deceive yourselves. For if someone merely listens to the message and does not
live it out, he is like someone who gazes at his own face in a mirror. For he
gazes at himself and then goes out and immediately forgets what sort of person
he was. But the one who peers into the perfect law of liberty and fixes his atten-
tion there, and does not become a forgetful listener but one who lives it out—he
will be blessed in what he does. (JAMES 1:22–25)

But you, as a person dedicated to God, keep away from all that. Instead pursue
righteousness, godliness, faithfulness, love, endurance, and gentleness. Compete
well for the faith and lay hold of that eternal life you were called for and made
your good confession for in the presence of many witnesses. (1 TIM. 6:11–12)

But you, dear friends, by building yourselves up in your most holy faith, by
praying in the Holy Spirit, maintain yourselves in the love of God, while antic-
ipating the mercy of our Lord Jesus Christ that brings eternal life. And have
mercy on those who waver; save others by snatching them out of the fire; have
mercy on others, coupled with a fear of God, hating even the clothes stained by
the flesh. (JUDE 20–23)

A Little Butter for the Bread

Jesus is the Word made flesh and in him is perfect peace—a state of untroubled, undisturbed well-being. Therefore, as his followers we are to encourage one another, in the midst of life's chaos and storms, with the living and powerful Word of God. As our Lord did, he spoke the Word and calmed the sea. Just as it was true then, it is still true today—his Word calms and he can speak it even through a donkey. His Word is alive and active and sharper than any two-edged sword. It is able to divide soul and spirit, joint and marrow. It judges the thoughts and attitudes of the heart. It is not to be merely idle words for us as Moses told the Israelites, it is to be our life. God's Word is a balm for every needy soul—and truly, what soul isn't needy?

—Beth H. Yoe

For us to grow in maturity, it's not enough to just read God's Word. We need to obey it and put it into practice. Much as an athlete builds physical muscles through repetition and conditioning, we build spiritual muscles by learning, obeying, and living God's Word. Sound Bible study transforms our lives by training our minds and hearts. Bible literacy protects us from error and increases our love for God himself. By giving us his Word and his Spirit, God has given us everything we need for spiritual maturity. Failure to grow is always our choice, never God's. What are we doing today to help us grow and mature as Christians?

—Donna Evans

Three things helped me as we went through, and continue to go through, crisis: prayer, the Word of God, and the encouragement of fellow believers.

—Greg Laurie

I have a Father in heaven who rules over the affairs of the nations and my focus is to be upon his kingdom. Earthly kingdoms rise and fall, and leaders come and go, but the kingdom of God cannot be shaken. When I think about the world in which our grandchildren are growing up, I find encouragement in considering Daniel. What a spiritual grounding he and his friends must have enjoyed enabling them to live as they did under the rule of a temporary kingdom in anticipation of one that is eternal. All the twists and turns of nations and leaders are under the jurisdiction of the Lord of history. When we cannot see God's hand in the present, it is not because he is absent but because he is working in a way yet to be revealed. One day the earth will be filled with the glory of God as the waters cover the sea (Hab. 2:14).

—ALISTAIR BEGG

ENDNOTES

Foreword

1. Eric Reed, "Six Reasons Young People Leave the Church," *Christianity Today* (Winter 2012), accessed March 4, 2021, http://www.christianitytoday.com/le/2012/winter/youngleavechurch.html.
2. William Wilberforce, *Real Christianity* (1829) (Portland, OR: Multnomah, 1982), 1–2.
3. See Robert Bork, *Slouching Towards Gomorrah: Modern Liberalism and American Decline* (New York: HarperCollins, 1996).

Introduction

1. Russell Moore, "Is Christianity Dying?" RussellMoore.com, May 12, 2015, https://www.russellmoore.com/2015/05/12/is-christianity-dying/.

Part One: KNOW

Chapter 1

1. Walter Donaldson, composer; Joe Young and Sam M. Lewis, lyricists, "How 'Ya Gonna Keep 'em Down on the Farm (After They've Seen Paree)?" (New York: Waterson, Berlin & Snyder, 1919).
2. Greg L. Hawkins and Cally Parkinson, *Reveal: Where Are You?* (South Barrington, IL: Willow Creek Association, 2007).
3. Christian Smith with Melinda Lundquist Denton, *Soul Searching: The Religious and Spiritual Lives of American Teenagers* (New York: Oxford UP, 2005), 118.
4. Tim Elmore, *Generation iY: Our Last Chance to Save their Future* (Atlanta, GA: Poet Gardener, 2010).
5. David Kinnaman with Aly Hawkins, *You Lost Me: Why Young Christians Are Leaving Church …and Rethinking Faith* (Grand Rapids, MI: Baker, 2012).
6. Barna Group, *Gen Z: The Culture, Beliefs and Motivations Shaping the Next Generation* (Ventura, CA: Barna, 2018).
7. Navigate 360, "New Poll Reveals American Teens Are Experiencing High Rates of Anxiety, Depression and Acts of Self-Harm," PRNewswire, January 13, 2021, https://www.prnewswire.com/news-releases/new-poll-reveals-american-teens-are-experiencing-high-rates-of-anxiety-depression-and-acts-

of-self-harm-301207541.html.

8. Joe Carter, "New Study: Frequent Churchgoers Have Better Mental Health," *The Gospel Coalition*, December 12, 2020, https://www.thegospelcoalition.org/article/frequent-churchgoers-better-mental-health/.

9. Carter, "New Study."

10. K. C. Madhav, Shardulendra Prasad Sherchand, and Samendra Sherchan, "Association Between Screen Time and Depression among US Adults," *Preventive Medicine Reports* 8 (December 2017) 67–71, https://reader.elsevier.com/reader/sd/pii/S2211335517301316?token=7269D033FA025B1C3951E51AF-8E5ED7E1C2E4FD7D63D22264F1C3E029480A77A426B858C9FE7A-B317EA5AAB2FAC10F4E.

11. James Sire, for example, identified seven basic questions for worldview in his book *Naming the Elephant: Worldview as a Concept* (Downers Grove, IL: IVP, 2004). In his list, he underscored the relentless question-asking of our species and how the answers to these questions shape our cultures and belief systems.

12. For an excellent analysis of the early church's effectiveness in its time, see Alan Kreider's *Patient Ferment of the Early Church* (Grand Rapids, MI: Baker, 2016).

13. Rod Dreher, *The Benedict Option: A Strategy for Christians in a Post-Christian Nation* (New York: Sentinel, 2017).

14. See, for example, the World Economic Council's challenge to remake the world's economies and political structures: "The Great Reset," World Economic Forum, accessed January 21, 2021, https://www.weforum.org/great-reset/.

Chapter 2

1. Elton Trueblood, *The Predicament of Modern Man* (New York: Harper & Brothers, 1944), 59–60.

2. Learn more about the exciting ways we are training the next generation at Impact 360 Institute (www.impact360.org).

3. See also Jonathan Morrow, *Welcome to College: A Christ-Follower's Guide for the Journey* (Grand Rapids, MI: Kregel, 2018). You can connect with me at www.jonathanmorrow.org.

4. Barna Group, *Gen Z*, 12. See www.GenZlab.com for the latest research and actionable insights as well as the forthcoming *Gen Z*, vol. 2.

5. *Gen Z*, 64.

6. *Gen Z*, 56.

7. *Gen Z*, 56.

8. *Gen Z*, 56.

9. *Gen Z*, 56.

10. *Gen Z*, 56.
11. *Gen Z*, 46.
12. *Gen Z*, 55.
13. Christian Smith and Patricia Snell, *Souls in Transition: The Religious and Spiritual Lives of Emerging Adults* (Oxford: Oxford University Press, 2009), 293.
14. Smith and Snell, 293.
15. See the 2020 Netflix documentary *The Social Dilemma*.
16. William Inge, quoted in John Stonestreet and Roberto Rivera, "Preach Christianity's Weird Stuff," Christian Post, December 14, 2020, https://www.christianpost.com/voices/preach-christianitys-weird-stuff.html.
17. For a helpful overview of the postmodern turn, its applications, and current power dynamics from a secular perspective, see Helen Pluckrose and James Lindsay, *Cynical Theories: How Activist Scholarship Made Everything About Race, Gender, and Identity—and Why This Harms Everybody*, first ed. (Durham: Pitchstone, 2020). For a distinctly Christian approach to addressing issues around racism see the excellent book by Miles McPherson, *The Third Option: Hope for a Racially Divided Nation* (New York: Howard, 2018).
18. See J.P. Moreland, *Scientism and Secularism: Learning to Respond to a Dangerous Ideology* (Wheaton, IL: Crossway, 2018).
19. See, for example, the excellent Thaddeus J. Williams, *Confronting Injustice without Compromising Truth: 12 Questions Christians Should Ask about Social Justice* (Grand Rapids, MI: Zondervan, 2020).
20. See "John Stonestreet, Ann Morse: The Sexual Revolution's Latest Victims Are Children Abused by Other Children," BCNN1, accessed January 20, 2021, https://blackchristiannews.com/2019/01/john-stonestreet-ann-morse-the-sexual-revolutions-latest-victims-are-children-abused-by-other-children/.
21. Mark Sayers, *Disappearing Church: From Cultural Relevance to Gospel Resilience* (Chicago: Moody, 2016), 15.
22. Nancy Pearcey, *Saving Leonardo: A Call to Resist the Secular Assault on Mind, Morals, and Meaning* (Nashville, TN: B&H, 2010).
23. For an interesting perspective on how this is affecting culture at large from a secular perspective, see Greg Lukianoff and Jonathan Haidt, *The Coddling of the American Mind: How Good Intentions and Bad Ideas are Setting Up a Generation for Failure* (New York: Penguin, 2019).
24. For accessible places to start, see my books, Sean McDowell and Jonathan Morrow, *Is God Just a Human Invention?: And Seventeen Other Questions Raised by the New Atheists* (Grand Rapids, MI: Kregel, 2010) and Jonathan Morrow, *Questioning the Bible: 11 Major Challenges to the Bible's Authority* (Chicago:

Moody, 2014).

25. Moreland, *Scientism and Secularism*, 39–40.

26. C.S. Lewis, *Mere Christianity* (New York: Simon & Schuster, 1996).

Chapter 3

1. See J.P. Moreland's *Scientism and Secularism* for more on this.

2. Barna Group, *Gen Z*, 64.

3. This section and that covering the theories of truth is taken from J.P. Moreland and William Lane Craig, "Theories of Truth and Postmodernism" in *Philosophical Foundations for a Christian Worldview* (Downers Grove, IL: IVP, 2003), 130–53.

4. Moreland and Craig, 135.

5. *Gen Z*, 64.

6. *Gen Z*, 65.

7. For further information, see J.P. Moreland's *Christianity and the Nature of Science* (Grand Rapids, MI: Baker, 1989) and *Scientism and Secularism* (Wheaton, IL: Crossway, 2018), John A. Bloom and David S. Dockery's *The Natural Sciences: A Student's Guide* (Wheaton, IL: Crossway, 2015) and John Lennox's *God's Undertaker: Has Science Buried God?* (Oxford: Lion, 2009).

8. *Gen Z*, 104.

9. Genesis 1:27; 5:1–2.

Chapter 4

1. Tawa J. Anderson, W. Michael Clark, and David K. Naugle, *An Introduction to Christian Worldview: Pursuing God's Perspective in a Pluralistic World* (Downers Grove, IL: IVP Academic, 2017), 8.

2. Barna Group, *Gen Z*.

3. See the summary statement with the graphic found in *Gen Z*, 12.

4. The remainder of this section draws heavily from *Gen Z*, 15–36.

5. See Jean Twenge, *iGen: Why Today's Super-Connected Kids Are Growing Up Less Rebellious, More Tolerant, Less Happy—and Completely Unprepared for Adulthood* (New York: Atria, 2017).

6. James Emery White, *Meet Generation Z: Understanding and Reaching the New Post-Christian World* (Grand Rapids, MI: Baker, 2017), 49.

7. David Kinnaman and Mark Matlock, *Faith for Exiles: 5 Ways for a New Generation to Follow Jesus in Digital Babylon* (Grand Rapids, MI: Baker, 2019), 69.

8. For more on the historical development of worldview thinking, see David K. Naugle Jr., *Worldview: The History of a Concept* (Grand Rapids, MI: Eerdmans,

2002).

9. James W. Sire, *Naming the Elephant: Worldview as a Concept*, 2nd ed. (Downers Grove, IL: IVP Academic, 2015), 20–21.

10. W. Gary Phillips, William E. Brown, and John Stonestreet, *Making Sense of Your World: A Biblical Worldview*, second ed. (Salem, WI: Sheffield, 2008), xi–xiii.

11. Michael W. Goheen and Craig G. Bartholomew, *Living at the Crossroads: An Introduction to Christian Worldview* (Grand Rapids, MI: Baker Academic, 2008), 4.

12. Smith's Cultural Liturgy series includes the following volumes: *Desiring the Kingdom: Worship, Worldview, and Cultural Formation* (Grand Rapids, MI: Baker Academic, 2009); *Imagining the Kingdom: How Worship Works* (Grand Rapids, MI: Baker Academic, 2013); *Awaiting the King: Reforming Public Theology* (Grand Rapids, MI: Baker Academic, 2017).

13. Timothy C. Tennent, *Invitation to World Missions: A Trinitarian Missiology for the Twenty-first Century* (Grand Rapids, MI: Kregel Academic, 2010), 347.

14. Andy Crouch addresses the need for entire families to have a rightly ordered approach to screens in *The Tech-Wise Family: Everyday Steps for Putting Technology in Its Proper Place* (Grand Rapids, MI: Baker, 2017).

15. Again, these particular spiritual practices apply as often to older generations as they do Gen Z. For a helpful book on this theme, see Justin Whitmel Earley, *The Common Rule: Habits of Purpose for an Age of Distraction* (Downers Grove, IL: InterVarsity, 2019).

16. For example, see the important studies by sociologist Mark Regnerus in *Forbidden Fruit: Sex & Religion in the Lives of American Teenagers* (New York: Oxford University Press, 2007), *Cheap Sex: The Transformation of Men, Marriage, and Monogamy* (New York: Oxford University Press, 2017), and *The Future of Christian Marriage* (New York: Oxford University Press, 2020).

Part Two: BE

Chapter 5

1. Barna Group, *Gen Z*.

2. *Gen Z*, 16–18.

3. See Freddie Sayers, "Why do British Teens Think Life is Meaningless?" in *Unherd* December 19, 2019, https://unherd.com/2019/12/why-do-british-teens-life-is-meaningless/.

4. I first heard this phrase from my friend Kevin Bywater.

5. See Carl Trueman, *The Rise and Triumph of the Modern Self: Cultural Amnesia, Expressive Individualism, and the Road to Sexual Revolution* (Wheaton, IL:

Crossway, 2020), 22–23.

6. See *Gen Z*, 55–58.

7. Charles Taylor, *A Secular Age* (Boston, MA: Harvard, 2007). For a helpful introduction to the idea of expressive individualism, see Trevin Wax, "Expressive Individualism: What Is It?" *The Gospel Coalition*, October 16, 2018, https://www.thegospelcoalition.org/blogs/trevin-wax/expressive-individualism-what-is-it.

8. C.S. Lewis, *The Four Loves* (San Francisco, CA: HarperOne; 2017). A helpful summary of the four loves can be found in Zach Kinkaid, "Four Types of Love," at *The Official Website of C.S. Lewis*, accessed March 11, 2021, https://www.cslewis.com/four-types-of-love/.

9. See Owen Strachan, "Back to Your Posts: A Response to Dalrymple on Marriage" in *Thought Life: A Patheos Blog*, November 27, 2012, https://www.patheos.com/blogs/thoughtlife/2012/11/back-to-your-posts-a-response-to-dalrymple-on-marriage/.

Chapter 6

1. Barna Group, *Gen Z*, 38–39.

2. *Gen Z*, 40–41.

3. *Gen Z*, 38.

4. *Gen Z*, 41.

5. Jamin Goggin and I develop this in our book, *The Way of the Dragon or the Way of the Lamb: Searching for Jesus' Path of Power in a Church that has Abandoned it* (Nashville, TN: Thomas Nelson, 2017).

6. See David Peterson, *Possessed by God: A New Testament Theology of Sanctification and Holiness* New Studies in Biblical Theology (Downers Grove, IL: IVP, 1995), 27.

7. For the most recent book-length discussion of the definitive nature of sanctification, see Don J. Payne, *Already Sanctified: A Theology of the Christian Life in Light of God's Completed Work* (Grand Rapids, MI: Baker Academic, 2020).

8. As Jacob Milgrom noted in his commentary on Leviticus, "Holiness is not innate. The source of holiness is assigned to God alone. Holiness is the extension of God's nature; it is the agency of God's will." Jacob Milgrom, *Leviticus: A Book of Ritual and Ethics* (A Continental Commentary) (Minneapolis, MN: Fortress, 2004), 107.

9. Gordan J. Wenham, *The Book of Leviticus* (Grand Rapids, MI: Eerdmans, 1979), 17.

10. K. Bo., "Sanctification" in *New Dictionary of Theology* edited by Sinclair B. Ferguson, David F. Wright, and J. I. Packer (Downers Grove, IL: IVP, 1988), 613.

11. Peterson, *Possessed by God*, 17.

12. Peterson, *Possessed by God*, 24.

13. See Peterson, *Possessed by God*, 36.

14. For a development of these notions, see John Walton, "Equilibrium and the Sacred Compass: The Structure of Leviticus," *Bulletin of Biblical Research* 11, no. 2 (2001): 293–304.

15. For a history of this notion in Reformed theology, see Angela Carpenter, *Responsive Becoming: Moral Formation in Theological, Evolutionary, and Developmental Perspective* (London: T&T Clark, 2019).

16. I think Eleonore Stump is right about this. See her, "The Non-Aristotelian Character of Aquinas's Ethics: Aquinas on the Passions," *Faith and Philosophy* 28, no. 1 (2011), 29–43. This does not mean that acquired virtue is irrelevant or not, in some sense, virtuous, however.

17. Dallas Willard, *Renovation of the Heart: Putting on the Character of Christ* (Colorado Springs, CO: NavPress, 2002), 22.

18. Willard, *Renovation of the Heart*, 23.

19. Willard, *Renovation of the Heart*, 82.

20. For an example, see Kyle Strobel, *Formed for the Glory of God: Learning from the Spiritual Practices of Jonathan Edwards* (Downers Grove, IL: IVP, 2013).

21. Dallas Willard, *The Great Omission: Reclaiming Jesus's Essential Teachings on Discipleship* (San Francisco, Harper One, 2014), 34.

22. Willard, *Renovation of the Heart*, 22.

Chapter 7

1. Kim Parker and Ruth Igielnik, "On the Cusp of Adulthood and Facing an Uncertain Future: What We Know about Gen Z So Far," Pew Research Center, May 14, 2020, https://www.pewsocialtrends.org/essay/on-the-cusp-of-adulthood-and-facing-an-uncertain-future-what-we-know-about-gen-z-so-far/.

2. Gretchen Livingston and Anna Brown, "Intermarriage in the U.S. 50 Years after Loving v. Virginia," Pew Research Center, May 18, 2017, https://www.pewsocialtrends.org/2017/05/18/intermarriage-in-the-u-s-50-years-after-loving-v-virginia/.

3. Monica Anderson and Jingjing Jiang, "Teens, Social Media & Technology 2018," Pew Research Center, May 31, 2018, https://www.pewresearch.org/internet/2018/05/31/teens-social-media-technology-2018/.

4. Chris Demaske, "Critical Race Theory," The First Amendment Encyclopedia, MTSU, accessed March 12, 2021, https://www.mtsu.edu/first-amendment/article/1254/critical-race-theory.

5. Richard Delgado and Jean Stefancic, *Critical Race Theory: An Introduction, Third Edition* (New York: University Press, 2001), 6–7.

6. Delgado and Stefancic, *Critical Race Theory*, 7–8.

7. George Yancey, *Beyond Racial Gridlock: Embracing Mutual Responsibility* (Downers Grove, IL: IVP, 2006), 69–70.

8. Alvin Plantinga, *Faith and Rationality: Reason and Belief in God* (Notre Dame: Notre Dame University Press, 1983), 87.

9. Editorial Staff, "What Does 'Imago Dei' Mean? The Image of God in the Bible," Christianity.com, accessed March 12, 2021, https://www.christianity.com/wiki/bible/image-of-god-meaning-imago-dei-in-the-bible.html.

Chapter 8

1. Rachel Gilson, *Born Again This Way: Coming Out, Coming to Faith, and What Comes Next* (Denmark: The Good Book Company, 2020), 22–23.

2. Gilson, *Born Again This Way*, 23.

3. Sara Moslener, *Virgin Nation: Sexual Purity and American Adolescence* (New York: Oxford University Press, 2015).

4. Linda Kay Klein, *Pure: Inside the Evangelical Movement that Shamed a Generation of Young Women and How I Broke Free* (New York: Touchstone, 2018).

5. Christine J. Gardner, *Making Chastity Sexy: The Rhetoric of Evangelical Abstinence Campaigns* (Berkeley, CA: University of California Press, 2011), 61.

6. See Matthew Saxey, "Do 'Church Ladies' Really Have Better Sex Lives?" Institute for Family Studies, November 16, 2020, https://ifstudies.org/blog/do-church-ladies-really-have-better-sex-lives.

7. See Sean McDowell, *Chasing Love: Sex, Love, and Relationships in a Confused Culture* (Nashville, TN: Broadman Holman, 2020).

8. Barna Group, *Gen Z*, 104.

9. *Gen Z*, 46–47.

10. *Gen Z*, 58.

11. Sean and Josh McDowell, *The Beauty of Intolerance: Setting a Generation Free to Know Truth & Love* (Uhrichsville, OH: Barbour, 2016), 98.

12. Sean McDowell, "How 'Passengers' Subverts the Sexual Revolution," SeanMcDowell.org, December 20, 2016, https://seanmcdowell.org/blog/how-passengers-subverts-the-sexual-revolution.

13. Rebecca Hawkes, "Passengers: Watch the New Trailer, Plus All You Need to Know about Jennifer Lawrence and Chris Pratt's Sci-fi Romance," *The Telegraph*, November 24, 2016, https://www.telegraph.co.uk/films/2016/09/20/passengers-trailer-plus-everything-you-need-to-know-about-jennif/.

14. Mark 7:21–22; Rom. 1:24–31; 13:13; 1 Cor. 6:9–10; Gal. 5:19–21; Col. 3:5–9; 1 Tim. 1:9–10; Rev. 21:8.

15. Sean McDowell and J. Warner Wallace, *So the Next Generation Will Know: Preparing Young Christians for a Challenging World* (Colorado Springs, CO: David C. Cook, 2019), 103–105.

16. Richard M. Davidson, *Flame of Yahweh: Sexuality in the Old Testament* (Peabody, MA: Hendrickson, 2007), 15–16.

17. Sean McDowell, "Does the Levitical Prohibition of Homosexuality Still Apply Today?" *Christian Research Journal* 38, no. 2 (2015), https://www.equip.org/article/levitical-prohibition-homosexuality-still-apply-today/.

18. McDowell, *Chasing Love.*

19. *Gen Z*, 28.

20. *Gen Z*, 15–24.

Chapter 9

1. Tim Flech, *Who Am I? A Peek-through-the-Pages Book of Endangered Animals* (Auckland, New Zealand: Blackwell and Ruth, 2019).

2. Sam Tschida, *Siri, Who Am I? A Novel* (Philadelphia, PA: Quirk Books, 2021).

3. The following statistics are drawn from *Gen Z: The Culture, Beliefs, and Motivations Shaping the Next Generation* (Ventura CA: Barna, 2018), especially chapter 2.

4. For a helpful resource on these questions, see *Understanding Transgender Identities: Four Views*, ed. James K. Beilby and Paul Rhodes Eddy (Grand Rapids, MI: Baker, 2019).

5. *Gen Z*, 46.

6. Ryan S. Peterson, "Created and Constructed Identities," in *The Christian Doctrine of Humanity: Explorations in Constructive Dogmatics*, ed. Oliver D. Crisp and Fred Sanders (Grand Rapids, MI: Zondervan Academic, 2018), 137.

7. Peterson, "Created and Constructed Identities," 140.

8. Peterson, "Created and Constructed Identities," 141.

9. Michael S. Horton, "Image and Office: Human Personhood and the Covenant," in *Personal Identity in Theological Perspective*, ed. Richard Lints, Michael S. Horton, and Mark R. Talbot (Grand Rapids, MI: Eerdmans, 2006), 181.

10. My thoughts here relate to the incredibly fruitful work of Horton in "Image and Office."

Part Three: LIVE

Chapter 10

1. Ryan Jenkins, "Top 4 Factors That Are Shaping Generation Z," *Inc.com*, August 22, 2017, https://www.inc.com/ryan-jenkins/meet-your-future-workforce-4-factors-shaping-gener.html.

2. Hanna Rosin, "The Overprotected Kid," *The Atlantic*, April 2014, https://www.theatlantic.com/magazine/archive/2014/04/hey-parents-leave-those-kids-alone/358631/.

3. Rika Swanzen, "Facing the Generation Chasm: The Parenting and Teaching of Generations Y and Z," *International Journal of Child, Youth, and Family Studies* 9, no. 2 (2018): 125–50, https://journals.uvic.ca/index.php/ijcyfs/article/view/18216.

4. Neil Howe, "Revisiting the Homeland Generation (Part 1 of 2)," *Forbes*, July 31, 2015, https://www.forbes.com/sites/neilhowe/2015/07/31/revisiting-the-homeland-generation-part-1-of-2/?sh=1e8f2f96a8ff.

5. Neil Howe, "Introducing the Homeland Generation (Part 2 of 2)," *Forbes*, October 31, 2014, https://www.forbes.com/sites/neilhowe/2014/10/31/introducing-the-homeland-generation-part-2-of-2/?sh=1f225e60cbb6, accessed January 8, 2021.

6. Swanzen, "Facing the Generation Chasm."

7. Howe, "Introducing the Homeland Generation (Part 2 of 2)."

8. Jenkins, "Top 4 Factors That Are Shaping Generation Z."

9. Libby Kane, "Meet Generation Z, The 'Millennials on Steroids' Who Could Lead the Charge for Change in the US," *Business Insider*, December 4, 2017, https://www.businessinsider.com/generation-z-profile-2017-9#theyve-been-given-much-more-leeway-than-previous-generations-5.

10. Kane, "Meet Generation Z."

11. Howe, "Introducing the Homeland Generation (Part 2 of 2)."

12. Leesa Beck and Alexis Wright, "iGen: What You Should Know About Post-Millennial Students," *College and University* 94, no. 1 (2019): 21–26.

13. Jean M. Twenge and Heejung Park, "The Decline in Adult Activities Among U.S. Adolescents, 1976–2016," *Child Development* 90, no. 2 (March/April 2019): 638–54.

14. Eric Hoover, "Meet the Members of iGen, and Help Them Get Off Their Phones," *The Chronicle of Higher Education* 64, no. 11 (November 5, 2017).

15. Barna Group, *Gen Z.*

16. Rosin, "The Overprotected Kid."

17. Jessica Grose and Hanna Rosin, "The Shortening Leash," *Slate*, August 6, 2014,

http://www.slate.com/articles/life/family/2014/08/slate_childhood_survey_results_kids_today_have_a_lot_less_freedom_than_their.html#lf_comment=197474576.

18. Rosin, "The Overprotected Kid"; Grose and Rosin, "The Shortening Leash."

19. Grose and Rosin, "The Shortening Leash."

20. Peter Gray, "The Play Deficit," *Aeon*, September 18, 2013, https://aeon.co/essays/children-today-are-suffering-a-severe-deficit-of-play.

21. Rosin, "The Overprotected Kid."

22. Gray, "The Play Deficit."

23. Gray, "The Play Deficit."

24. Kyung Hee Kim, "The Creativity Crisis: The Decrease in Creative Thinking Scores on the Torrance Tests of Creative Thinking," *Creativity Research Journal* 23, no. 4 (2011): 285–95.

25. Grose and Rosin, "The Shortening Leash."

26. Barna Group, *Guiding Children To Discover the Bible, Navigate Technology and Follow Jesus* (Ventura, CA: Barna, 2020); Karen Zraik, "Teenagers Say Depression and Anxiety Are Major Issues Among Their Peers," *New York Times*, February 20, 2019, https://www.nytimes.com/2019/02/20/health/teenage-depression-statistics.html.

27. Barna Group, *Guiding Children*.

28. Erica D. Shifflet-Chila et al., "Adolescent and Family Development: Autonomy and Identity in the Digital Age," *Children and Youth Services Review* 70 (2016): 364–68.

29. Betty-Ann Cyr, Steven L. Berman, and Megan L. Smith, "The Role of Communication Technology in Adolescent Relationships and Identity Development," *Child & Youth Care Forum* 44 (2015): 79–92.

30. *Guiding Children*, 19.

31. *Guiding Children*, 19.

32. *Gen Z.*

33. *Guiding Children*, 17.

34. Sarah M. Coyne et al., "Parenting and Digital Media," *Pediatrics* 140, no. s2 (November 2017), s112–s116.

35. *Guiding Children*, 65.

Chapter 11

1. See The Westminster Shorter Catechism, question 1, https://www.apuritansmind.com/westminster-standards/shorter-catechism/, accessed March 16, 2021.

2. Philip Cushman, *Constructing the Self, Constructing America: A Cultural History*

of Psychotherapy (Boston, MA: DeCapo Press, 1996).

3. See J.P. Moreland, *Love Your God with All Your Mind: The Role of Reason in the Life of the Soul* (Colorado Springs, CO: NavPress, 2012), 101–11.
4. Tracy Francis and Fernanda Hoefel, "'True Gen': Generation Z and Its Implications for Companies," McKinsey & Company, November 12, 2018, https://www.mckinsey.com/industries/consumer-packaged-goods/our-insights/true-gen-generation-z-and-its-implications-for-companies.
5. *Gen Z*, 15–16.
6. *Gen Z*, 38.
7. *Gen Z*, 38–39.
8. Dallas Willard, *Renovation of the Heart: Putting on the Character of Christ* (Colorado Springs: NavPress, 2002), 53.
9. Willard, *Renovation of the Heart*, 56.
10. Barna Group, *Gen Z, vol. 2: Caring for Young Souls and Cultivating Resilience* (Ventura, CA: Barna, 2021), 18.
11. *Gen Z*, 43. The data show that 60 percent of engaged Christians said that "professional and educational achievement is very important to me," whereas only 42 percent of all other Gen Z members affirmed this statement.
12. Willard, *Renovation of the Heart*, 210.
13. Daniel Doriani, *Work: Its Purpose, Dignity, and Transformation* (Phillipsburg, PA: P&R, 2019), 96.
14. Doriani, *Work*, 96.
15. Willard, *Renovation of the Heart*, 210.
16. Kinnaman and Matlock, *Faith for Exiles*, 146.
17. See Timothy Keller with Katherine Leary Alsdorf, *Every Good Endeavor: Connecting Your Work with God's Work* (New York: Dutton, 2012).
18. Kinnaman and Matlock, *Faith for Exiles*, 146.
19. *Gen Z vol. 2*, 40.
20. Brian Bosché and Gabrielle Bosché, *The Purpose Factor: Extreme Clarity for Why You're Here and What to Do About It* (New York: Post Hill, 2020), 110.
21. Bosché and Bosché, *The Purpose Factor*, 51.
22. *Gen Z vol. 2*, 33. Seventy-three percent of respondents agreed that seven-and-a-half hours was a fair estimate of daily recreational screen time.
23. See Angela Duckworth's bestselling book entitled *Grit: The Power of Passion and Perseverance* (New York: Scribner, 2016).
24. Gallup Poll of 1,016 adults in the United States, United Kingdom, Canada, France, Japan, and China; February 19–21, 2001.

Chapter 12

1. Robert Greenleaf, *Servant Leadership: A Journey into the Nature of Legitimate Power and Greatness* (Mahwah, NJ: Paulist, 1977), 27.
2. C. Gene Wilkes, *Jesus on Leadership: Timeless Wisdom on Servant Leadership* (Nashville: LifeWay, 1997), 5.
3. *Gen Z*, 15.
4. Twenge, *iGen*, 15.
5. Jean M. Twenge, "Have Smartphones Destroyed a Generation?" *The Atlantic*, September, 2017.
6. Twenge, *iGen*, 291.
7. *Gen Z*, 36.
8. Henry Blackaby, *Spiritual Leadership: Moving People on to God's Agenda* (Nashville: Broadman & Holman, 2001), 17.
9. Blackaby, *Spiritual Leadership*, 19.
10. Blackaby, *Spiritual Leadership*, 20.
11. Wilkes, *Jesus on Leadership*, 15.
12. Willard, *Renovation of the Heart*, 142.
13. *Gen Z*, 40.

Chapter 13

1. See Christian Smith and Melissa L. Denton, *Soul Searching: The Religious and Spiritual Lives of American Teenagers* (Oxford University Press, 2009). By "moralistic therapeutic deism," the authors mean that a divine being exists and had a hand in the universe's beginning but stays at a distance from human activity (deistic). This being wants people to be good to each other (moralistic) and will be involved in their lives only when they ask for help (therapeutic).
2. Her name is Robbie Castleman. She led the chapter at FSU for several years. Robbie would eventually become a professor at John Brown University and the author of several books.
3. Peter Kreeft, *Between Heaven and Hell: A Dialog Somewhere Beyond Death with John F. Kennedy, C. S. Lewis & Aldous Huxley* (Downers Grove, IL: IVP, 1982).
4. Steven D. Smith, *Pagans and Christians in the City: Culture Wars from the Tiber to the Potomac* (Grand Rapids, MI: Eerdmans, 2018).
5. H. Richard Niebuhr, *Christ and Culture* (New York: Harper & Row, 1951).
6. H. Richard Niebuhr, *The Kingdom of God in America* (Middletown, CT: Wesleyan University Press, 1988), 193.
7. William P. Young, *The Shack* (Newbury Park, CA: Windblown Media, 2007).

Postscript
1. Rod Dreher, *Live Not by Lies: A Manual for Christian Dissidents* (New York: Sentinel, 2020), 162.
2. Willard, *Renovation of the Heart*, 31.

CONTRIBUTORS

Phil Alsup (Ed.D, Southern Baptist Theological Seminary) serves as Executive Director of Impact 360 Institute. Before joining Impact, Phil served at Lifeway Christian Resources as Director of Adult Enrichment Training & Events and Manager, Student Camps, as well as various student ministry roles in the local church. He also serves as an Affiliated Professor of Leadership at North Greenville University. Phil, his wife, Vicki, and their three children live in Peachtree City, Georgia.

Hunter Baker (Ph.D., Baylor University) serves as dean of arts and sciences and professor of political science at Union University in Jackson, Tennessee. He is the author of three books, including *The System Has a Soul* (2014), has contributed chapters to several others, and has written for a wide variety of print and digital publications. Hunter is the winner of the 2011 Michael Novak Award conferred by the Acton Institute and has lectured widely on religion and liberty. In addition to his work at Union, Baker has served as an associate editor for the *Journal of Markets & Morality* and as a contributing editor for *Touchstone: A Journal of Mere Christianity*. He is also a research fellow of the Ethics and Religious Liberty Commission.

John D. Basie (Ph.D., Baylor University) serves as Director of the Masters Experience at Impact 360 Institute in Pine Mountain, Georgia. He also holds a faculty appointment with North Greenville University as an Affiliated Professor of Leadership. John has served in various leadership capacities in Christian higher education since 1997. One of his gifts is coaching undergraduates, graduate students, and young professionals in a process to identify their strengths and God-given callings. He also has experience in the for-profit business sector as a certified executive coach and practitioner of various coaching assessments. John is a member of the Evangelical Theological Society. His publications include *Your College Launch Story: Six Things Every Parent Must Do* (2016). He resides in Pine Mountain, Georgia, with his wife of nearly 25 years, Marana, and their three teenage children. John and his family are members of St. Andrews Presbyterian Church (PCA) in Columbus, Georgia.

Dana L. Bort (M.A., Talbot School of Theology, Biola University) is pursuing a Ph.D. in Holocaust and Genocide Studies through Gratz College, after having served as guest professor and leader of women's retreats at Impact 360 Institute. Prior to this she worked with college students in the U.S. and abroad for eight years in campus ministry.

Ed Bort (M.A., Talbot School of Theology, Biola University) is currently the Senior Associate Director and Faculty Chair at Impact 360 Institute. He has served on the Fellows team for 10 years. Before coming to Impact 360 Institute, he served with Cru and taught Biblical Worldview and New Testament Survey at a prestigious Christian high school in California. His education is in Philosophy of Religion and Ethics. Ed and Dana have three wonderful children, Elijah, Elise, and Victoria. They make their home in Fayetteville, Georgia.

Gene C. Fant (Ph.D., University of Southern Mississippi) currently serves as president of North Greenville University (SC). He is a long-time leader in Christ-centered higher education, having served as an academic leader and professor at Mississippi College, Union University, and Palm Beach Atlantic University. He has served as a contributing author to *First Things* and *The Chronicle of Higher Education*. Dr. Fant is author of *The Liberal Arts: A Student's Guide* (2012). He and his wife, Lisa, have two grown twin children, and they live in Tigerville, South Carolina.

Nathan A. Finn (Ph.D., Southeastern Baptist Theological Seminary) serves as Provost and Dean of the University Faculty at North Greenville University in Tigerville, SC. Nathan teaches courses primarily in the fields of theology, church history, and leadership. He is the author or editor of ten books and has written over fifty book chapters, journal articles, and other scholarly and semi-scholarly essays. He is also an ordained minister who preaches regularly in local congregations. Nathan has been married to Leah for over twenty years and is the father of four children. He enjoys drinking coffee, playing golf, hiking, and rooting for the Atlanta Braves.

Sean McDowell (Ph.D., Southern Baptist Theological Seminary) is an Associate Professor in the Christian Apologetics program at Talbot School of Theology, Biola University. Sean is the cohost for the "Think Biblically" podcast, which is one of the most popular podcasts on faith and cultural engagement. He is the author, coauthor, or editor of over twenty books including his most recent, *Chasing Love: Sex, Love, and Relationships in a Confused Culture*. Sean has an apologetics blog that can be read at seanmcdowell.org. He has been married to his wife, Stephanie, since 2000. They have three children and live in San Juan Capistrano, California.

J.P. Moreland (Ph.D., University of Southern California) has for decades served as a discipler of disciplers. He has been on staff with several churches, as well as with Cru. JP is currently Distinguished Professor of Philosophy at the Talbot School of Theology, Biola University. He is the author of many publications, including his recent book *Scientism and Secularism: Learning to Respond to a Dangerous Ideology* (2018). He and his wife, Hope, have two grown daughters. They live in Yorba Linda, California.

Jonathan Morrow, (D.Min., Talbot School of Theology, Biola University) has been equipping students and parents in biblical worldview, apologetics, and culture since 2007. He is the Director of Cultural Engagement and Student Discipleship at Impact 360 Institute and an adjunct professor of apologetics at Biola University. He is the author of several books, including *Questioning the Bible: 11 Major Challenges to the Bible's Authority* (2014), and also contributed to the *Apologetics Study*

Bible for Students. Jonathan and his wife have been married for eighteen years and live with their three children near Atlanta. Connect with him at jonathanmorrow.org.

Melissa Pellew is Co-Chapter Director and Community Apologist with Ratio Christi at Winthrop University (Rock Hill, SC) and in Ratio Christi College Prep ministry to youth. Through the ministry of Ratio Christi, she is equipping students to defend the Christian faith, as well as engaging unbelieving and skeptical students on the truth of Christianity using history, science, and philosophy. She regularly speaks at conferences and events on a variety of apologetic and worldview issues. She has also been involved in biblical racial unity advocacy and pro-life activism in various leadership and training capacities for the last 15 years.

Stephanie Shackelford (Ed.D., Northeastern University) is the author of *You on Purpose: Discover Your Calling and Create the Life You Were Meant to Live* (2021). She is a Senior Fellow at the Barna Group, primarily studying vocation and calling. In 2012, she founded a career coaching company and has since helped hundreds of students, recent graduates, and working professionals live into their purpose. Stephanie received her M.Ed. and B.S. from Vanderbilt University, where she is also an Adjunct Instructor. She lives with her husband and two children in Atlanta. Learn more at StephShackelford.com.

Jacob Shatzer (Ph.D., Marquette University) is associate professor of theological studies, associate dean in the School of Theology & Missions, and assistant provost at Union University in Jackson, Tennessee. Jacob reads and writes at the overlap between theology and ethics, publishing most recently in the areas of transhumanism and theological anthropology. Jacob and his wife, Keshia, have four children ranging from five to twelve years old. They live in Jackson, Tennessee.

John Stonestreet, (M.A., Trinity Evangelical Divinity School) serves as president of the Colson Center for Christian Worldview. He's a sought-after author and speaker on areas of faith and culture, theology, worldview, education and apologetics. John is the daily voice of *BreakPoint*, the nationally syndicated commentary on the culture founded by the late Chuck Colson. He is also the voice of *the Point*, a daily one-minute feature on worldview, apologetics, and cultural issues. Before coming to the Colson Center in 2010, John served in various leadership capacities with Summit Ministries and was on the biblical studies faculty at Bryan College (TN). John has coauthored five books: *A Practical Guide to Culture*; *A Student's Guide to Culture*; *Restoring All Things*; *Same-Sex Marriage*; and *Making Sense of Your World: A Biblical Worldview*. He and his wife, Sarah, have four children and live in Colorado Springs, Colorado. Connect with John at BreakPoint.org or follow him on Twitter @jbstonestreet.

Kyle Strobel, (Ph.D., University of Aberdeen) is associate professor of spiritual theology at Talbot School of Theology, Biola University. He is the coauthor of *Where Prayer Becomes Real: How Honesty with God Transforms Your Soul* (with John Coe) as well as the books *Beloved Dust* and *The Way of the Dragon or the Way of the Lamb* (with Jamin Goggin). Kyle has also written the book *Formed for the Glory of God* on Jonathan Edwards's view of spiritual formation. Kyle serves on the preaching team of Redeemer Church.

John W. White, III (J.D., Cumberland School of Law at Samford University) is cofounder and president of Lifeshape® and Impact 360 Institute. Passionate to encourage and develop people who intentionally impact global culture, he is deeply committed to cultivating leaders who follow Jesus. Along with his wife, Trudy Cathy White, John served 20 years with the International Mission Board in the country of Brazil and in service at the Richmond global headquarters. Proud parent of four children and grandparent to fifteen grandchildren, John enjoys time with family and serving as a member of Woolsey Baptist Church. His stated life focus is, "to know and love God with all my heart, mind and body— and to become more like Him in attitude and character each day."